Pierre Le Moyne d'Iberville

Iberville's Gulf Journals

TRANSLATED AND EDITED BY
Richebourg Gaillard McWilliams

WITH AN INTRODUCTION BY
Tennant S. McWilliams

The University of Alabama Press
Tuscaloosa

The University of Alabama Press
Tuscaloosa, Alabama 35487-0380
uapress.ua.edu

Original publication of this book was assisted by a grant
from the National Endowment for the Humanities.

Cataloging-in-Publication data is available from the
Library of Congress.
ISBN: 978-0-8173-0539-0 (paper)
ISBN: 978-0-8173-8529-3 (electronic)

To

Dorothy Schultz McWilliams

out of love

and in admiration of her skill

in criticizing writing.

Contents

Acknowledgments

I am grateful to the Bibliothèque Nationale in Paris and to the Library of Congress for making available to me microfilm copy of historical material necessary in the preparation of this book.

Some years ago the American Council of Learned Societies provided funds for me to do nothing but study the French in America during the period 1698 to 1763. Out of the money not spent on travel or on the purchase of documents during that year of study I still had some A.C.L.S. funds; on these I was permitted to draw to pay for microfilm of documents in Paris Archives, among which were the films of the three Gulf Journals which Iberville had dictated on the occasions when he returned to France during the years 1699–1702. In addition Birmingham-Southern College gave me several grants of money to provide time for me to study further about the culture of the French on the Gulf Coast and in the Lower Mississippi Valley.

Rucker Agee, my friend for many years, repeatedly encouraged me in my writing by his enthusiasm about my subject; and I am deeply indebted to him, the donor, and to Ruth Spence, the curator of the Rucker Agee Map Collection housed in the Birmingham Public Library.

Richebourg G. McWilliams, Jr., has assisted in my search for maps of the Gulf Coast and has obtained for me valuable information on the history of the Choctawhatchee Bay area.

Jay Higginbotham, of Mobile, kindly helped me locate maps.

Frances White-Spunner, of the Mobile Public Library, was always helpful and persistent in searching for books I needed.

Dr. William Thomas, Professor of Geology, first mentioned mud lumps to me, which led me to write the proof that there never was a barrier of "petrified trees" blocking the mouth of the Mississippi River.

Burk McWilliams, as a geologist, assisted me greatly by drawing maps which clarified certain areas of the Mississippi Delta, and also provided photography and information about mud lumps.

Amelia Walston of Birmingham and Janet Bolton of Mobile have been most skillful as typists for me, and have always been kind indeed.

Monique Cesari Martin and Mrs. David Vest, being French ladies, guided me through several French passages difficult for them and certainly for me.

William Livingston, Circulation Librarian at Spring Hill College, showed great kindness to me.

Dr. Howard H. Creed graciously agreed to go by and examine for me the configuration of the Old Pass at Destin, Florida.

Margaret Hughes, formerly head of the Birmingham-Southern College library, and Viola Harper, Reference Librarian of the University of South Alabama library, have both been important to me in my research.

James M. Babcock, one-time chief of the Burton Collection of the Detroit Public Library, made it possible for me to obtain microfilm of the Edith Moodie English translation of Iberville's Gulf Journals, which I collated with my own English translation.

The reference librarians at Florida State University, Tulane University, and the University of Southern Illinois, Edwardsville, most pleasantly gave assistance during my research.

Dr. John Francis McDermott, whom many consider the dean of American scholars in Mississippi Valley French culture, has been a good and encouraging friend ever since I began to do research and to write in this field.

Dr. Douglas F. Munch photographed several of the illustrations appearing in this book, and I appreciate his enthusiastic and capable assistance.

Finally, I am very grateful indeed to Tennant S. McWilliams for writing an introduction for "Iberville's Gulf Journals."

R. G. M.

Avertissement au Lecteur

I have tried to avoid destroying the tone of Iberville's dictation. There are a few long and awkward sentences in the French text which I have translated without improvement. Many proper nouns are spelled in several different ways just as they appeared in the manuscripts of the Journals.

R. G. M.

Introduction

Pierre LeMoyne d'Iberville and the Competition for Empire

TENNANT S. McWILLIAMS

Europe's expansion into the new world during the sixteenth, seventeenth, and eighteenth centuries was a story of power alignment and cultural transmission as well as dramatic individual effort. Spain had her *conquistadores,* France her *coureurs de bois,* and England her sea dogs. Isolated from the authority of home governments, tempted by the abundance of gold, fur, and fish in the new world, these adventurers so vital to national policies of expansion developed their own personal creeds of conquest and colonization. Their individual exploits not only represent a humanistic theme essential in Europe's movement westward but heighten the analyses of cultural institutions of the era. It is within such a multidisciplinary light that one can experience the Gulf coast adventures of Pierre LeMoyne d'Iberville.

Iberville's father was Charles LeMoyne, who arrived in New France (Canada) in 1641 as an indentured servant, lived as a missionary, fur trader, and Indian fighter, and died in 1685 one of the wealthiest, most powerful citizens in Montreal. He and his wife, Catherine Thierry, produced thirteen children. Although all eleven boys saw battle in the French conquest of Canada, it was Pierre, born around 1661, who overcame a lack of formal education and the social stigma of a paternity suit to develop his reputation as the first Canadian hero.[1]

---

[1]Iberville's family background and early years are summarized in Nellis M. Crouse, *LeMoyne d'Iberville: Soldier of New France* (Ithaca, N.Y., 1954), pp. 1–14. On the problem of dating Iberville's birth, see Guy Frégault, *Pierre LeMoyne D'Iberville* (Montreal, 1968), p. 37.

King William's War, known in Europe as the War of the
League of Augsburg, provided much of the background for
Iberville's early exploits. When William III of England resisted
Louis XIV's invasion of the Rhenish Palatinate, hostilities
inevitably broke out between French and English colonials in
North America.[2] By that time, Iberville had already had some
four years of experience in the Hudson Bay area fighting on
behalf of the Compagnie du Nord and its strategy to obstruct
the English fur trade.[3] So in 1690, with King William's War one
year under way, he was named second in command under
Count Frontenac and helped lead the defeat of the English at
Corlaer (Schenectady, New York), one of the most brutal
massacres of the colonial wars. Iberville's growing reputation
as a shrewd tactician and a cruel fighter led to another ad-
vancement in 1694, when he commanded the attack against the
English at York Fort on the Hudson Bay. There he routed the
enemy (though the English reclaimed the fort the following
year) and captured a considerable number of furs, which he
sold for his own personal gain.[4] Next he had the task of
expelling the English from New Foundland, an area of great
importance in the fishing industry. In some four months of
raiding during 1695 he not only destroyed thirty-six English
settlements in New Foundland, killing 200 and imprisoning
700, but managed on his own to sell 200,000 quintals of cod.
These victories, at least for the government of France, were
short-lived. Following the general pattern of Anglo-French
conflict in North America, Iberville's return to Hudson Bay
resulted in reinstitution of English control over the New
Foundland fisheries.[5] His last activities in the northern section

---

[2]The standard work on the colonial wars is Howard H. Peckham, *The Colonial
Wars* (Chicago, 1964).
[3]Herbert Eugene Bolton and Thomas Maitland Marshall, *The Colonization of
North America, 1492-1783* (New York, 1920), pp. 260-67; Crouse, *d'Iberville*,
pp. 14-66.
[4]W. J. Eccles, *Canada under Louis XIV, 1663-1701* (Toronto, 1964), pp. 196-99;
idem, *France in America* (New York, 1969), pp. 90-117; Crouse, *d'Iberville*, pp.
67-117.
[5]This account of Iberville's ravaging of New Foundland is taken from *Diction-*

of the continent, in 1697, bore similar fate. In the forty-four-gun *Pelican* he defeated England's fifty-six-gun man-of-war, the *Hampshire*, a naval duel guaranteeing French control of the Hudson Bay, and then took the important trading post Fort Nelson (Fort Bourbon). Yet that same year the Treaty of Ryswick, ending King William's War, virtually ignored French advances in Canada and reflected instead developments in the European theater. The Hudson Bay, where Iberville had become known as "the most famous son of New France," ironically remained *status quo antebellum* and an area under no nation's effective control until 1763, when England would gain clear title to Canada.[6]

Although many citizens of New France felt frustrated over such unrewarded sacrifices in the cause of French colonialism,[7] Iberville did not. For him, fame, personal gain, and the adventure of fighting were ends in themselves. So with a whetted appetite and a desire for action in warmer climates, this soldier of fortune, now thirty-seven years old, responded enthusiastically to his new assignment: the northern littoral of the Gulf of Mexico.

The Gulf had been an area of concern for Louis XIV for some fourteen years. In 1684 he had sent the explorer LaSalle to establish a colony at the mouth of the Mississippi; his goal was to control the Mississippi Valley fur trade and provide a base for defense against Spanish and English encroachment. Although LaSalle had located the mouth of the Mississippi two years earlier by traveling out of Canada down the river, in 1684 a series of setbacks—sea wrecks, disease, hostile Indians, and

ary of Canadian Biography, s.v. "d'Iberville, LeMoyne" (hereafter cited as *DCB*). See also Eccles, *France in America*, p. 100; Crouse, *d'Iberville*, pp. 119–38.
[6]Crouse, *d'Iberville*, pp. 138–54; Eccles, *France in America*, pp. 100–07, 178–208; Francis Parkman, *Count Frontenac and New France under Louis XIV* (Boston, 1880), pp. 391–93. Signed in 1763, the Treaty of Paris, ending the French and Indian War (the Seven Years War), provided that France cede to England all claims to Canada, Acadia, Cape Breton, and the islands of the St. Lawrence.
[7]Eccles, *France in America*, pp. 107–08.

ultimately mutiny—defeated his efforts to locate the river
mouth from the Gulf. Others proposed to continue the search.
It was not until the Treaty of Ryswick, however, and a five-
year cessation of hostilities between France and England, that
Louis XIV could again focus on the project.[8] Iberville, whose
reputation as a fighting man had spread to France, was selected
in 1697 to resume the endeavor. Pontchartrain, French Minister of Marine, gave strong but unencumbering instructions: Go
to the Gulf of Mexico, locate "the mouth [of the Mississippi
River,] . . . select a good site that can be defended with a few
men, and block entry to the river by other nations."[9] When
news of Iberville's charge reached Madrid in early 1698,
Andrés de Arriola was ordered out of Vera Cruz to fortify the
Spanish post at Pensacola, where the Frenchman was expected to land. As Herbert Eugene Bolton observes, the movement was timely: Iberville was two months behind Arriola.[10]
What happened when Iberville reached the Gulf coast and
during the next four years of his operations from Pensacola to
present-day New Orleans can be experienced through Iberville's own words. After writing daily logs, he later, in France,
dictated to a scribe three journals covering the Gulf exploits.
Although the journals were intended as official reports for the
French Minister of Marine, they provide a microcosm of the
competition for empire and a chronicle, in fascinating detail, of

---

[8]In 1690 LaSalle's brother, the Abbé Cavelier, called for the renewal of the
Mississippi project and four years later Tonty actually filed in his own interests
for permission to do so. In 1697 Sieur d'Argaud asked for a territorial grant
between Florida and New Mexico, and the Gulf and the Illinois River. Among
all these requests was the argument that France needed to block Spanish
advances in North America. See Bolton and Marshall, *Colonization,* p. 275;
DCB, s.v. "Cavelier de La Salle, René-Robert."
[9]*DCB,* s.v. "d'Iberville, LeMoyne."
[10]Bolton and Marshall, *Colonization,* pp. 275–76. See also Irving A. Leonard,
"Pensacola's First Spanish Period (1698–1763)," in James R. McGovern, ed.,
Colonial Pensacola (Hattiesburg, Miss., 1972), pp. 28–31; and Jack D. L.
Holmes, "Dauphin Island's Critical Years: 1701–1722," *Alabama Historical
Quarterly* 29 (Spring and Summer 1967): 39–43.

what daily life was like as a representative of the old world encountered life in the new world. This book permits the journals to appear in their first scholarly translation into English.[11]

Journal 1 (December 31, 1698 through May 31, 1699) picks up the expedition as it approached the Gulf coast one month out of Brest, France. After observing Spanish installations at Pensacola, Iberville moved his three ships down the coast to the entrance of Mobile Bay, where he used a longboat to search for evidence that the river emptying into the bay might be the east branch of the Mississippi; it was this branch, he reckoned, that LaSalle had followed to reach the Gulf in 1682. Finding no such evidence in Mobile Bay, he relocated his base of operations off an island on the south side of Mississippi Sound, now called Ship Island. Here, with safe anchorage in deep water, he moved ashore once again in longboats and canoes to reconnoiter for the Mississippi's mouth. Exploring on the north shore of the sound, Iberville made his first contact with the local Indians, who greeted his men with a "belly-rub" ceremony. On this shore, too, Iberville first encountered the word *Malbanchya*, the name several southern tribes used for the Mississippi River. As he explored the coastline inside the Chandeleur Islands, he found what appeared to be a headland of black rocks that he feared would wreck his small boats—the obstruction that had kept Spanish navigators and perhaps LaSalle from entering the mouth of the Mississippi. With increasing seas, he faced a choice of running before the wind, risking conditions that could capsize his boats, or making a run for the shore where the black rocks stood. He chose the latter course, and, partly by luck, emerged through the East Pass of the Mississippi (now

---

[11]For a summary English-language version of Iberville's Gulf activities, see Crouse, *d'Iberville*, pp. 155–241. Crouse's account does not appear to be based on Iberville's journals but upon two secondary versions by Benjamin F. French and Pierre Margry. In the Burton Collection of the Detroit Public Library there is an English translation (unpub. MS.) of Iberville's Gulf journals rendered by Edith Moodie, a British translator.

called the North Pass) and into twelve to fifteen feet of muddy
and white water, what LaSalle had described as "toute bourbeuse et blanche." This led Iberville to suspect that the Malbanchya might be the Mississippi.[12]
    Iberville then journeyed up the river in search of conclusive
evidence that it, indeed, was the Mississippi. At every Indian
village, he inquired about LaSalle and his companion, Henri de
Tonty; he was especially interested in locating the Quinipissas
tribe mentioned in LaSalle's records. The higher he went
upriver, the more he decried the writers of false narratives of
this area. At a point slightly above the Houmas' upper landing,
he decided, in low spirits, to turn back. The only fork the
Indians could tell him about was downriver, where a small
distributary parted from the main stream. Although this
branch was clogged with roots and logs, Iberville had to determine if this might be considered an east fork of the river.
Sending the bulk of the party on downriver under M. de
Sauvole, he took four men and an Indian guide to explore the
unknown distributary. The side journey disclosed two lakes,
now called Maurepas and Pontchartrain, and, with considerable portages, a rough passage to his Ship Island anchorage.
There was no mistaking this course for a navigable fork of the
Mississippi. Yet when Iberville rejoined the rest of the excursion party at the ships, his disappointment turned to excitement
with the news that the larger group had discovered a letter left
by Tonty for LaSalle, dated "Village of Quynpyssa, April 20,
1685." They had obtained the letter from the chief of the
Mougoulachas. It proved that the mysterious Quinipissas were
in fact the Mougoulachas, which in turn proved that Iberville
had found the Mississippi River, which was the Malbanchya as

---

[12]For more on the discovery of the mouth of the Mississippi from the Gulf,
especially on the role of mud lumps in frustrating Spanish and French expeditions, see Richebourg Gaillard McWilliams, "Iberville at the Birdfoot Subdelta," in John Francis McDermott, ed., *Frenchmen and French Ways in the
Mississippi Valley* (Urbana, Ill., 1969), pp. 127–40. See also Irving A. Leonard,
trans. and ed., *Spanish Approach to Pensacola* (Albuquerque, N.M., 1939), pp.
9–10.

well as what the Spanish called the Río de la Palizada. Having discovered the Mississippi by navigation through the Gulf of Mexico, Iberville erected a fort on Biloxi Bay, naming it Fort Maurepas. The fort was garrisoned with some eighty men, including Iberville's brother, Jean-Baptiste LeMoyne de Bienville. Leaving the fort under the command of Sauvole, Iberville, on May 3, 1699, sailed out into the Gulf for France.[13]

In France, Iberville was awarded the cross of the Order of Saint-Louis, the first man of Canadian birth to receive such an honor. Still, he failed to convince authorities that they should launch immediately into a full-scale colonial activity in Louisiana. France's limited financial resources and her need to avoid offending Spain, a nation connected to France in the complicated issue of Spanish succession and a nation that also claimed Louisiana, prompted French officials to reject Iberville's plea. Nevertheless, Iberville's argument that French presence on the Gulf coast was needed to block English expansion beyond the Carolinas showed a prescience confirmed by the War of the Spanish Succession to begin in 1702; and even before this time, in 1699, his views so impressed authorities that they reassigned him to the Gulf. Iberville was to explore further and to indulge in covert activities designed to discourage English influence.[14] To a leader who had fought in the Hudson Bay and along the Atlantic coast and who simply hated the English, this must have been a welcome instruction. And in the back of his mind he no doubt hoped that further exploration ultimately would result in a major effort at colonization when the international scene was right.

Iberville headed back to the Gulf in October 1699. What happened to him and his men with these new orders is re-

[13]Sauvole's career is traced in Jay Higginbotham, "Who Was Sauvole?" *Louisiana Studies* 7 (1968): 144–58; and in idem, trans. and ed., *The Journal of Sauvole* (Mobile, 1969). Tonty's life is summarized in *DCB*, s.v. "Tonty, Henri (de)"; Bienville's many adventures are recorded in *DCB*, s.v. "De Bienville, Jean-Baptiste LeMoyne." The founding of the Biloxi base is considered in Jay Higginbotham, *Fort Maurepas: The Birth of Louisiana* (Mobile, 1968).
[14]Crouse, *d'Iberville*, pp. 196–202.

counted in Journal 2 (December 22, 1699 through May 28, 1700). On arriving off Biloxi in January 1700, he received news that an English corvette had made its way twenty-five leagues up the Mississippi. Although Bienville had bluffed the vessel out of the river, reports of English activity confirmed Iberville's suspicion and pointed up the need for a second French fort, this one on the lower Mississippi, to prevent the vessels of unfriendly powers from going upstream. He also learned that during his absence two French missionaries, Father Montigny and Father Davion, had come out of Canada to work among the Taensas and the Tonicas Indians, and the latter had reported that English agents were living among the Chickasaws. Anxious about this news, Iberville assigned Bienville to select a site for the second fort, one that would not flood. What ultimately came of this mission was the construction of Fort Boulaye, commonly called Fort Mississippi. Although the fort flooded on occasion, sometimes by as much as several inches, it endured and became the scene of much activity: Pierre-Charles LeSueur stopped there on his way to exploit the mineral potential of the upper Mississippi; so too did Juchereau de St. Denis, the French diplomat to the Indians, as well as Tonty and many other Canadians and Frenchmen looking for work at the new posts.[15]

Needing to explore the Mississippi higher and to learn more about the Indians of the region and their contact with the English and the Spanish, Iberville left the river fort and journeyed to the Natchez and the Taensas. Bienville, who had acquired considerable knowledge of Indian languages during his years on the Gulf coast, accompanied his brother. In his visits among the Taensas, Iberville also benefited by the guidance and translation of Father Montigny. From these three men come vivid portraits of Indian life in the Mississippi Valley of the early eighteenth century. Especially interesting is the

---

[15]For information on the French missionaries François Jolliet de Montigny and Albert Davion see footnotes on page 109. St. Denis appears in *DCB*, s.v. "Juchereau de St. Denis, Louis." Le Sueur's life is sketched in *DCB*, s.v. "Le Sueur, Pierre-Charles."

account of five Taensas women who, desiring to appease the
gods and find greater social status within their community, cast
their suckling children into a fire. Also noteworthy, for what it
reveals about different cultures in intersection for the first time,
is an account of conflict that developed when Father Montigny
persuaded the Taensas to forsake their custom of killing persons close to a chief who had recently died.[16] Although Iberville
thrived on these experiences and wanted more, his personal
activities were limited by sickness. Hence, when his energy
lapsed, he sent Bienville with twenty men to explore areas
difficult to traverse. Bienville's report of Indians to the west of
the Mississippi River stands as an important documentary
report in Journal 2.

The second exploration concludes with two dramatic events.
In heading out the East Pass of the Mississippi on the way to
his ships, Iberville's smack struck one of the black rocks or
"petrified trees" which was even with the surface of the water.
Although the vessel struck athwart, it cleared without scraping
badly. The rocks that had discouraged two nations from Mississippi exploration, Iberville concluded, were nothing more
than mud.[17] Back at his ship, Iberville discovered that during
the excursion upriver, Spaniards (considered less of a threat
than the English) had come in force to drive his garrison away.
Yet when the Spanish commander found two well-armed
French frigates at Ship Island, he did no more than write an
injunction against further fortifications and sail proudly away,
only to wreck his main ship on Chandeleur Island, losing
everything, even clothes. The Spaniards then had to subdue
their pride and accept food and clothing from Iberville's men.
Such were the ways of international conflict in early eigh-
teenth-century America.

By late May 1700 Iberville was on his way back to France;
the voyage (but not the Journal) included a slight detour to
New York, where the soldier of fortune peddled some nine

[16]Richebourg Gaillard McWilliams, "Iberville and the Southern Indians," *The Alabama Review* 20 (1967): 243–62.
[17]See McWilliams, "Iberville at the Birdfoot Subdelta," p. 139.

thousand pelts bought from Canadian trappers working the
Mississippi Valley.[18] In France from August 1700 to September 1701, Iberville again lobbied for a stronger French commit-
ment to Louisiana. The development of the fur trade there
helped draw Canadians southward as a check against English
expansion. The founding of a strong naval base at Mobile
represented a logical response to Spain's continued hostility
toward French presence along the Gulf coast—a hostility that
had not eased even though Louis XIV's grandson, Philip V,
had taken Bourbon influences to the throne of Spain in 1700.
Such a base also would protect French interests against Spanish expansion if for some unforeseen reason war developed
between the two nations. Iberville must have been persuasive.
The crown called for still another expedition, this one to establish a permanent colony on the Gulf, and also to continue
building anti-British sentiment among the Indians.[19] Iberville
left France on September 29.

Journal 3 (December 15, 1701 through April 27, 1702) traces
this third and final expedition. Iberville made landfall at Pensacola with the hope that the Spanish, in a spirit of cooperation
stemming from their new crown, would at least provide him
with civilized refuge while he completed recovery from an
abscess in his side. He found the Pensacola base in wretched
condition and the Spanish soldiers openly hostile to what they
perceived to be intrusion on the part of the French. Still, for
two months Iberville was allowed to rest at Pensacola on board
his ship, during which time—and directly under the eye of the
Spanish—he supervised the establishment of a major French
base.

Because of the shallow water between Ship Island and Fort

---

[18]*DCB*, s.v. "d'Iberville, LeMoyne"; Crouse, *d'Iberville*, pp. 219–21. For unknown reasons, while Iberville was at New York he devoted one full month to
taking soundings of the harbor. Some have suggested that he was accumulating
data with an eye to the day when France might have New York. It also is
possible that Iberville, out of intense dislike for the English, was indulging in a
bit of harassment.

[19]*DCB*, s.v. "d'Iberville, LeMoyne."

Biloxi, as well as the unhealthy conditions of these low-lying spots, Iberville had orders to place his new effort twenty-six leagues north of Massacre Island (now Dauphin Island) up Mobile Bay, on the high ground overlooking the Mobile River, at a location on the west bank called Twenty-Seven-Mile Bluff. Bienville, the new commandant at Biloxi, was instructed to move everything from his fort to a way station on the south side of Massacre Island, where a snug little harbor had been located and a warehouse was to be constructed. Satisfying this command, Bienville proceeded up the Mobile River to the prescribed bluff to deposit four families Iberville had brought from France and to lay the basic construction for a colony. With the project two months underway, Iberville had recovered sufficiently at Pensacola to join the operation. After inspecting the completed warehouse at Massacre, he proceeded up the bay to the mouth of a small river, Rivière-aux-Chiens (now Dog River), where he established a second way station. At Twenty-Seven-Mile Bluff he found the work moving smoothly. Fort Louis de la Louisiane, he announced, would be the name of this settlement; it would be called La Mobile.[20]

The remainder of the expedition—some three months—Iberville devoted to food, lodging, and Indian relations. Corn, he hoped, could be grown easily on fields once used by Indians. Even more corn might be found through trading with Indians. The commander tried but failed to find a stream with sufficient power to run a sawmill. Although his Indian operations had the clear strategy of blocking an expansion of British influence in the area, they also demonstrate certain aspects of Indian life along the Mobile and Alabama rivers. On one of the islands in the Mobile River, Iberville gave an Indian a gun in return for directions to a hidden place where gods were supposedly located. The guide did indeed show the way to five figures made of plaster, but would approach them only by walking backwards and, at that, would move no closer than ten feet from the idols. Yet if there were incidents indicating the Indians' cultural isolation, there also were episodes foreshadowing Euro-

---

[20]See Jay Higginbotham, *Old Mobile: Fort Louis de la Louisiane* (Mobile, 1977).

pean conquest. Chickasaws and Choctaws, whom the British had manipulated into war, were invited through a visit by Tonty to come to La Mobile for a peacemaking conference. Iberville's purpose was to weld these groups into an effective counter to the English. Increasingly knowledgeable on the subject of Indian practices, the commander decided on a long speech delineating the reasons for peace: His main point, delivered through Bienville's translation, was that the English had encouraged Chickasaws to attack Choctaws as a means of weakening Chickasaw power, and when that power was sufficiently reduced, the English would wipe out the Chickasaws or sell them as slaves in the Indies. His plea was eloquent and followed by valuable gifts. It also was futile. The Chickasaws would remain within British hegemony and, in fact, defeat French soldiers on two subsequent occasions. Ignorant of this pending failure, Iberville departed from La Mobile in April 1702 with a certain buoyancy. He had met his charge, he thought, and in returning to Pensacola to prepare for the voyage to France he also managed to acquire for his personal disposal a large load of beaver pelts brought out of the Mississippi Valley by Canadian voyageurs. The soldier of fortune rarely missed an opportunity.

Iberville did not return to the Gulf coast. After three years in France, he completed his fascinating career with a Caribbean tour de force. The War of Spanish Succession pitted England against France over the future of the Spanish crown; Iberville was assigned to assault the British island of Nevis, where he made prisoners of the entire population, over seven thousand, and looted ruthlessly.[21] That same year, 1706, he died suddenly at Havana after what may have been a bout with malaria.[22] His wife, Marie-Thérèse Pollet, and his five children

---

[21]Crouse, *d'Iberville*, describes the Nevis assignment, pp. 253–65.

[22]It is conjecture that Iberville died of malaria or of yellow fever. As Guy Frégault writes, "Une autre question se pose au sujet de ce qui a amené sa mort. L'opinion générale est qu'il succomba à une épidémie. Ce n' est pas avec les documents que nous avons que nous pouvons l'affirmer de façon absolument catégorique" (*D'Iberville*, p. 272). Cf. Crouse, *d'Iberville*, p. 266; Higgin-

were left with thirty years of court proceedings as the French government attempted to recoup the small fortune that Iberville had accumulated while mixing questionable business with French expansion.[23]

Writings on the career of Pierre LeMoyne d'Iberville generally have failed to treat the man in broad historical perspective. Before the 1940s, there were some ten studies of Iberville, recently described as "religio-nationalistic panegyrics."[24] Then in 1944 a Canadian scholar, Guy Frégault, published *Iberville le conquérant*, a scholarly if at times melodramatic assessment.[25] Ten years later Nellis M. Crouse, of Cornell University, offered *Le Moyne d'Iberville: Soldier of New France*, the best full-length English language biography of Iberville. Yet the most searching analysis of Iberville's significance is Bernard Pothier's essay, "Le Moyne d'Iberville," published in 1968 in the *Dictionary of Canadian Biography*. Pothier calls for a redefinition of "the place of Iberville in the context of North America in the 17th and 18th centuries." Iberville's Gulf journals should be read with an eye to that goal.

The Gulf journals permit an appreciation of Iberville within the broad, comparative-culture perception of early American history. Recent comparative scholarship has focused on Spanish, Portuguese, English, and, to an extent, French institutions that developed in the new world after initial exploration and settlement, especially labor and agricultural institutions. Much could be gained, however, from a similar approach to the

---

botham, *Old Mobile*, p. 284. Whatever disease killed Iberville struck quickly. He died aboard his flagship on July 9, 1706, having made his will in the presence of a notary and having received the rites of the church. On the same day he was buried in the parochial church of San Cristoval, the church record listing him as "El General Don Pedro Barbila." The precise burial site remains unknown, for the church was removed in 1741.

[23]*DCB*, s.v. "d'Iberville, LeMoyne."

[24]*DCB*, s.v. "d'Iberville, LeMoyne," where a list of early writings on Iberville can also be found.

[25]Frégault's *Iberville le conquérant* was revised as *Pierre LeMoyne D'Iberville* (Montreal, 1968).

experiences of the early explorer-colonizers such as Iberville.[26]
While the Caribbean offers an ideal setting for such study, it
being an area that the powers occupied simultaneously, so does
the northern littoral of the Gulf of Mexico.[27] Indeed, one
following Iberville cannot but notice that French, Spanish, and
English were in the same area at the same time and after the
same thing: empire.

Iberville's journals, moreover, provide examples of how such
comparative study might proceed. His Indian observations,
besides aiding the ethnologist's search of certain tribes at specific points in time, support the classic account of English and
French reactions to the red man: Englishmen killed the Indian
or pushed him westward; Frenchmen attempted to use him in
anti-English diplomacy, and when that failed usually left him
alone.[28] The journals also suggest a diplomatic comparison.
Although "defensive expansion" has long been considered an

[26]Much of the groundwork for a comparative approach to early American
history was established through a powerful dialogue of the 1930s and 1940s:
See Herbert Eugene Bolton, "The Epic of Greater America," *American
Historical Review* 38 (1933): 448–74; and Edmundo O'Gorman, "Do the
Americas Have a Common History?" in *Points of View*, no. 3 (Washington,
1941), pp. 1–10. This seminal exchange is continued in Lewis Hanke, ed., *Do
the Americas Have a Common History? A Critique of the Bolton Thesis* (New
York, 1964); and in John J. Tepaske, ed., *Three American Empires* (New York,
1967). On specific comparative problems, see for example David W. Cohen and
Jack P. Greene, eds., *Neither Slave Nor Free: The Freedman of African Descent
in the Slave Societies of the New World* (Baltimore, 1972); Eugene Genovese and
Elizabeth Fox Genovese, "The Slave Economies in Historical Perspective,"
Journal of American History 66 (1979): 12–13, 17–18. For illustration of a
comparative approach to early Gulf coast history, see James T. McGowan,
"Planters without Slaves: Origins of a New World Labor System," *Southern
Studies* 16 (1977): 5–26; and Jack D. L. Holmes, "Naval Stores in Colonial
Louisiana and the Floridas," *Louisiana Studies* 7 (1968): 295–309.
[27]Tepaske, *Three American Empires*, p. 5; and idem, "French, Spanish, and
English Indian Policy on the Gulf Coast, 1513–1763: A Comparison," in
Ernest F. Dibble and Earle W. Newton, eds., *Spain and Her Rivals on the Gulf
Coast* (Pensacola, 1971), p. 9.
[28]Tepaske, *Three American Empires*, p. 5; Tepaske, "Indian Policy," p. 36. See
also Wilcomb E. Washburn, "The Moral and Legal Justification for Dispos-

important aspect of Spain's North America strategy, Iberville's experience shows that France used the same tactic, and against both Spain and England.[29] In this comparative light, Iberville's personality warrants probing, too. Iberville represented, not a culture evolving rapidly toward parliamentary rights, such as England possessed, but instead a society still firmly committed to absolute political and religious authority. Hence in "uncivilized" America, Iberville presided over his expedition with a French absolutism considered harsh next to an English colonizer's participatory decision-making. Climate and geography are still other factors which the comparing observer will notice in these journals. Although European colonizers encountered a spectrum of rough terrain below the Río Grande—deserts, mountains, jungles—in North America they had a less difficult time.[30] Granted, Iberville found unpleasant winters in Canada, unpredictable water levels on the Gulf coast, and ultimately may have died because of the mosquito. Still, he moved with relative ease through the bays and rivers of the Gulf coast and found plentiful food. As a result he and other Frenchmen, not to mention Spaniards, quickly infused the Mississippi Valley and the Gulf coast with their own cultures, an influence that lasted long after formal English control came to North America.[31]

sessing the Indians," in James Morton Smith, ed., *Seventeenth Century America: Essays in Colonial History* (Chapel Hill, 1959).

[29]Herbert Eugene Bolton, *The Spanish Borderlands* (New Haven, 1921), pp. 207–08, 234–35, 255–58; idem, "Defensive Spanish Expansion and the Significance of the Borderlands," in John Francis Bannon, ed., *Bolton and the Borderlands* (Norman, 1964), pp. 32–66. For an examination of the long term significance of "defensive expansion" in France's Gulf policy—although this term is not employed—see Donald J. Lemieux, "The Mississippi Valley, New France, and French Colonial Policy," *Southern Studies* 17 (1978): 50–53, 56.

[30]Tepaske, *Three American Empires*, pp. 3–4.

[31]The enduring impact of the French influence along the Gulf coast is illustrated in Samuel Wilson, Jr., "Gulf Coast Architecture," in Dibble and Newton, eds., *Spain and Her Rivals*, pp. 78–126; and in Marie S. Dunn, "A Comparative Study: Louisiana's French and Anglo-Saxon Cultures," *Louisiana Studies* 10 (1971): 131–69. A good guide for related research materials is

In short, a reassessment of the expeditions of early Gulf coast colonizers such as Iberville—not just Frenchmen, but other Europeans, too—poses a provocative application of the comparative approach to early American history. Especially through their journals and memoirs might one find clues to the evolution of a perplexing heterogeneity and internationalism in the culture of the American South. Equally important, this particular social science endeavor, unlike some, would be exciting history, for it would be drawn from day-by-day accounts of rugged individual Europeans as the old world extended its ways into America.[32]

Ernest F. Dibble and Earle W. Newton, eds., *In Search of Gulf Coast History* (Pensacola, 1970).
[32]Alfred B. Thomas, a Bolton student, ponders related implications of Gulf coast history in "Gulf Coast Colonial History: An Overview," in Dibble and Newton, eds., *Spain and Her Rivals*, pp. 1–8; and in "Colonial United States History: A New Point of View," an address delivered to the Alabama Alpha chapter of Phi Beta Kappa, The University of Alabama, April 9, 1963 (copy in possession of Tennant S. McWilliams, Birmingham, Alabama).

Iberville's Gulf Journals

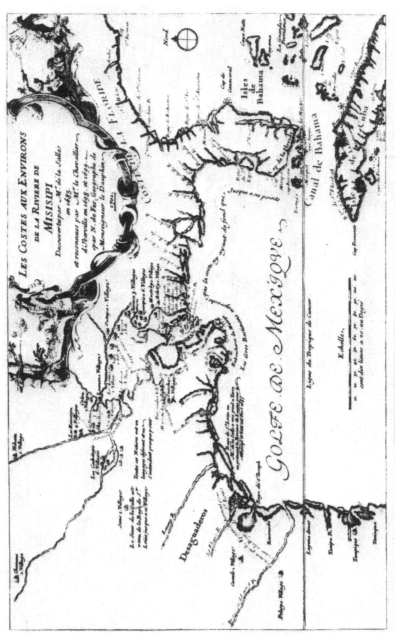

(Photographic reduction by Dr. Douglas F. Munch)

The First Voyage
to the Mississippi

THE JOURNAL OF THE *BADINE*

JOURNAL OF THE VOYAGE MADE
BY d'HIBERVILLE TO THE
SOUTH COAST OF FLORIDA IN 1699

I AM TAKING LEOGANNE as my point of departure.[1] I sailed from there on December 31, 1698, at nine o'clock at night.

The first day of the year 1699 we are at noon at north latitude 19°12' and longitude 301°.[2] I am about 10 leagues west of

---

[1]To take a departure means to sail; but, in the language of navigation, it can mean to begin dead reckoning by fixing one's position while the ship is still within sight of land. Léogane is on the north shore of the southwest peninsula of Haiti, a few miles west of Port-au-Prince. Haiti was called St. Domingue by the French.

[2]The MS. gives the figure 301° of longitude, which is the correct longitude measured east from Tenerife in the Canary Islands. European navigators commonly used Tenerife as their prime meridian before the present use of Greenwich. Iberville is calculating his longitude east around the earth from Tenerife. The Margry text erroneously prints "30 degrees" longitude; see Pierre Margry, *Découvertes et Établissements des Français dans l'Ouest et dans le Sud de l'Amérique Septentrionale (1614–1754)*, 6 vols. (Paris, 1879–1888), 4:131.

Leoganne, 2 leagues out from land, and 1½ leagues off Gouen-ave.[3]

January 2nd, 1699. At noon I am at 18°30′ north and 301°14′ longitude. About six o'clock at night we are 2½ leagues off Nypés,[4] where I have a smack buying fowls for the sick. I sent it from Leoganne for that purpose on December 28th. Immediately after noon, I sent my Biscayan to notify the smack to come out of the harbor and catch up with me. The wind is north, blowing directly into this cove, where the seas are quite heavy and where one should by no means run the risk of anchoring ships unless there is great need. The smack being unable to get underway, I remained under sail all night, along with the *Marain*[5] and the other smack, 3 leagues out from this haven. The *François* sailed on, and we no longer could see it at eight o'clock in the morning. My smack and my Biscayan have caught up with me, bringing 138 fowls, which cost twenty-five livres. They were unable to get more. We are becalmed. On all our ships we have a great many sick, several men being sick of the plague.

The 3rd. At noon we are at 18°40′ and 301°2′ longitude. I am

---

[3]The prominent island northwest of Port-au-Prince and only a few miles out is named Île de la Gonâve or Gonaïves, in the gulf of the same name. For geographical names mentioned here and later as the expedition proceeded along the south coast of Cuba, I have used "West Indies," Atlas Plate 23, Map of the National Geographic Society, 1962; also *The Royal Illustrated Atlas of Modern Geography* (London, 1819), in the Rucker Agee Map Collection of the Birmingham Public Library.

[4]MS.: "Nypés" surely must be related to the Petit Trou de Nippes, which appears to have been formed by the two Cayemites, islands farther west along the shore between Léogane and Cap Dame Marie. The anchorage in question provided access to chickens raised close by. I do not know of any connection that Nippes has with Nipe, the name of the bay on the northeast shore of Cuba, a bay that Admiral Samuel Eliot Morison refers to as one of the best harbors in the world. See *Admiral of the Ocean Sea* (Boston, 1942), p. 264.

[5]The correct spelling of the name of the companion frigate accompanying the *Badine* is *Marin*, but I am leaving the MS. spelling unchanged. The *Marin*, commanded by La Rochefoucault de Surgères, was armed with thirty-odd guns and carried a crew of 130 men. (Guy Frégault, *Iberville le conquérant* [Montreal, 1944], pp. 272–73 and n. 27.) This officer's name is usually given as M. de Surgères or Surgère.

some 4 leagues off the island, to the west of the Caymite[s]. These two islands are each at least 2 leagues long, 1½ leagues from each other, and, apparently, half a league from the big island of St. Domingue. We are finding nothing but calms. Along the land we see a ship sailing east and, 6 leagues north, a vessel sailing west-southwest, at six o'clock at night. We observe that it is the *François,* clearing before the north wind,[5] about which people have much to say in this region.

January 4, 1699. At noon I am at 19° north latitude and 300°30' longitude. Cape St. Nicolas[7] lies 18 leagues northeast by north of us and Cape Dame Marie[8] to the southwest by south. We can see the east end of the island of Cuba, to the east, or at least see high land. From the end of this island to the north-northwest, for more than 15 leagues from here, all the land that I can see of these islands is quite mountainous and, apparently, wretched country. The wind is in the northeast— light wind. The *François* has caught up with us again. We find that the currents are bearing us to the north very fast. Le Vasseur, the master of the big smack, is quite sick, and so is a man by the name of Bourjois, a Canadian.[9] On my ship I have two others badly sick of the plague, and fully ten, besides, sick of fever.

---

[6]A felicitous phrase of the sea taken from the Moodie translation of Margry's *Découvertes et Établissements des Français.* Bernice C. Springer, Chief of the Burton Historical Collection, Detroit Public Library, to Viola W. Harper, Reference Librarian of the University of South Alabama Library, February 22, 1971.
[7]On Guillaume de L'Isle's "Carte du Mexique et de la Floride," 1703, Cape St. Nicolas is shown as the northwest tip of Haiti.
[8]MS.: "Cap d'amarie," a rather good phonetic spelling of Cap Dame Marie, which is the name of the western tip of the southwest peninsula of Haiti and is the northwest point of the tip, as shown on modern maps. The Margry text is corrupt at this passage (4:132).
[9]Surely the name of this sick Canadian must have been Bourgeois, as Margry gave it (4:132). Jacques Bourgeois (1621–1701), a surgeon, founded a large family with his wife and ten children at Port-Royal; still, it cannot be stated with any certainty that the sick Canadian was a member of this family. See the *Dictionary of Canadian Biography,* hereafter cited as *DCB,* s.v. "Bourgeois, Jacques (Jacob)."

The 5th. In these twenty-four hours I find that I have sailed west 3°50' and north 14 leagues 5';[10] consequently, I ought to be at latitude 19°23' and 299°44' longitude. The wind has been in the northeast and east. Light wind. We are running 3 leagues off the island of Cuba. That land appears to be mountainous and arid all along.

The 6th. At noon I found, by my corrected course, that I had sailed west 8° and north 35 leagues; therefore, I should be at latitude 19°30' and longitude 297°57'. At ten o'clock in the morning we were 3 leagues south of Santiaugue,[11] which I find to be at 19°40' north. We could make out quite clearly the towers on the walls defending the entrance to the harbor, which is a small river, at the mouth of which ships anchor. The town is a league farther inland on the bank of the river. This place seems to be a flat country extending for about 4 leagues along the sea and 2 leagues inland, as far as the mountains. The copper mountains[12] are some 4 leagues west of Santiaugue. They are the highest in the vicinity. It is said that they are quite productive and are about 3 leagues from the sea.

January 7th. My corrected course gives me by dead reckoning latitude 19°45' and longitude 296°30'. We are 4 leagues off the island. The land is, all along, quite elevated and mountainous. The coast runs always west, and no point at all juts outward, as far as I can tell. The wind has been east-northeast. Yesterday evening we saw three ships 3 leagues west of us, sailing south as if bound for Jamaica.

The 8th. At noon I find that during these twenty-four hours I have sailed west 18 leagues, by my reckoning, which gives me by dead reckoning latitude 19°37' and longitude 295°35'. In taking the altitude of the sun, using the land 2 leagues from me

[10]MS.: "3 degrés 50 m. nord 14 L⋅ 5m." I do not understand this mixture of degrees, leagues, and minutes.
[11] Santiago de Cuba. On G. de L'Isle's "Carte du Mexique et de la Floride," 1703, the name is written "Sant Iago."
[12]Being 4 leagues west of Santiago would put them in the Sierra Maestra mountains. On the maps I am using I have not been able to find a name in this area suggestive of copper.

as the horizon, I got 19°17'. Cape Cruz[13] lies 3 leagues to the northwest of me. It is low land, on a level with the water, and one can see it from the deck from 3 leagues out. A ship is visible, anchored to the west of the land, about 1 league off shore. On all the charts Cape Cruz is shown at 19°50' at most or 19°45', and I find it at only 19°30' at most, so that the south coast of the island of Cuba is shown to be at least 15' farther north than it is. The distance from Santiaugue to this Cape Cruz I calculate to be only 50 to 55 leagues, the direction being west and west by south. I do not, by any means, find that all these lands are shown in their true longitude; therefore, I am going to take Cape Cruz as my point of departure and my meridian.[14]

The 9th. By my corrected course, beginning with the meridian of Cape Cruz, and by my latitude at noon, 19°18', I find that I have sailed 34 leagues west-southwest and that I am, therefore, at latitude 19° and am 1°46' west of Cape Cruz. At two in the afternoon we sighted Little Cayman[15] from the main-top, about 6 leagues west-northwest of us; therefore, by my reckoning, I shall find the south coast at 19°8' and the east end 2°4' west of Cape Cruz. This island is believed to be at 19°30' north. I do not know what to believe, for Cape Cruz is believed to be 25' farther north than it is. Sailing from 3 leagues off Cape Cruz, steering west by south, I passed 2½ leagues to the south of this island; and M. de Chasteaumorand,[16] to whom I have

[13]The most southerly part of Cuba, a large cape jutting prominently out into the Caribbean Sea at a point 200 miles west of the Windward Passage.
[14]But Iberville was to use Cape Cruz only a short while as his meridian. Cabo San Antonio, at the west end of Cuba, was to serve him longer.
[15]Cayman (Sp. *caiman*) originated from the Carib Indian language. It was used by Indians and Spaniards for several American crocodiles of tropical waters and by the French for alligators. Little Cayman and Cayman Brac lie northeast by east of Grand Cayman, the three islands being almost due west of Cape Cruz, at a distance of some 170 miles, and almost due south of the Bahía de Cochinos (the Bay of Pigs).
[16]The captain of the *François,* a French warship that convoyed Iberville's frigates and the two smacks until they were safely beyond the English and the Spaniards, was the Marquis Joubert de Châteaumorant et de la Bastide. Nellis

just spoken, asking him what bearing he would give it, told me that this island bore 15 leagues west-southwest of them, and we have found it 5 or 6 leagues to the west-northwest. Whereupon he told me that the currents had carried them south, which I doubt. I have found my reckoning accurate in locating this island farther south in proportion to other lands. M. de Grafes,[17] who has had experience with those charts, assures me that he has taken an altitude from above it giving 19°30′ north, and tells me besides that this island lies 40 leagues west by south of Cape Cruz. This gave me a bearing 24′ farther south than Cape Cruz. This is a contradiction and cannot be so, for Cape Cruz is no more than 19°25′ or 30′ at most. He assures me that he has noticed that the currents ordinarily run west-northwest, which, on this course, can make a difference of 2 or 3 leagues farther north if one runs this course with a fair wind, especially since the currents are inconstant and unknown.

The 10th. At noon my corrected course gives me, by dead reckoning, latitude 19°55′ and 3°16′ west of Cape Cruz. The wind is south-southwest and southwest with fog.

The 11th. At noon I found that during these twenty-four hours I ran 17½ leagues west by south, which gives me, by dead reckoning, latitude 19°45′ and 4°12′ west of my meridian. The wind has shifted from southwest to west and northwest. We took two reefs in our topsails. This morning I hoisted my Biscayan aboard. I have it on one side and my other longboat on the other; the middle of the ship is clear.

The 12th. At noon my corrected course for these twenty-four hours gives me, by dead reckoning, latitude 20°4′ and longitude

---

M. Crouse, *Lemoyne d'Iberville: Soldier of New France* (Ithaca, N.Y., 1954), p. 167; and Marcel Giraud, *Histoire de la Louisiane Française,* vol. 1, *Le Règne de Louis XIV (1698–1715),* (Paris, 1953), p. 357.

[17]Laurent de Graff, a famous corsair who was brought along on the Iberville expedition from St. Domingue because he was supposed to have knowledge of Gulf waters. Frégault, *Iberville,* pp. 292–93; Ducasse au Ministre de la Marine, January 13, 1699, in Margry, 4:93; and M. de Chasteaumorant au Ministre de la Marine, June 23, 1699, in Margry, 4:103.

4°55' west of Cape Cruz. These twenty-four hours the wind has shifted from north to north-northeast, the weather being overcast as it is in Canada during autumn. We feel a little cold—enough to put on woolen jackets in place of linen. From the 12th to the 13th. At noon I have found that I have run northwest 2°30' and 28⅓ leagues north; therefore, I am at latitude 21°, and 6° west of my meridian. The wind has been north-northeast, a rather fresh gale.

The 14th. At noon my corrected course gives me, by dead reckoning, latitude 21°20' and longitude 6°15' west of Cape Cruz. At noon I am 1½ leagues east-southeast of Cape Corriente,[18] where I took the altitude: 21°18'. To a depth of 1 league back from the shore, this coast is so low—without high ground from Philippe Bay[19] to Cape Corriente—that, from the sea, it can be seen from the deck no farther out than 3½ leagues at most. One league east of Cape Corriente stands a quite noticeable hook of white sand. From the cape to this sandy hook the coast lies east and west; and from this hook to Philippe Bay the coast runs about 12 leagues northeast by east. Cape Corriente is a low point on which is visible a mound of

---

[18]Cape Corriente or, in Spanish, Cabo Corrientes was the last prominent point that Iberville would sight before coming to Cabo San Antonio at the west end of Cuba. On the course set for Cape Corrientes the two smacks had proved to be such poor sailors that Châteaumorant and Surgères had towed one each with the *François* and the *Marin*. (M. de Chasteaumorant au Ministre de la Marine, June 23, 1699, in Margry, 4:104). The word *smack* as a translation of *traversier* is taken from Edith Moodie's translation of Margry. I had been planning to use *transport* as the translation but abandoned that word because it connotes troop-carrying, whereas the *traversiers* in question were supply ships. Many writers have used *traversier* itself, and a few have used *ferry*, which is a poor choice because ferries are boats that make regular short crossings of rivers and small bays; Iberville's *traversiers*, of course, sailed the Atlantic Ocean. For the problem of understanding French names for small craft, see N. M. Miller Surrey, *The Commerce of Louisiana during the French Régime, 1699–1763* (New York, 1916), pp. 55–81.

[19]Phillip Bay may be the waters of the west end of the Golfo de Batahanó, which are bounded on the south by six to eight islands marked Cayos de San Felipe on the "West Indies" map of the National Geographic Society, 1962.

bleak stones piled on top of one another, rising 12 or 15 feet, upon which stands a cross. Here a lookout stays in time of war. The seashore is a barren, rocky country,[20] with few trees, but trees are visible 1 league inland.

From Cape Corriente the coast runs north-northwest for 1 league and north-northeast for 2½ leagues, forming a bay; and the land runs west-southwest to within 2 leagues of Cape San Antonio. It appears to me that one has to run only some 10 or 11 leagues west and west by south from Cape Corriente to get to Cape San Antonio. We passed the night without making headway with a fair wind from the east-northeast, the pilot of the *François* keeping close to the land and I 10 leagues out.

The 15th. From noon till eight o'clock last night I was 1 league to the south of Cape San Antonio, at latitude 21°30′ and longitude 6°45′ west of Cape Cruz.[21] All night we lay to, the *François* expecting to double this cape. At seven o'clock in the morning Cape San Antonio lay 1 league east of us. Coming from Cape Corriente, one can run close to this cape, half a league out, and less, as far as 1 league from Colorado Point,[22] off which there are shoals 1 league and 1¼ leagues out, which one can come close to by sounding. From Cape San Antonio to Colorado Point the coast keeps turning from north by west to north by east for the 2½ leagues from one to the other. All these lands are low. There is no danger. Leaving Cape San Antonio at night, steering a course north by west, you clear Colorado

---

[20]MS.: "Le rivage de la mer est un pais plé, de roche, peu de boys." Margry, 4:137 reads, "Le rivage de la mer est un pays plat, de roche, peu de bois." I can only guess at the meaning of the MS. word *plé*, which conceivably can be a shortened form of *pelé*, "bald" or "bare." Possibly Margry's *plat*, which means flat or low or shallow, is correct. Perhaps taking *plé* as *plein*, Edith Moodie gave "is full of rocks, with few trees."

[21]Iberville is using Cape Cruz as a temporary meridian for the last time. The next time he gives the longitude, he will write "longitude 5′ west of Cape San Antonio, which I am taking as my meridian of departure."

[22]I cannot find a point named Colorado in the area, but I do find the Archipiélago de los Colorados. The point in question may be the southern or western point of the first of the islands that Iberville would see in the archipelago.

Point, that is, the reefs, if you are afraid to steer a north-north-westerly course. At noon I am at latitude by observation 21°57′ and longitude 5′ west of Cape San Antonio, which I am taking as my meridian of departure. The cape lies 9 leagues south by east of me. One league south of the cape I took a sounding of 150 fathoms, no bottom. The wind has been east-northeast. I find Cape San Antonio at 21°30′ north, and on all charts it is marked 22°.

The 16th. I am at latitude 23°58′ and longitude 30′ west of the cape. The wind has been in the east and northeast, light wind, calm. Every day the sun is bright and the weather clear. I have observed the variation at sunset and sunrise, which I find to be no more than 1° northwest.

Saturday, January 17, 1699. My corrected course gives me, by dead reckoning, latitude 23°50′ north and 36′ west of Cape San Antonio. The wind has been southeast to south, light wind and calm.[23]

The 18th. My corrected course gives me, by dead reckoning, latitude 24°56′ and 59′ west of Cape San Antonio. The wind has been south-southwest, fine weather, light wind. I took a sounding and found no bottom at 215 fathoms of water. My corrected course, from the 18th to the 19th, at noon, gives me, by dead reckoning, latitude 25°54′ and 1°25′ west of Cape San Antonio. The wind has been south and southwest, light wind, bright sunshine, a few clouds. I took a sounding—no bottom at 213 fathoms.

My corrected course, from the 19th to the 20th, gives me, by dead reckoning, latitude 26°34′ and 1°42′ west—from Cape San Antonio, 2°15′ west.[24] The wind has varied from east to west, through the south, with mist, rain, thunder, and lightning. A rather fresh gale has been blowing, particularly from the

---

[23]After the words, "the wind has been southeast to south," Margry has added "beau temps, clair, sans nuage," which is not in the MS. Margry, 4:138, entry for January 16, 1699.

[24]I cannot explain why there should be two temporary meridians given here: 1°42′ west and 2°15′ west.

west-southwest, so that I could carry no more than the main
topsail and the two courses.

January 22, 1699. My corrected course gives me, by dead
reckoning, latitude 28°38′ north and 2°18′ west of Cape San
Antonio. At midnight the wind from the west fell. The seas
were quite heavy from the southwest and west. We saw some
big gulls, white and gray, and the sea was covered with small
Portuguese men-of-war. A light fog came on out of the southwest and west, covering all the sky, and the wind freshened
from the southeast, light wind. At 200 fathoms of line we found
no bottom.

The 23rd. At noon my corrected course gives me, by dead
reckoning, and observation, 29°25′ north and longitude 2°20′
west of Cape San Antonio. At eight o'clock last night, at 29°, I
took a sounding and found bottom at 170 fathoms, at 6 feet per
fathom. The wind in the south, foggy, I hove to and drifted
north for 2 leagues and then north-northeast. I found only 108
fathoms, bottom of black mud. At daybreak we got underway,
the wind northwest and north. I steered north-northeast and
east-northeast, taking soundings hourly. Within the course of
1¼ leagues to the east-northeast, the depth diminished from
100 fathoms to 15 fathoms.[25] Down to 70 fathoms the bottom is
mud, and from 70 up to 40 sand and mud, and down to 28 pure
fine sand mixed with grains of all colors. At four-thirty in the
afternoon I sighted land to the northeast, 8 leagues from me.
Upon dropping anchor, I hailed the *Marain* and told them to
run on toward the land till sunset. They told me that they had
sighted a point running west-northwest and east-southeast.
They took a sounding and got 28 fathoms of water, at 5 feet to
the fathom. I anchored in 28 fathoms of water at latitude 29°33′

---

[25]Margry, 4:140: " . . . l'eau a diminué de cent brasses à quinze brasses." This
seems to be a reasonable correction of the MS.: " . . . de 15 brasses, de cent
brasses," which makes no sense in its context.

north and 2°12′ west of Cape San Antonio.[26] After nightfall, I observed fires northwest by north, 20 leagues inland. I believe it is prairies that the Indians are burning off at this season for the buffalo hunt. We caught three reds[27] and two sharks. January 24, 1699. At noon I am at latitude 30° north and 2°18′. The land appears to me to be 2½ leagues north, ranging[28] east and west as far as one can see. This morning at daybreak we got underway. The *Marain* bore up to the west-northwest for 3 leagues toward the little smack; it had not been able to overtake us. I crowded on sail to the north-northwest to go and find the land, the wind being east-northeast. I ran north-northwest for 9 leagues. I sighted land from the masthead at a distance of 5 leagues and am in 18 fathoms of water, 6 feet [to the fathom]. At noon in 17 fathoms, the bottom of sand, gravel, and ooze. At first sight of these lands one sees sand dunes, which look very white. To the north of me a medium-sized

---

[26]The name Rivière des Indios identifying Iberville's landfall was written in a report to the ministry by Admiral Chasteaumorant who, in his battleship, convoyed the Iberville expedition.

Later, in 1699 when Iberville was visiting the Bayogoula Indian village on the bank of the Mississippi River, he referred in a letter to the ministry to his landfall "at the Rivière des Indios" (Margry, 4:106). Indian River must have been a fairly well-known landmark, for two captains of English ships, separating in the Gulf of Mexico, chose the Rivière des Indios for a rendezvous (Margry, 4:361). Du Bois' map *La Floride* [1736] gives this river running from north to southwest as a current (obviously) running through what is now called Choctawhatchee Bay, and uses the name "R. de S. Roch ou des Indiens." (This possibly was copied from a 1717 map by N. de Fer.) The map *La Floride* also shows "C. Blanc" on the outside of the barrier reef, and the January 24th entry in Iberville's Journal gives his anchorage "directly south by east of Cape Blanc."

It is interesting that modern maps show Rocky Bayou where one might expect to have found "R. de S. Roch ou des Indiens." St. Roch, a Frenchman, was a miracle-worker who lived in the fourteenth century.

[27]These three fish may have been channel bass. In Louisiana French, perhaps drawing on Canadian French, a channel bass is called "un rouge."

[28]Margry, 4:140: "La terre me paroist rouge au nord, à deux lieues et demy, courant à l'est et à l'ouest, à la vue." The word *rouge* is Margry's misreading of MS. *ranger*.

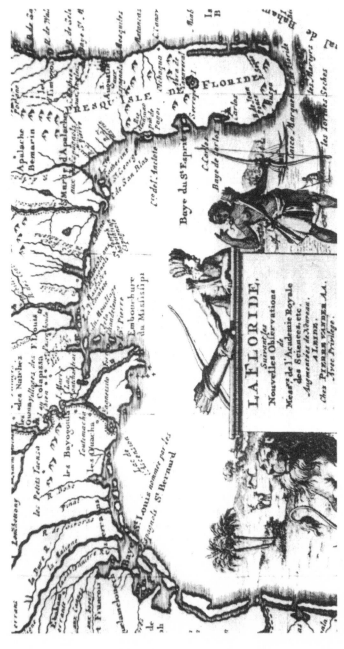

East of Pensacola can be seen a river named "R. de S. Roch ou des Indiens" and, just east on the Gulf Coast, "C. Blanc." These were landmarks the Iberville expedition had in mind as they approached land. (From Abraham Du Bois, *La geographie moderne* . . . [1736]. Section of a map from the Rucker Agee Map Collection, Birmingham Public Library)

river is visible. For 3 leagues I have run along the coast, 1½ leagues out, in 8 fathoms of water. The wind was from the offing. The seashore appears to be covered with rather tall trees, behind which there are prairies. The fire we saw last night is north of me, fully 10 leagues inland. At four o'clock in the afternoon I see two big columns of smoke 3 leagues east and about 3 leagues inland. At sunset I anchored directly south by east of Cape Blanc, 1½ leagues out, in 11 fathoms, gray sand, quite fine. The other ships and the smacks are 1 league farther out, where they were becalmed. My Biscayan went on half a league shoreward from me. I had a cannon shot fired to attract the Indians to the seashore, so that I can see them tomorrow if I do not have a fair wind to sail west.

January 25, 1699. My corrected course gives me, by dead reckoning, latitude 30°9′ north and 2°40′ west of Cape San Antonio. This morning at daybreak we got underway. I sent the Sieur Desourdys[29] with my Biscayan to take soundings in the mouth of the river at Cape du Sable or Cape Blanc.[30] I had brought the ship to within one-third of a league, in 28 fathoms.[31] It has looked to me like a mouth 200 yards wide, obstructed by two reefs on which there is 3 feet of water. The inside looks like

---

[29]Probably François Desjordy-Moreau de Cabanac was the same person as the Sieur Desjordy-Moreau, an ensign on the *Badine* (Margry, 4:50), whose name was spelled several ways, Sourdy being used sometimes instead of -jordy. He was born at Carcassonne in 1666 and died at Trois-Rivières, Canada, in 1726. If François and the ensign on the *Badine* were the same man, one wonders how he ever found the time to make a voyage to France and to Louisiana, for he was a very active man in Canada (*DCB*, s.v. "Desjordy Moreau de Cabanac, François (Sourdy)."

[30]When he had brought the *Badine* within one-third of a league of Cap Blanc (or Cap du Sable), into 28 fathoms, Iberville estimated that the mouth of the river (pass is more accurate) was 200 yards wide. Observe that Iberville was not only thinking of the pass as the River des Indios, but thinking of the shore (*contre-côte* or barrier island) as being Cap du Sable or Cap Blanc. Not a word hints that he was looking from the masthead across Choctawhatchee Bay.

[31]MS.: "28 brasses." Margry, 4:141: "dix-brasses."

a big bay[32] or salt lake that extends 2 or 3 leagues east-north-east and 2 leagues west, being separated from the sea by a strip of land that is nothing but sand dunes with trees on them, to all appearances joined to the mainland. Two and a half leagues [west][33] of the mouth, I again saw a kind of lake separated from the sea by sand dunes 100 to 200 yards wide, with shrubby trees upon them, particularly a few low pines. From these dunes to the mainland, the lake is perhaps 2 leagues wide. For 4 leagues I ran on along these dunes, 1 league out in 9 fathoms of water, and night caught me. I anchored in 9 fathoms. This coast shows very good soundings: 10 and 11 fathoms 1½ leagues out; 9 at 1 league out; 8 at one-third of a league; 7 at half a league; 5 at one-quarter of a league. The mainland, which I see beyond this lake, looks very fine, quite level, covered with tall trees, the ground elevated enough to be visible from the deck 6 leagues out. The wind has been east. Toward the afternoon the weather changed and became foggy. In many places these sand dunes can easily be seen from the deck 4 leagues out. During heavy winds from the south-southeast and the southwest, when the seas are heavy, they pass over these sand dunes. We are seeing numbers of gulls along the shore.

January 26, 1699. I am, at noon, at latitude 30°7' and 2°50' west of Cape San Antonio. It was foggy all night; we could not get underway till seven o'clock in the morning. Although it was foggy, I hugged the land, one-third of a league out in 8 fathoms, the two smacks and the Biscayan going in advance and between us and the land. At nine o'clock we sighted two ships anchored on this lake and saw the mouth of a river. When the fog thickened until we could not see one another, I had the ship brought to anchor. At three o'clock in the afternoon it lifted, and we saw a flag ashore that looks white to us. A longboat

---

[32]Here is a good description of Choctawhatchee Bay that gives proof that Iberville was not thinking of the north shore of that bay as having a white point aimed south, but of Santa Rosa Sound at the outlet where Destin, Florida, now begins.

[33]The MS. lacks *ouest*, but Margry, 4:141, has put this essential word into his text.

came out to identify us, and several cannon shots were fired on shore. Because the weather was foggy, we could not send anyone to the shore. The distance from this river to the one at Cape Blanc must be 10 to 11 leagues, east and west.

The 27th. In the morning I sent my longboat ashore with M. de Lescalète[34] to see what people had occupied the place and tell them that we had need of wood and water and that we wanted to go in and be sheltered from squalls from the south and be in a safe place while awaiting our wood and water. He found them to be Spaniards who had come from Vera Cruz three months earlier to establish themselves at this harbor, which they call Pensacola; they had acted upon information they had that people were to come there from Europe. They number some three hundred men,[35] who are busy erecting their buildings. So far, they have no more fortification than a square palisade the height of a man, at 1 league from the mouth of the river, on the left side. The commandant wrote M. de Chasteaumorand that he would have wood and water provided for him and that he could come inside to get shelter from the wind without entering the port, as he was forbidden to let any foreign nation come there, and that he was sending M. de Chasteaumorand a pilot in case he was obliged to come in. M. de Chasteaumorand answered that night through the commandant's major, who had come on board his ship, and thanked him for his courtesies, and told him that he would be obliged to come in to take shelter from the bad weather.[36]

The 28th. In the morning we went and took soundings in the entrance, M. de Surgère and I. The *François*'s rowboat went, too, with M. de Grafes. We found this entrance to be quite good: the least water we found was 21 and 22 feet over a shoal

---

[34]The Sieur Lescalette was lieutenant commander on the *Badine*. See "Liste des officiers de Marine choisis pour servir sur la *Badine*, armée à Rochefort," June 10, 1698, in Margry, 4:50.

[35]Margry, 4:143: "trois cents hommes." I cannot tell whether the MS. has 300 or 360.

[36]From this sentence as given by Margry, thirty-seven words of the MS. were dropped (Margry, 4:143).

extending a cable's length, beyond which one does not find less than 32 to 33 feet of water. Here one can anchor sheltered from bad weather, out of the range of a twelve-pound cannon at the fort. To get into this harbor coming from the east, you must follow the shoreline in 25 to 30 feet of water until you have the fort to the north and north by east; then you are to look for some sand bars over which you always see waves breaking. They are on the point on the port side as you come in. Approach them to within half a cable's length, where you will find 22 feet of water. Run north-northeast until you have gone past the bars. Here you can anchor in safety, in 30 and 35 feet of water, getting the fort from the northeast as far around as the north-northwest. You can get past the fort by partly doubling Croix Point[37] to starboard when entering, where there is a bar, on which there is no more than 18 feet of water, whereas in the channel there is 25 feet. This river is fully a league wide at its mouth, and the channel is one-third of a league, [safe] for bringing in a ship of 14-foot draft. From the fort to Croix Point, half a league. This Croix Point is the sandy point of that tongue of land, or barrier island,[38] I found, which extends from a point 8 leagues from here as far as the mouth of this harbor, or bay, which appears to go back 3 leagues inland. The water in it is salty. Two or three small rivers empty into this lake. The water is salty everywhere in this bay, from which few currents flow out.

After we had come back to our ships about noon and had got the *Marain,* the *Badine,*[39] and the two smacks underway to go

---

[37]The western end of Santa Rosa Island, at Pensacola Bay. *Croix* means "cross." That Iberville found no inlet and no outfall of water from the sound behind this long island along which he was sailing is in itself strong proof that the last outfall, where he first sighted the Florida coast, has to be a pass at Destin.

[38]The French word is *contre-coste (-côte),* which is not the mainland and its shore but an outer coast, a counter coast, such as the outer edge of the Great Barrier Reef. The barrier island here carries the name Santa Rosa Island; it extends from Pensacola to the pass at Destin.

[39]The *Badine,* a frigate of 30 guns and a crew of 150 men, served as Iberville's

in, M. de Chasteaumorand sent for us to inform us that the commandant had written him that he could not let him go in and that he would have wood and water brought to him. After making several protests about our desire to go in in order to have ourselves in a sheltered place and to obtain fresh provisions for our crews, we made the decision to go out and look for another harbor.

The 29th. All day there has been a calm, with mist.

The 30th. In the morning—wind in the east, light wind, almost calm—we got underway and steered a west-southwesterly course for 9½ leagues, up until six o'clock in the evening; therefore, I am at latitude 29°58' north and longitude 3°50' west of Cape San Antonio. Sailing from a point 1¼ leagues off Pensacola, in 7 fathoms of water, and setting the course west by south and west-southwest, I found all along 8 to 9 fathoms. At noon, 5 leagues out from Pensacola, I found a shoal. Always keeping the same course, at 1¼ leagues off shore, at 30°6' north, where I find 3⅓ fathoms, I steered southwest for 4 cable-lengths and again found the depth of 9 fathoms. I went west again until I got 6 fathoms, and from there I kept on the west-southwest course. Toward evening, 9 leagues out from Pensacola, I was forced to steer southwest by west and south-southwest to get into 6 fathoms; and at six o'clock in the evening I dropped anchor in 7⅓ fathoms, fully 2 leagues off shore. I notice that, when I steered southwest by south, I repeatedly found the same depth, 5½ fathoms for 1 league; when steering south for 2 cable-lengths, I found 7⅓ fathoms. The weather was misty. From a distance I could not sight land to the west. I think I am not far from La Mobilla.[40] We are seeing a number of ospreys and black porpoises.

---

flagship on this first voyage to the Mississippi. See Crouse, *d'Iberville*, p. 165.

[40]This spelling of the name of the river and of the identical name of the bay occurs several times in the entries Iberville wrote in his journal while he was for the first time in the vicinity of Mobile Bay, using Spanish maps (Margry, 4:149). The Spanish spelling of place names shows in a report to the Minister of Marine: e.g., after M. de Lescalette had found the entrance to the river at the

The 31st. We got underway about six o'clock in the morning, the weather a little overcast, wind in the southeast. We ran west-southwest for 3½ leagues; therefore, I am at latitude 29°54' and 4°4' west of Cape San Antonio. At noon I dropped anchor in 45 feet of water, approximately [2 leagues][41] south-southeast of the east point of the mouth of La Mobilla. One league southeast of where I am lying at anchor, coming from 10 fathoms on a northwest course, I found 9, 8, and 7 fathoms over a distance of one-quarter of a league, and 9, 8, and 8 fathoms, of 6 feet to the fathom, bottom of sand, mud, and gravel.

I sent M. de Lescalète to shore in the Biscayan and my brother and M. Dejourdys in the big smack and Vilautré in the little one, with the two feluccas to sound the entrance to this bay where we are anchored. We find a current coming out of it which sets to the south at an eighth of a league per hour. M. de Chasteaumorand sent to my ship for me three cows, which he had got at St. Domingue, and twelve sacks of corn. The three other cows have died.

February 1st. The longboat and the feluccas returned to the ship. M. de Lescalète sounded a part of the channel, finding 5 fathoms 1 league from shore. He passed over a bar, on which he found only 2 fathoms. The bad weather prevented him from sounding this channel better. He thinks there may be a pass. Toward evening I went ashore with M. de Sauvole[42] and my

---

place of the landfall, Chasteaumorant recalled the event thus: "Il fit le signal d'une, qui me parut estre celle qui est appelée sur la carte, que vous m'avez fait l'honneur de m'envoyer, la Rivière des Indios." M. de Chasteaumorant au Ministre de la Marine, June 23, 1699, in Margry, 4:106.

[41]MS.: "environ au suds sudest de la pointe de Lest de L'entrée de la mobilla." Obviously the distance out has been dropped just after *environ*. Fortunately Iberville gave that distance in a report: "deux lieues au large de l'entrée de la Mobile, où nous mouillasmes l'ancre par huit brasses d'eau." D'Iberville au Ministre de la Marine, June 29, 1699, Margry, 4:117.

[42]For the little that is known about M. de Sauvole, see *The Journal of Sauvole*, trans. and ed. Jay Higginbotham (Mobile, 1969).

brother De Bienville[43] in my longboat. The *François*'s rowboat came, too. We slept ashore.

The 2nd. It rained for a part of the night and up till nine o'clock in the morning, when the rain stopped. We went and sounded the channel, wind in the southeast. About two o'clock in the afternoon, it started raining again, very hard, with a quite brisk gale and such fog that we could not see our ships. I took soundings as far as that bank with the depth of 2 fathoms, following the reef from the east, where I put up a stake. Because my sailors were too tired to row out to the ships, I went on to the land and spent the night, on an island 4 leagues in circuit.[44] Here we had much trouble in making a fire, my crews were so exhausted. The *François*'s rowboat reached the ships.

---

[43]Jean-Baptiste Le Moyne, commonly called by his seignorial name, Bienville, who was the second to bear this title among the sons of Charles Le Moyne de Longueuil et de Châteauguay (*DCB*, s.v. "Le Moyne De Bienville, François"), exercised the highest and longest command of all the Le Moyne brothers who came to the Gulf Coast to live. Yet he was at times in disfavor with the ministry because he was suspected of graft, namely, using the king's ships and the king's stores to make money for himself. The regulations he was accused of violating were established to prevent graft, which was common enough among officers at the beginning of the eighteenth century. A commissary of the Marine, Martin d'Artaguiette, was sent to Louisiana along with a new governor, De Muy, to investigate charges made against Bienville by respectable people. The new governor died before he reached La Mobile, but the commissary not only arrived safely but conducted his investigation with some formality. He could not get evidence that justified a recall of Bienville or other punishment. Iberville, too, although he had been dead for several years, was brought into the investigation. For some charges against the brothers Bienville and Iberville, see Giraud, *Histoire*, 1:113–20.

[44]This estimate of the distance around Massacre Island (now Dauphin) is shockingly inaccurate, having no value other than as some evidence that Iberville hardly went farther west in Mississippi Sound than Cedar Point. Four leagues, 10 to 12 miles, would be less than the distance from Fort Gaines west around Little Dauphin to a line crossing the island at the public bathing beach and back to Fort Gaines along the south shore. The estimate becomes even worse when one remembers that Petit Bois Island and the 6-mile pass between Dauphin and Petit Bois were both merely an extension of Massacre Island

The 3rd. I remained on the island, which I am naming Massacre because we found on it, at the southwest end, a spot where more than sixty men or women had been slain. We found the heads and the rest of the remains along with some of their household belongings. As none of these have yet rotted, it appears that this occurred no more than three or four years ago.[45]

Last night there was a heavy wind from the southeast, which at four o'clock in the morning shifted to the west-northwest, heavy wind and heavy seas. As we were unable to go to our ship, four of my Canadians went hunting and killed eighteen bustards,[46] several ducks, and one raccoon. And in the Biscayan, I crossed over to the point on the mainland, which is 3½ leagues north by west of this island. I followed the shore for 4 leagues, running north by east. Here I went ashore and climbed to the top of a white oak, and I observed that the land

---

when Iberville made his calculation. The excuse for such a poor estimate is that the sky was overcast and rain was falling during a big part of Iberville's visit to the bay. He should have corrected this estimate of 4 leagues in circuit as soon as he sailed west along the south shore of the long island, but he did not return to the error in his logbook.

[45]By 1711 the French were moving their little capital of Louisiana from Twenty-Seven-Mile Bluff. Possibly the villagers who lived on Massacre Island, at Port Massacre, or just Massacre, had formed a dislike for the word and wanted a new name for the island, the harbor, and the little village. The reasons for the change are not fully clear, but in 1711 Bienville and Martin d'Artaguiette changed the name to Dauphine for the island and Dauphin for the port. Bienville said that several persons "consider the name of Massacre as harsh." In the letter reporting this change, Bienville does not state that the name is to pay honor to any particular dauphin or dauphine of France, as Peter J. Hamilton believed was the intention. (Bienville to the Minister, October 27, 1711, and Hamilton, *Colonial Mobile* [Mobile, 1952], p. 91.) *Dolphin*, a fish, is the same word as *dauphin*.

[46]Fr. *outarde*, "bustard," is Mississippi Valley French for the Canadian goose. In American English *bustard* should mean "big bird." Both *outarde* and *bustard* are derived from L. *avis tarda*, "slow bird." John Francis McDermott, *A Glossary of Mississippi Valley French, 1673–1850* (St. Louis, 1941), p. 110.

ran in the same direction for 3½ leagues, where I could make out a cape, at the tip of which the land bends northwest. The east side of the river (for I do not doubt that it is a river, the water being so brackish) was 4 leagues east of me and appeared to me to lie north-northwest and east-southeast as far as the eye could see and possibly rejoins the shoreline of the east point, where I spent the first night, which is about 4½ leagues from the point lying to the east of me. From the island to the mainland I found only 15 feet of water, and this pass appears to me to be obstructed to the southwest by several islands, most of them wooded. I found all kinds of trees, oak, elm, ash, pines, and other trees I do not know, many creepers, sweet-smelling violets,[47] and other yellow flowers, horse-beans like those in St. Domingue, hickories of a very thin bark, birch (the high ground not being subject to flooding),[48] traces of Indians and some huts, from which they had moved on no more than six days before. I fired several musket shots to make myself known, and I made pictures on trees, of a man shown carrying a calumet of peace and having three ships, just as I had come there. I returned to my ship at sunset.

---

[47]He saw these flowers on February 3, 1699. A year later, on February 10, 1700, Father Paul du Ru, who was on the Mississippi River with Iberville, reported in his journal that violets had bloomed and buds were swelling on the trees. Paul du Ru, *Journal of Paul du Ru*, trans. and ed. Ruth Lapham Butler (Chicago, 1934), p. 10.

[48]Although in this entry for February 3, 1699, he gives no indication of his real purpose, Iberville is reconnoitering the Mobile Bay area for no casual observations: He wants to find out whether the current and the color of the water, the height of the land above sea level, and the kinds of trees are similar to what he had learned about conditions in the area of the mouth of the Mississippi. He brought with him the false idea that the Mississippi River forked, and he wished to see for himself whether the Mobile River could possibly be the east branch of the Mississippi. In the long entry for March 22, 1699, the reader may find some of the thoughts that passed through Iberville's mind when he first reconnoitered Mobile Bay—thoughts that he did not put into his journal until fifty-one days after he ascended Mobile Bay.

The 4th. Wind in the north-northwest, fine weather. I set out to sound this channel, which I found to be very good, as the depth was 36 feet all along as far as a bar 3 cable-lengths' wide, on which I found only 12 or 13 feet of water at low tide. I noticed that the tides were northeast and southwest and rose no more than 2 or 3 feet vertically on the high seas. Half a league west-southwest of the point on the east side of the mouth is a little sand island, one-fourth of a league in circuit, with grass on it. Between this island and Massacre Island one finds only 6 feet of water.[49] The islands are one-third of a league apart, to the south-southeast. I came back to my ship, bringing wood and some hay for the cattle I have. On all these islands plenty of fresh water is found. When we were on board, we saw columns of smoke up the river, perhaps 15 leagues from us, and others along the coast, 4 leagues away. About three o'clock I weighed anchor and ran 3 leagues west-southwest, all along in 9, 8, 10, and 10 fathoms of water. Here I anchored at seven o'clock at night, wind in the north, light wind, fairly cool.

The 5th. At noon, I am, by observation, at latitude 29°55' north and 4°20' west of Cape San Antonio and in 30 fathoms of water. Massacre Island, the main part of it, is northeast of me. Viewed from the mizzen-top, it is possibly 6½ or 7 leagues away. I reckon it to be at 3°10' west and the east point at the entrance to La Mobilla to be at 30°12'.

I see land, which I judge to be an island, 5 leagues northwest

---

[49]This was the day of the best weather for sounding that Iberville had had at Mobile Bay; yet in sounding the waters from Sand Island to Dauphin Island, he made the biggest mistake of his first voyage to the Gulf. He must have taken soundings on a straight line toward the east end of Dauphin, for he failed to locate the deep water between Pelican Island and Dauphin—a tight little harbor that three years later was to become the port when the French abandoned Fort Maurepas on Biloxi Bay and moved to Twenty-Seven-Mile Bluff. Pelican Bay would have been a far better anchorage than the Ship Island anchorage. The Pelican Bay harbor has had an unfortunate history, however; a storm in 1717 closed the pass into the harbor and blocked two ships inside, and the hurricane Camille delivered the *coup de grâce* to both Pelican Island and Port Dauphin in 1969.

of me, and other land to the north-northwest, 5 leagues away, which appears to me to be joined to the mainland on the east. These islands to the north are at 30°6' north and longitude 4°30' from my meridian. I judge it to be a sand island with a few trees on it; it is possibly 4½ leagues long. From La Mobilla Point to this island the course is approximately southwest by west for 7 leagues. Starting from 2 leagues south of La Mobilla Point and steering west by south, one would, I believe, pass close to it. The Spanish charts I have show the east point of La Mobilla at 30°45' north. At noon the wind shifted and became southwest by west; I tacked north for 2½ leagues and at night anchored in 9½ fathoms of water. The middle of the island lies about 1½ leagues northwest of me. About noon I had 13 fathoms. The depth has gradually diminished. When sighting the island from the deck, I had 11½ fathoms, the bottom all along being muddy sand. From where I am anchored, Massacre Island lies due northeast of me. I observe that the mainland is connected with the shoreline, which is almost joined to this island, being separated from it by a third of a league. It is a spit of sand, without trees except for a little brushwood and some shrubby trees; and beyond it there is a lake of salt water. La Mobilla Point lies east-northeast of me.

The 6th. In the morning, calm. I sent M. de Lescalète and my brother toward the land to see whether west of this island they could find a way in to an anchorage. At noon the wind shifted to the southeast, light wind. We got underway and steered west by north for about 2½ leagues, all along in 9, 10, and 8 fathoms of water. Here I dropped anchor at seven o'clock at night, 2 leagues out, wind in the south, the bottom being a gray muddy sand. We are catching a great many fish.

February 7th. In the morning about six o'clock, wind in the southwest, we weighed anchor in order to tack and fetch the west end of the island, where we saw our longboat. It came back to the ship about noon. We reached the west end of the island, which lay 1½ leagues north of us. Here we anchored in 7 fathoms of water, the bottom mud. One league and a half west of this island, an island is visible, about 2 leagues long, and

to windward of that one, another just as big. Three leagues
south of us one is visible, without trees, sandy, quite flat. Our
smacks could not go farther than a league beyond us. We are at
latitude 29°54' north and 4°48' west of Cape San Antonio.
The 8th. In the morning M. de Surgère, Sauvole, Desourdys,
and my brother Bienville went off in the Biscayan and the two
feluccas to take soundings between the islands lying northwest
and west-northwest of us, to see whether there wasn't a way in.
I am sending the big smack, too, to take soundings between the
island south of me and the one to the north. Wind northwest
and west.

The 9th. Wind southeast, misty. I set sail, and the other
vessels, too, and came on and anchored 1¼ leagues south-
southeast to seaward of the island, in 33 feet of water. This
island is unwooded sand dunes. About eight o'clock at night my
brother came back to the ship in the felucca to inform me that,
between the two islands lying northwest and west-northwest,
there was a pass with 24 feet of water, which the Sieur
Desourdys had sounded. Wind in the southeast, light wind.
Every day the weather is fine, warm but with a light wind that
is quite cold. We are seeing a great many bustards and snow
geese.[50]

February 10th. About seven o'clock in the morning, wind in
the southeast, we set sail and steered northwest for 3 leagues.
We came in, under shelter of an island or the point of an
island,[51] where we are protected from winds from the south-
southwest, south-southeast and east by the island and from the
northeast and north and northwest by the mainland, 3½
leagues from us, and from the west and southwest by an island
2 leagues away. We have found no less than 23 feet of water,
and we are anchored a cannon's shot off the island in 26 feet of
water. The *François,* being unable to come in, is anchored at
the entrance.

The 11th. We warped a little farther east and put our animals

---

[50]Margry, 4:151: "Nous voyons beaucoup d'outardes et d'oyes sauvages."
According to Charles Upson Clark, *oyes sauvages* means snow geese or blue
geese (*Voyageurs, Robes Noires, et Coureurs de Bois* [New York, 1934], p. 345).
[51]Ship Island.

ashore, and we have men busy rigging up the Biscayan that M.
de Surgère has on his ship, and I am making ready to leave
with the Biscayans and go and discover the Myssysypy. For a
part of the day it was misty.

The 12th. At noon we saw a column of smoke to the
northeast, 5½ leagues from here, on the shore of an island.
The 13th. I crossed over to the land 4 leagues north of here in
my Biscayan, with eleven men, and my brother in a bark canoe
with two men. I went ashore and there found two trails of
Indians made yesterday, which I followed overland with one
man,[52] my brother coming along in the bark canoe, and the
Biscayan following half a league behind us, to avoid frightening
the Indians. I followed them 2 leagues, going in an easterly
direction; here night caught me, and I made camp. From the
ships over to this land it is fully 4 leagues, due north. Between
the two, I found 16 feet of muddy water. The approach to the
shore is quite shallow: half a league off shore, 4 feet of water.
This coast runs west by south and east by north. The trees here
are very fine, mixed: We are seeing many plum trees in bloom;
tracks of turkeys; partridges, which are no bigger than quail;
hares like the ones in France; some rather good oysters.

February 14th. I continued to follow the tracks of the Indians, having left at the place where I spent the night two axes,
four knives, two packages of glass beads, a little vermilion; for I
was sure that two Indians who came at sunrise to watch me
from a distance of 300 yards would come there after we left. A
league and a half from the spot where I spent the night, walking
as on the day before, I noticed a canoe crossing over to an
island and several Indians waiting for it there. They joined five
other canoes, which crossed over to the land to the north. As
the land where I was was separated from them by a bay 1
league wide and 4 leagues long, I got into my canoe and

---

[52]The Journal of the *Marin,* in the entry for Saturday, February 14, 1699,
makes reference to an Indian whom Iberville apparently brought along from
Canada: "M. d'Iberville, son Sauvage, et le Père Anastase au long de la terre
ayant fait une demy-lieue, M. d'Iberville et son Sauvage aperceurent trois
Sauvages" (Margry, 4:238). This is a part of what Iberville did when he first
attempted to communicate with the local Indians on Biloxi Bay.

pursued the canoes and overtook them as they were landing on the shore. All the Indians[53] fled into the woods, leaving their canoes and baggage. I landed 500 yards beyond them and went across land with one man to their canoes, where I found an old man who was too sick to stand.[54] We talked by means of signs. I gave him food and tobacco; he made me understand that I should build a fire for him. This I did and, besides, made a shelter, near which I placed him along with his baggage and a number of bags of Indian corn and beans that the Indians had in their canoes. I made him understand that I was going half a league from there to spend the night. My longboat joined me there. I sent my brother and two Canadians after the Indians who had fled, to try to make them come back or to capture one. Toward evening he brought a woman to me whom he had caught in the woods 3 leagues from there. I led her to the old man and left her, after giving her several presents and some tobacco to take to her men and have them smoke.

The 15th. Three of those Indians and two women, having been met by one of my Canadians, came along to sing the calumet of peace to me. The old man died about ten o'clock in the morning. One of those men sang, carrying a little plank of whitened wood, which he held up in the air, offering it to me. I met them at their canoes, where they made a sagamité of Indian corn to feast us; I sent for something with which to feast them, in return, and gave them presents of axes, knives, shirts, tobacco, pipes, tinderboxes, and glass beads. More of their men joined them. They went off and spent the night half a league from there.

The 16th. In the morning, during foggy and rainy weather, I went overland and joined them. There I found only ten men with their weapons, entirely naked, wearing *braguets*.[55] All

---

[53]Iberville estimated the number of these Indians to be more than fifty, including women and children. D'Iberville au Ministre de la Marine, February 17, 1699, in Margry, 4:101.

[54]The Journal of the *Marin* (Margry, 4:238) says of the old man: "Il avoit une jambe pourrie." The Marquis de Châteaumorant reported that the old man had been wounded in the leg by a wild animal (Margry, 4:112).

[55]For a man, the *braguet* was a loin flap; for a woman, it was somewhat like an

their canoes and baggage were gone, indicating to me that they were suspicious of me. We smoked together all over again, although I never smoke. I persuaded three to go aboard our ships, having left with the Indians my brother and two Canadians as hostages. I got to my ship at two o'clock in the afternoon. There they were greatly astonished at all they saw. I had some cannon shots fired for them, which they greatly wondered at.

The 17th. At noon I went back and joined my brother and brought the three Indians back, who belong to the nation of the Annochy and Moctoby.[56] They are 3½ days from their village. They mentioned to me the name of a village of their neighbors, Chozeta.[57] They are on a river the mouth of which is 9 leagues east; they call it Pascoboula.[58] I gave them several presents to take to their nations. They assured me that there are 4 fathoms of water in their river.

At six o'clock in the evening I got to the place where my brother was. Here I found a chief of the Bayogoula with twenty-one of his men and some Mougoulascha,[59] who had got

---

apron, to the hem of which tassels were sometimes attached. Whenever the woman walked or danced, the agitation of the tassels made her body appear sinuous.

[56] Annochy is another name for the Biloxi Indians, recorded by Iberville here as well as by the Marquis de Châteaumorant, who recorded the spelling Anaxis (Margry, 4:113 and 172, and Frederick Webb Hodge, *Handbook of American Indians North of Mexico*, 2 vols. [Washington, D.C., 1907 and 1910], 1:148). The Moctoby (MS.: "Moctaby") were associated with the Bilocchy and Pascagoula Indians on the Pascagoula River; they may have been of Siouan linguistic stock. See Hodge, *Handbook*, 1:917.

[57] Gatschet believed that the people of the village Chozeta were Choctaws. Hodge, *Handbook*, 1:293.

[58] The name *Pascagoula* came from Choctaw *paska*, "bread," and *okla*, "people," hence "bread people" (Hodge, *Handbook*, 2:205). The site of the homes of the Pascagoula was 2½ days by canoe up the Pascagoula River in Mississippi. It is unknown whether they were of Siouan or Muskhogean linguistic stock. Iberville was the first to observe and record the presence of this small tribe, a bare remnant. He heard the name as Pascoboula and thus recorded it.

[59] The Bayogoula and the Mugulasha were domiciled in the same village on the west bank of the Mississippi River 64 leagues above the mouth. The chief of the Mugulasha seems to have been the chief or a chief of the Quinipissas. There were some hundred cabins and 400 to 500 souls in this village. In 1700 the

there as early as yesterday evening. They live on the bank of
the Myssysypy and, being on a hunt on this side, came on at the
noise of the cannon to see who we were. They caressed my
brother many times; he gave them some tobacco and feasted
them that night. They wanted to know whether he had come in
the canoe they saw he had and whether he was of the people of
the Upper Myssysypy, which in their language they call Malbanchya. He told them yes.

When we got to where my brother was, the chief or captain
of the Bayogoula came to the seashore to show me friendliness
and courtesy in their fashion, which is, being near you, to come
to a stop, pass their hands over their faces and breasts, and
then pass their hands over yours, after which they raise them
toward the sky, rubbing them together again and embracing
again. I did the same thing, having watched it done to the
others. They did the same thing to the Annocchy, their friends.
After our meeting and amenities on both sides,[60] we went to my
brother's tent, to which all the Bayogoula made their way to
show friendliness to me and all my men, all embracing one
another. I had them smoke, and together we all smoked an iron
calumet I had, made in the shape of a ship with the white flag
adorned with fleurs-de-lis and ornamented with glass beads.
Then [I gave it to them][61] along with a present of axes, knives,
blankets, shirts, glass beads, and other things valued among
them, making them understand that with this calumet I was
uniting them to the French and that we were from now on one.
I feasted them with sagamité made with plums and had them
drink brandy and wine, of which they took very little, marvel-
ing greatly at the brandy that we set on fire. About eight o'clock

---

Bayogoula suddenly attacked the Mugulasha and reduced their numbers
greatly. Hodge, *Handbook,* 1:954, and John R. Swanton, *The Indians of the
Southeastern United States,* Bureau of American Ethnology Bulletin 137
(Washington, 1947), p. 95.

[60]The Journal of the *Marin* (Margry, 4:239) has this account of the amenities
observed by these coastal Indians: "Nous les embrassames, frottant leurs
ventres. On leur donna à fumer et des présens de toute manière." From these
Indians the French had quickly learned the amenities to show to other Indians.

[61]From the Burton text, which has the sense demanded here. Iberville gave the
calumet to the Bayogoula Indians, but Margry (4:155) lacks the pronoun

at night the chief and seven others came and sang the calumet
to me, giving me a present of three of their blankets made of
muskrat, making me the ally of four nations west of the
Myssyssypy, which are the Mougoulascha, Ouascha,[62] Toutymascha,[63] Yagueneschyto;[64] and, east of the river, of the Bylocchy,[65] Moctoby, the Ouma,[66] Pascoboula, Thecloël,[67]

---

object or "ce calumet": "Après quoy je leur donnay avec un présent de
haches . . ." This calumet will be seen again.

[62]The Washa Indians were a small tribe on Bayou Lafourche in Louisiana,
probably of Muskhogean stock, living near the Chaouacha, or Chawasha, with
whom they later united. They were induced to settle on the Mississippi River, 3
leagues above New Orleans. After the Natchez Massacre in the winter of
1729, the Chawasha were treacherously attacked by Negro slaves and at least
seven or eight men were killed and the town destroyed. This calculated
barbarity was instigated by the French because, after the massacre at Fort
Rosalie, the French in New Orleans were nervous about the possibility of the
Indians and Negro slaves' forming a plot to massacre other Frenchmen. An
attack on the Chawasha by Negro slaves, even though they were forced into it,
would prevent plotting. See Swanton, *Indians*, pp. 108–09.

[63]This seems to be one of the varied spellings given for the name of the
Chitimacha Indians. Hodge, *Handbook*, 1:286.

[64]Here is either another name for a part of the Chitimacha tribe or the name of
a tribe related to them or affiliated with them. Swanton gives the name as
Yakna-Chitto, "Big Country" (*Indians*, pp. 119–20).

[65]Bylocchy and Bilocchy were early spellings the French wrote for the name of
this tribe of Siouan linguistic stock living on the Pascagoula River, first
reported by Iberville in the documents here translated. He and others used the
spelling Bilocchy, and other spellings were common until the name was finally
stabilized as Biloxi. Gatschet, who visited a remnant of the tribe in 1886, made
the convincing argument that these Indians were of Siouan linguistic stock
(Hodge, *Handbook*, 1:147–48). These Indians gave their name to three settlements: Old Biloxi, now Ocean Springs; Bilocchy, a settlement on a small
stream between New Orleans and Lake Pontchartrain; and New Biloxi,
which the French built in 1718, on the site of present-day Biloxi. See Swanton,
Indians, p. 97.

[66]Oumas or Houma or Huma is the name of a Choctaw tribe living 7 leagues
above the mouth of the Red River and on the east bank of the Mississippi.
Huma means "red." Their emblem was the red crawfish. In 1699 they had 140
huts and 350 families. The famous red pole, *bâton rouge*, marked the dividing
line between their land and the land of the Bayogoula. Hodge, *Handbook*, 1:577.

[67]Thecloël is another name for the Natchez Indians, the spelling usually being
Théloël or Théloelles, even Chéloëlles, unless what I read as *Ch* in the MS. is
nothing other than a *T* wearing a crown. The dominant name of 1699 gave
place quickly to Natchez or Nadchés. Hodge, *Handbook*, 2:36.

Bayacchyto,[68] Amylcou.[69] At my camp they sang till midnight, and my men sang with them.

February 18th. When we showed the Indians some maps in order to learn where the east fork of the Myssysypy was, we decided that they were indicating that it was the Pascoboula River, which they marked for us. I later learned that they wished to show that, from that river, they went to the Myssysypy by way of rivers that connect with one another. I made them understand that I was going in my longboat to the mouth of it to take soundings and that I would come back and join them. My brother and three men, in the bark canoe, would stay with them. The chief of the Bayogoula came to me to tell me that he was going hunting for buffalo and turkeys and in four nights would be back at the place where I had slept the first time I went ashore and that there we would feast one another. I set out for the Pascoboula River, which I could not get to because of a head wind. I turned back, expecting to find the Indians again and keep them from going hunting and persuade them to come with me to the west branch, for I could not see how this Pascoboula River could be big enough to have sufficient water at its mouth, which broadened too much. I found that they had gone. I spent this night ashore.

The 19th. At noon I proceeded to my ship with all my men to get ready to set out for the west branch of the Myssysypy upon the arrival of the Indians. That day I got 16 casks of wine from M. de Chasteaumorand for 150 livres; 10 small barrels of flour; 97 pounds of butter, so that I would not lack provisions, not knowing what I would do on the coast.

The 21st. At noon two columns of smoke became visible at the rendezvous I had given the Bayogoula. I had four cannon shots fired to let them know that I saw them, although the rendezvous was not until tomorrow.

February 22nd. We set out, M. de Surgère and I, to go to the rendezvous in the two Biscayans. We got there about noon. We

---

[68]Identified by Hodge (*Handbook*, 2:137) as a name of Bayou Chicot, a Choctaw village near present-day Cheneyville, in St. Landry parish, Louisiana.

[69]Little is known about the Amylcou other than what Iberville wrote in this passage. Hodge, *Handbook*, 1:49.

found nothing there. The columns of smoke came from fires sweeping through the woods.

The 23rd. A high wind blew from the north, too strong for us to sail in the longboats, and lasted all day of the 24th.

The 25th. M. de Surgère returned to his ship, and I sent my brother in the bark canoe to within 2½ leagues of the rendezvous to see whether he could get any news of the Indians. He found two of them and two women. One, an Annocchy, came with him to see me and spent the night with us. He made me understand that the Bayogoula had gone back and had spent only two nights with them and that they had made some columns of smoke, which we had seen, to notify us that they had set out from there during the morning, the wind being right for them to go to the Malbanchya, and they had no provisions at all.

The 26th. I sent the Indian back to his camp, and I came on to my ship, having ordered MM. Desourdys and Lavilautré, sent by M. de Surgère to me in the two feluccas, to go 6 leagues east and examine the Pascoboula River and take soundings of it and proceed from there to the ship. I got to the ship at two o'clock in the afternoon and made ready to set out tomorrow.

The 27th. I set out from the ships with two Biscayans and two bark canoes with the Sieur de Sauvole, a sublieutenant on the *Marain,* and my brother, and the Recollect father, and forty-eight men, with provisions for twenty days, to go to the Myssysypy, which the Indians of this area call Malbanchya [and the Spaniards call the Palisade].[70] Wind in the southeast with rain and drizzle. I steered south to make some islands that were visible there; and, running along the shore for 6 leagues, in 4 and 5 feet of water all along, I ran along the island of grass and sand and passed through bays and by hooks covered with grass and rushes but without trees. Seven leagues south of the ships I passed between a rocky island and a grassy one, 1,000 yards apart. They become covered during high tides. The rocky one is rather free of shoals; 2 cable-lengths from it there is 18 feet of water. I see other islands to the northeast, east, and southeast, where I hear the seas breaking to seaward, making

[70]Words deleted in the MS. but still legible and important enough to be retained.

a great deal of noise on the bars. From these islands, to follow the shore and avoid running by any river, I set the course southwest by south for 3 leagues along these islands. I spent the night on a very low island covered with grass; it becomes flooded like all the others.

The 28th. At noon I came to an island one-quarter of a league in circumference, 4 leagues from the place where I spent the night, near a point where the shore runs west-northwest, into a bay extending 2½ leagues into the land. This point is in latitude 29°35' north. From this point, which is flooded land, I came on and spent the night at a little island 3 leagues to the southwest. One league out from these islands I found 6 and 8 feet of water. I believe that farther out are islands that I am failing to see.

March 1st. It rained and thundered all day, and a heavy wind blew from the southeast. I stayed at this island , which has been almost covered with water. We find no trees here, no fresh water—no more than on the other islands and shores by which I have passed. On all these islands we are killing raccoons, which live here off shellfish.[71] Their fur is reddish brown.

The 2nd. Wind in the north and northeast. We left and proceeded along the islands. After steering south for 6½ leagues, I passed between a point and an island which is 2 leagues east of the point and which may be 3 leagues in circumference and is bare of trees. Between the two, half a league off the point, I found 18 feet of water; I do not doubt that farther out there is more. From this point I steered south-southeast, crossing a bay 2 leagues wide that extends 3 to 4 leagues inland. I ran on this course along the shore, 1½ leagues out, in 12 and 15 feet of water, for 10 leagues, wind north-northeast and heavy and the seas so high that I could not keep to seaward, nor could I run for the shore, the water in the area being too shallow. I remained at sea, lying to with my long-boats, my canoes being aboard them, and heavy seas often

---

[71]*Chat sauvage* is Mississippi Valley French for raccoon. On Biloxi Bay and near Bayou La Batre, Alabama, are two islands named Cat Island for the many raccoons. These animals can open oysters with their claws and teeth. The zoologist Dr. Dan Holliman, who is well acquainted with the animals

spilling into our longboats.[72] After I had held the southeast
course for three hours in order to double a rocky point, as night
was coming on and the foul weather continuing, so that we
could not endure without going to the shore during the night
lest we perish at sea, I stood for those rocks in order to run
ashore by day to save my men and longboats. When drawing
near to the rocks to take shelter, I became aware that there
was a river. I passed between two of the rocks, in 12 feet of
water, the seas quite heavy. When I got close to the rocks, I
found fresh water with a very strong current.

These rocks are logs petrified by the mud and changed into
black rocks, which withstand the sea.[73] They are countless,
above water, some big, others small, separated from one another by distances of 20 yards, 100 yards, 300 yards, 500 yards,
more or less, running southwest. This made me know that here
was the Palisade River, which appears to me to have been
rightly named;[74] for, when I was at its mouth, which is 1½

living on Mississippi Sound, has told me that, in wading along the shores of the
sound, he has come across three dead raccoons, drowned, their claws still
caught in oyster shells. They endanger their lives when they feed on oysters on
a rising tide.

[72]French longboats, having no decks, carried a strip of tarpaulin to lash to the
gunwales in heavy seas. The Journal of the *Marin* (Margry, 4:245–46) describes this protection against shipping seas as "une toile goudronnée d'environ
un pied de haut, au-dessus de nostre bord, que nous estions obligés de tenir
pour empescher la mer de s'embarquer."

[73]Margry (4:159) carries the passage thus: "Ces roches sont de boys pétrifié de
la vase et devenues roches noires, qui resistent à la mer." The MS. is slightly
blurred, but I read "pétrifiées avec de vaze." For evidence that there was no
palisade, although the Spaniards named the Mississippi "Rio de la Palizada,"
no black rocks, and no petrified trees, but a field of mud lumps, see my article
"Iberville at the Birdfoot Subdelta: Final Discovery of the Mississippi River,"
in *Frenchmen and French Ways in the Mississippi Valley*, gen. ed. John Francis
McDermott (Urbana, 1969), pp. 127–40. Whoever was keeping the Journal of
the *Marin* at that time came along in the second Biscayan longboat right behind
Iberville, but he does not report seeing black rocks or petrified trees. He wrote:
"Nous aperceusmes une passe entre deux buttes de terre qui paroissoient
comme de petites isles. . . . Nous passames entre ces buttes de terre" (Margry,
4:246). The MS. has, "Ces roches sont de boys petrifiées avec de vaze," which
Moodie rendered as, "These rocks are trees petrified by the mud and turned
into black rocks."

[74]Not until his second voyage to the Mississippi did Iberville learn that the river

leagues in from these rocks, it appeared to be entirely obstructed by the rocks. At its mouth there is only 12 to 15 feet of
water where I came in, which seemed to me to be one of the
best passes, where the waves were breaking least. Between the
two points of the river I found 10 fathoms, the river being an
eighth of a league wide, the land low and flooded, covered with
reeds as thick as one's finger and 10 to 15 feet tall. I ascended
the river 1½ leagues and there made camp among the reeds, the
river being 350 fathoms wide, the current strong enough to take
one 1⅓ leagues per hour, the water quite muddy and white.[75]
When lying on these reeds, sheltered from the foul weather, we
feel the pleasure there is in seeing ourselves protected from an
obvious peril. It is a jolly business indeed to explore the sea-
coasts with longboats that are not big enough to keep to the sea
either under sail or at anchor and are too big to approach a flat
coast, on which they run aground and touch bottom half a
league off shore. It is rather cold, although not freezing. Two
cable-lengths out from these rocks there is 7 and 8 fathoms of
water, at 6 feet to the fathom. The water from the river does
not blend with the salt water for three-quarters of a league to
seaward, at most, where there is 18 to 20 fathoms. I found the
mouth of the river 28 leagues south of the place where the ships
are and at 28°45′ north. Ships can come and anchor at the
mouth of this river, one-third or one-half a league out, and take
on fresh water without any risk, which would be a very great

had been incorrectly named Río de la Palizada. See the Journal of the
Renommée (the first of her voyages), the entry for April 13–14, 1700, which tells
how Iberville had an experience that showed him the mistake he made in
thinking there were black rocks or petrified trees out from the East Pass, now
called North Pass. The passage in question is printed in Margry, 4:423. It
appears in this volume in Iberville's second journal.
[75]MS.: "le courant fort a faire 1 Lieue ⅓ par heure, L'eau toute bourbeuse et
blanche." These were important words written by Iberville, for the speed of the
current and the color of the water indicated that the Malbanchya was the
Mississippi River. Had not La Salle himself told Iberville that he would not fail
to recognize the Mississippi "par le courant qui en sort et l'eau blanche et
bourbeuse"? D'Iberville au Ministre de la Marine, June 18, 1698, in Margry,
4:53–54.

convenience to corsairs that cruise against ships out of Vera Cruz, which usually come close enough to be seen from these shores.

March 3rd. Mardy Gras day, wind in the northeast, so that I cannot take soundings to locate the passes of this river; however, I do not believe that there are any more. I went up the river, finding it quite deep: at a longboat's length from the bank, 20 feet of water; in the middle, 48 and 50 feet of water. Two leagues and a half above the mouth it forks into three branches: The middle one is as wide as the one through which I entered, being 350 to 400 fathoms wide; the other, which flows along the land to the southwest, does not appear to be so big. All this land is a country of reeds and brambles and very tall grass. Above the forks the river is some 550 fathoms wide, gradually becoming narrower as one goes upstream, until it is no wider than 300 fathoms. The very low land is covered with reeds, clumps of alder within them, short, and as big as the leg and the thigh, and that in certain spots. Six leagues upstream, trees begin to appear, especially on the left side going upstream, which are alders as big as a man's body and 30 to 40 feet high. From the forks up to 6 leagues inland, the river is rather straight, running northwest 5° north; then it winds west for 2 leagues and again runs northwest. I came on and spent the night at a bend it makes to the west, 12 leagues above the mouth, on a point on the right side of the river, to which we have given the name Mardy Gras. I had two canister shots fired to give notice to the Indians, if there were some in the vicinity. There is no indication that any came. I climbed to the top of a nut tree as big as my body, but saw nothing other than canes and bushes. The land becomes inundated to a depth of 4 feet during high water. I made the decision to go upstream as high as the Bayogoula to see whether I could get news of the Quinypyssa,[76] whom the

---

[76]When La Salle had an encounter with the Quinipissa Indians in 1682, they were living on the west side, a few leagues above the present site of New Orleans. Aware of this encounter, Iberville sought for them in vain. His most frustrating experiences were his failure to locate these Indians and to find the

narratives mention, locating them 25 leagues from the sea.
The 4th. The wind in the east, blowing from across the land,
we went on upstream and made about 8½ leagues, coming to
several bends the river makes to the west-northwest and north-
northwest, where the wind helped us, the river being still as
wide as usual. At a distance of 2 or 3 leagues from where we
encamped and where we now are, we can see the sea or a lake
that runs, like the river, west-northwest. The river is separated
from this lake by a quarter-league's width of land. The ground
is getting a little higher and during times of overflow does not
become flooded more than 1½ feet. We are seeing all sorts of
trees on the left side of the river; in a number of places there is a
border of woods a quarter of a league wide, and beyond it are
prairies and clumps of trees. I have noticed that the waters are
swollen, for they are carrying along many trees. The water is
only 2½ feet below flood stage. I spent the night on the right side
of the river.

The 5th. Fog was on the river as late as nine o'clock. Calm.
We started off at six-thirty, rowing along the bank in a slight
wind, which helps us at the bend[s]. The river makes many
bends above a point 12 leagues from the sea. It would take
ships a long time to ascend this river, for each bend would
require wind from a particular direction. Today the bends have
shifted from west to southwest and northwest and north.
About noon we discovered a fire on the left side of the river, in
prairies, and we noticed that an Indian had passed along. The
ground gets higher and higher but becomes inundated to 1½
feet. It is possible that, 1 league back from the river, it does not
become inundated at all. We made 6 to 7 leagues today.

---

east fork of the Mississippi. He was seeking proof that the Malbanchya was the
Mississippi and that he was on the east fork by which La Salle and Tonty had
gone down to the sea in 1682. When he learned from a letter left with the
Mugulasha that the Quinipissa were indeed the Mugulasha, he was satisfied
that he had discovered the entrance to the Mississippi from the Gulf of Mexico.
Still, the identity of the Quinipissa and the location of the sites they occupied in
1699 are, in my opinion, relatively obscure. See Hodge, *Handbook*, 1:137, and
Swanton, *Indians*, pp. 176–77.

The 6th. All morning there was fog and no wind. We have gone on from place to place with great difficulty. The number of uprooted trees in the river make it quite rapid: At many points we have difficulty in making headway. My brother, with the two canoes, keeps to one side of the river, watching for some trace of Indians. At noon I took the altitude with a quadrant, which I had made for this purpose, and I am now at 30° north,[77] and I am at the first bend the river makes east-northeast. It has made one bend as far over as east, at the end of which I made camp on the right side of the river. Today I made 6½ leagues. The trees and the ground are getting higher and are subject to 8–10-inch overflow. I have not yet noticed any walnut tree or fruit tree whatsoever other than, at the seashore, some patches of blackberries almost ripe enough to eat. On the trees the leaves are big. We are seeing here a good many vines that have already bloomed. I had two canister shots fired from swivel guns.

The 7th. It has been calm all day. We are going on upriver, finding that the river bends a great deal from northeast to southwest, through the north and the west: Over a distance of 2 leagues it will make two and three bends. Two leagues from the place where we spent the night, I came across six canoes of Indians, who put in to the bank. I landed below them and went by land to them. One Indian stayed with his canoe; the others fled. We rubbed each other after their manner, about which I have already spoken. He told me that he was an Annocchy and that the Bayogoula and the Annocchy I had seen at the Annocchy's bay, near the ships, to whom I had given presents and a calumet of peace, were back at the village of the Bayogoula. I gave a present of knives, glass beads, and axes to him and his comrades, whom he summoned. They gave us buccaned buffalo meat and bear meat. I asked them for a man to guide me to the Bayogoula, and they gave me one. They count

---

[77]MS.: "30 degrés O nord." I cannot explain the *O* before *nord*. Margry, 4:163, gives "30 degrez ouest-nord," which I find just as meaningless, for *ouest-nord* is not a point of the compass.

it 3½ days from here to their village, which can amount to some 24 leagues. I came on and made camp that day 6½ leagues from my last camp, near one of their camp sites, where there are ten huts thatched with palmettos; near it, at a point on the right side of the river, is a small redoubt as high as a man, made of canes in the form of an oval, 25 yards wide and 55 long, having a few huts inside. They lead us to believe that a short while ago some of their men were killed and that the Chicacha[78] and the Napyssa[79] did it, but I have since learned that there is no war at all between them. The Quinypissa and Bayogoula are not on visiting terms because of some pique between the two chiefs. That is what they call war, according to what the Ouma have led us to believe. All the ground here becomes inundated a foot deep as far back as half a league in the woods, where I went. Both banks of the river, almost the entire distance above the sea, are so thickly covered with canes of every size—one inch, two inches, three, four, five, and six in circumference—that one cannot walk through them. It is impenetrable country, which would be easy to clear. Most of the canes are dry; when set on fire they burn readily and, when burning, make as loud a report as a pistol shot. A person who did not know that and was not watching them burn would think it to be a skirmish. These canes have roots three and four feet in the ground, which look like a puppet.

The 8th. The wind has been in the north-northwest, frustrating us at the bends considerably and driving the water so hard

---

[78]The Chickasaws lived mainly in northern Mississippi, near the headwaters of the Yazoo and the Tombigbee rivers. They were a Muskhogean tribe and perhaps the best fighters of the tribes of Muskhogean stock. Because the French were close to the Choctaws and because the English in Carolina successfully cultivated an alliance with the Chickasaws, the Chickasaws were from time to time at war with the French, who never were able to defeat them. The population of their villages was about six thousand and their warriors numbered about two thousand during the time of the French settlement of the Gulf Coast. Hodge, *Handbook*, 1:260–62.

[79]The Napissas were a tribe closely associated with the Chickasaws and probably were at last absorbed by them. Hodge (*Handbook*, 2:28) has only the little information recorded by Iberville.

that the current is faster than a quarter of a league per hour. We made only 4½ leagues and camped on the right side of the river. My men are getting very tired.

The 9th. The wind has been northwest, delaying us considerably. Two leagues from the place where we stopped for the night, the Indian I have with me pointed out to me the place through which the Indians make their portage to this river from the back of the bay where the ships are anchored. They drag their canoes over a rather good road, at which we found several pieces of baggage owned by men that were going there or were returning. He indicated to me that the distance from the one place to the other was slight. The Indian picked up a bundle from there. He told me that it is two nights more to the village. Today we made 5½ leagues. From here to the sea[80] it may be 50 leagues. I camped on the left side of the river.

March 10th. We have had a calm all day. Today the river has made many bends, from north to southwest and west, still keeping its course west by north. I must have made at least 5 leagues, and I camped on the right side of the river. The country becomes inundated everywhere to a depth of a foot. There are fine, tall trees, many canes.

The 11th. It has rained all day, and I have stayed here. Toward evening two sailors from the longboat of the *Marain* went out to shoot two ducks within a cannon-shot from camp, along the bank of the river. They did not come back and apparently have got lost. I have had shots fired from muskets and the swivel guns.

The 12th. I sent eight men in different directions to search for them, above and below the camp and back from the river, firing musket shots; but they did not find them. They found their trail in the canes and, beyond, in the hardwood forest, in which they followed them a long time but lost their trail. Along the river the woods are so full of canes that one cannot make any headway until half a league back from the river, beyond the hardwood

---

[80]MS.: " . . . au bas de la mer." Here the penman telescoped "à la mer" and "au bas de la rivière." The meaning is clear enough.

forest and the canes. Three quarters of a league back from the river the land does not become inundated. I spent the whole day waiting for those men, who are two Bretons from the *Marain*. The longboat that I had sent 2 leagues upriver to pick up the men who were searching for the two others took soundings in the middle of the river and found all along 90, 100, and 120 feet of water.

The 13th. Calm. On the left, 4 leagues from our camp site of last night, I found a river 200 yards wide, flowing from the west, which the Indian I have with me called the Ouacha River. A league and a half beyond, I found two Indian canoes: One was Ouacha, in which there were five men and two women, who were on their way home; the other was Bayogoula, with three men and one woman, who sold me some Indian corn, which I am beginning to need. The Ouacha's canoe went on its way to their village, two days from here, and the other returned to the Bayogoula, near here, to announce our coming. Toward evening it thundered, as often occurs here during winter.

The 14th. I decamped at six o'clock in the morning. Three leagues from our camp site and 1 league from the landing for the Bayogoula village, I met a wooden canoe, or pirogue, as such boats are called in the islands of America, in which were four men of the Mogoulacha nation who were coming to bring the calumet of peace to me, singing after their fashion. When we came up to them, they offered it to me to smoke on behalf of their nations. Then the bearer of the calumet came into my longboat, and we proceeded to the village landing about noon; and the Mogoulacha, whom I had in my longboat, sang as we drew near, raising his calumet as high as he could as a mark of joy and assurance.[81] When we drew close to the landing, the

---

[81]The Journal of the *Marin* tells that the detachment met on this same day a canoe of Indians, among whom was an old man who had survived scalping. Wearing a bearskin about him and having smeared his face with muck to make himself handsome, he bore a three-foot calumet embellished with bird feathers of various colors. He was the deputy of the chief of the Mugulasha. (Margry, 4:255–56.) This scalped deputy seems to be the same man whom Iberville describes as bearing a calumet and identifies as a Mugulasha.

Bayogoula and the Mogoulascha, who are two nations joined
together and living in the same village, were on the river bank
and sang when we arrived. When we left the boat, the two
chiefs of each nation came before me and greeted me in their
fashion, which I have already described, grasping me under the
arms as though to help me to walk, and escorted me on to some
bear skins spread out in the midst of their people. When I sat
down they gave tobacco to me and to all my men, whom they
heartily embraced. The calumet[82] I had given the Bayogoula
rested on two forked sticks two feet high in the middle of the
assembly, where a man of that nation domiciled with them
stood with his eyes fixed on it and without moving from it. They
had sagamité brought for me and all my men to eat, made of
Indian corn, and some of their bread. The afternoon was
devoted to singing and dancing. The chief of the Mougoulascha
had a hooded great-coat of blue serge from Poitou, which he
told me Tonty[83] had given him as a present when he passed by;
and he told several things, some of them by signs. I understood
many of their words, which I had taken down in writing the
first time I saw them; at least, my brother did: He was making
himself understood fairly well, having applied himself to the
task with the guide I had got on the river [whom my brother
kept in his canoe].[84]

---

[82]This is the iron calumet, in the shape of a ship, that Iberville gave the
Bayogoulas on February 17, 1699, when he was first getting acquainted with
tribes on Biloxi Bay, all from the surrounding area. The grammar of that
sentence written on February 17, 1699, called for an "it" or "this calumet," but
the necessary word was dropped by the penman. This passage proves that the
bracketed addition in my text is warranted in the entry for February 17.
Journal of the *Badine*, in Margry, 4:155.

[83]Henri de Tonty, called Le Bras Coupé as well as La Main de Fer, had lost a
hand while fighting for France against the Spaniards. This lieutenant of La
Salle's knew the Mississippi from the Illinois to the subdelta better than any
other French leader in 1699. His devotion to La Salle as expressed in the letter
recovered from Indians may be the most moving detail in these journals. This
loyal and capable man died at La Mobile (Fort Louis de la Louisiane) during
the small yellow fever epidemic of 1704, after the *Pélican* brought infected
mosquitoes as well as young girls to Île Massacre. No one now knows the site
of the cemetery at Twenty-Seven-Mile Bluff in which Le Bras Coupé is buried.

[84]This bracketed clause was deleted in the MS., but is still legible.

We talked a great deal about what Tonty had done when he stopped by and about the route he had taken and about the Quinypyssa. They told me there were seven villages in that nation eight days' travel overland east-northeast of this village. I could not get from them any information about the fork mentioned in the relations, by way of which I wanted to go down to the sea, in order to know both branches. They told me that the Malbanchya did not fork at all and that Tonty, in going down and in coming back, had gone by no other route than the one by their village. This I could not make square with the relations people had written about their travels,[85] particularly the Recollect, whom I thought I should have the most faith in. The Indians made maps of the whole country for me, indicating that from their village Tonty had gone among the Oumas. All that put me in great difficulty: The season urged me to return, I was 90 leagues away from the ships, and I had yet to establish a post and look for a place suitable for that purpose. The *Marain* was running short of provisions; and, when I left him, Surgère asked me for authorization to leave in six weeks if I was not back; my men were growing weary of rowing on and on against a strong current. I would come back time and again to the Recollect Father's relation, which he wrote about this river; I found it difficult to believe that he could have been such a rogue as to publish a hoax to all France, even though I well knew that in many passages in his relations he had told lies in what he said about Canada and Hudson Bay,[86] in which he had lied with impunity. I made up my mind to go to the Ouma, five days' travel from here, believing that these Indians, who were not good friends of the Quynypyssa, could, out of jealousy, be hiding the truth from me to keep me from going to the Quyny-pyssa and that, if I should turn back from the Bayogoula without proof that Tonty had stopped there, other than the proof I had, people would tell me in France that I had not gone

---

[85]MS.: "Ce que je ne pouvois faire cadrer avec les relations qu'ils en avoient fait." The pronoun *en*, of vague reference, seems to me to refer to travels or routes taken.

[86]MS.: "la baye du d'udsson."

up the Myssysypy, as I had not found the Quinypyssa 30 leagues from the sea or the Tangibao[87] the writers of relations mentioned, whom they had found pillaged and slain when they passed by. The Bayogoula told me that the Ouma were the ones that had destroyed the village of the Tangibao, which was one of the Quynypyssa's seven villages and that now they are only six, as the Ouma had carried off the remnant families of Tangibao and brought them to their village, where they still are [and where I shall see them];[88] and that their village never had been on the bank of the Myssysypy. At eight o'clock at night all the Indians withdrew to their village, which is a quarter of a league from the river bank, where the land does not become inundated. The intervening land does become inundated, to the depth of a foot, during high water. Four of the Indians stayed to spend the night with us.

The 15th. At daybreak three men came to bring me some tobacco to smoke ceremoniously and to place my calumet back on the two forked sticks, where one man stayed to guard it. At eight o'clock in the morning I went to their village along with the Sieur de Sauvole, the Recollect Father, and my brother, and two of my Canadians. A quarter of a league from the river I came to the village, close to which flows a little creek from which they get drinking water. It was surrounded by a palisade made entirely of canes an inch apart and ten feet high, without a door that closes. They came to the entrance of the village to receive me and escorted me before the hut of the Mougoulacha, where they had us sit down on cane mats[89] in very hot sun-

---

[87]Often spelled Tangipahoa as the name of the tribe and as the name of a river on which the tribe once resided. Perhaps the Tangipahoa were only a village of Acolapissas. The name was important to Iberville solely because Tonty had reported them as living on the Mississippi in 1682. Their village had been burned just before La Salle's party reached it, and dead bodies were lying about, owing, according to the Bayogoula, to an attack made by the Humas. Hodge, *Handbook*, 2:685.

[88]Deleted in the MS. but still legible.

[89]The MS. has "sur des queles de cannes." Margry (4:169) changed it to "sur des clayes de cannes," which I have translated "on cane mats" because it was the Indians' custom to use these or skins for seats for their visitors.

shine. There I gave them a present, a large one for them, of axes, knives, mirrors, needles, shirts, and blankets; they gave me a present, too, one of their most precious possessions, which was twelve deer skins, very big ones, most of them worm-eaten, which I gave to my men to make shoes. They feasted us with sagamité made of bread. While they were dividing their presents, I went for a walk in the village with the chief of the Bayogoula, who took me into their temple, on top of which were figures of animals, such as of a cock painted red. At the door there is a lean-to 8 feet wide and 12 long, supported by two big posts with a cross-beam, which serves as a girder. Beside the temple door are several figures of animals, such as bears, wolves, birds; on this side is the figure of one they call *choücoüa-cha,* which is an animal that has a head like a suckling pig's and as big, hair like a badger's, gray and white, a tail like a rat's, paws like a monkey's, and under the belly has a pouch in which it generates its young and suckles them. I have killed eight, which I examined thoroughly. The door of the temple is 3 feet high[90] and 2½ wide. The chief had it opened by a man and went in first. It was a hut built like all the others in which they are housed, dome-shaped, 30 feet in diameter and round, daubed with mud as high as a man's head. In the middle were two logs of dry, worm-eaten wood, laid end to end and burning. At the far end was a platform on which were several bundles of the skins of deer, bear, and buffalo, which were offerings to their god in the form of this *choücoüacha,*[91] which was depicted in several places in red and black. There was a bottle of thick glass that Tonty had given to these people. That is all I saw in the temple. From there I went through their village and huts,

---

[90]MS.: "3 pieds de haut." I know that it is often difficult to distinguish the figure 3 from an 8; but I read a figure 3 and know, anyhow, that doors to Indian houses were small and low. But Margry has (4:170): "La porte du temple a huit pieds de haut."

[91]The logic of the context calls for "offerings to their god [a singular noun] in the form of this choücoüacha"; but the MS. has "presens offerts a leurs dieux soubz la figure de ce choücoüacha."

constructed, like the temple, with a lean-to adjoining, some big, others small, roofed with split canes joined together quite neatly; there are no windows. These huts get their light from above through a hole 2 feet in diameter and are without paving or flooring except sand and dry dirt. Their beds are on four posts, raised 2 feet above ground, with crosspieces of red wood nearly as thick as one's arm, on which a mat is spread, made of small canes bound together in such a fashion that they are quite straight but not very soft. For furnishings they have only a few earthen pots, which they make nicely enough, fine and well wrought. All the men go around naked, without being self-conscious about their nakedness. The women wear just a *braguet*, made from bark, most *braguets* being white and red. The *braguet* is made of a number of strands of bark spun and woven together, eight inches wide for the top part, which covers their loins; the lower part is in foot-long tassels reaching down to above the knees. With the *braguet* the women are sufficiently concealed, as the tassels are in constant agitation. Many girls six to seven years old wear no *braguet* whatsoever; they conceal themselves with a small wad of moss held by a string passing between their thighs and tied to a belt they wear. I have not seen a single pretty one. They wear their hair in a twist around the head. In this village there were 107 huts and 2 temples; and there were possibly about 200 to 250 men and few women and children. The smallpox, which they still had in the village, had killed one-fourth of the people. They place the bodies of their dead on platforms around their village, quite close to it, raised 7 feet above the ground, wrapped in cane mats and covered by a cane mat shaped like the roof of a house. This stinks badly and attracts many buzzards to the neighborhood.

These Indians are the most beggarly I have yet seen, having no conveniences in their huts and engaging in no work. Some wear a kind of cloak made from bark woven tolerably well, such as a coarse linen made of bleached hemp would be in France. All the men have nimble, well-made bodies, agile figures, but are not much inured to war, I think. They wear their hair short and tattoo their faces and bodies. Blackening the teeth is a charm in the women; they blacken them with a herb crushed into a paste, which they put in their mouths. The teeth stay black for a while and become white again. The young girls are careful in doing that, so that their faces are clean. The bodies of some are tattooed and their faces and breasts marked with black.

In their village they have some cocks and hens. Their fields are not big, considering the number of people they have. The ground in the vicinity is fairly level. The country is very fine, with tall trees, all kinds mixed except pines. I saw some wild apple trees and some peach trees. There are neither strawberries nor raspberries nor mulberries. I returned to camp to join my men, the whole village escorting me, singing the while. We spent the rest of the day entertaining one another, singing and dancing. I had some canister shots fired for the Indians, which caused them great wonder. I could not learn anything about what I wanted to know. By observation I found that the latitude of this village, which is on the left side of the river going upstream, is 31°2' north.

The 16th. At eight o'clock in the morning I set out for the Ouma to see whether I could get information about the fork that Tonty, in his relation, says he took. The chief of the Bayogoula left in the boat with me and had a canoe follow in which there were eight of his own men to guide us. Today I have made 7½ leagues. Three leagues from their village, on the left going upstream, there is a creek by way of which they go in canoe to the Outymascha[92] and the Magenescito,[93] three days' travel west from here. Six leagues and a half above their village, on the right side of the river, they pointed out to me the stream they take to go to the Annocchy, whom they call

---

[92]Not mentioned by Hodge or Swanton.

[93]Hodge, taking this to be an error for Yagenechito, gives the little information available about the small tribe living within some association with the Chitimacha on Bayou Lafourche. They were still in existence as late as 1706 (Hodge, *Handbook*, 2:982, and Swanton, *Indians*, p. 120). The name is sometimes given as Yakna-Chitto.

Bylocchy. They call this stream Ascan[t]hya, and it flows to the sea, into the bay where the ships are.[94] The Myssysypy flows into it. That is the only branch they are acquainted with. The river has wound in and out a great deal since their village. The farther I go upstream, the more advanced I find the country: Grapes are grown as big as snipe shot and bigger; there are a great many vines along the river. The land becomes inundated one foot; I do not know whether it is the same thing back from the river.

The 17th. Five leagues and a half from our last stop for the night we came on the right side of the river to a little stream in which the Indians informed us that there were great numbers of fish. Here I had nets set out but caught only two catfish. The Indians having stopped 2 leagues below to hunt bear, where they say there are a great many, my brother stayed with them. This stream is the dividing line between the Ouma's hunting ground and the Bayogoula's. On the bank are many huts roofed with palmettos and a maypole with no limbs, painted red, several fish heads and bear bones being tied to it as a sacrifice.[95] The area is extremely fine.

The 18th. My brother and the Indians overtook me, the Indians having killed nothing; my brother killed one bear. Two leagues from our last camp I found an island 1 league long, the first one that I have discovered in the river. Two leagues from the island, on the right side, I found high ground rising 50 feet

---

[94]MS.: " . . . s'y jette dedans." It is accurate to say that the Ascanthia or Iberville River, later called Bayou Manchac, flowed into the bay where the ships were, but only in the sense that the current of the little stream flowed through the lakes Maurepas and Pontchartrain before flowing into Lake Borne.

[95]This pole is the famous *bâton rouge* for which a city is named. The MS. describes this red pole as having "testes de poisson et oss d'ours" attached to it. The first *s* of *oss* is made in the old style, like an *f*. Margry (4:173) does not follow the MS. exactly: he has "testes de poissons et d'ours." The passage is dated March 17, 1699. On the same day, whoever was keeping the Journal of the *Marin* merely mentioned the height of the pole, "trente pieds," and some fish bones on it (Margry, 4:263).

straight up—sandy land for 2 leagues, like at Étampe;[96] the
other bank was flat like everywhere else. Six leagues and a half
from our last camp we found a creek 6 feet wide that runs out
of the Myssysypy River. The Indians told me that, if I could get
my longboats through it, I would shorten my journey by one
day's travel. I sent my brother by canoe to see whether that
was possible. He told me that it could be done with a little work.
There is a distance of 500 yards where I found a raft of trees 30
feet high that the high waters had piled on top of one another,
blocking the way through. I put the men to work to clear a way
350 yards long and made the portage with everything I had in
my longboats; and with pulleys I had the boats dragged from
the other side and launched on the river,[97] after a great effort,
owing to the rain and the muddy ground, on which one could
not keep his footing. I finished this work at nine o'clock at night
by the light of torches made of canes bound together, and
proceeded to the other bank of the river and spent the night,
where my brother, with the two bark canoes, had gone to set up
the tents and prepare supper for everybody. We are all living on
Indian corn that I bought at the Bayogoula village. With corn
we make sagamité, as we do not have any provisions other
than 200 pounds of bread in each longboat, which I am saving
for the return journey.

The 19th. Today we made fully 6½ leagues and came at night
to the left side of the river and made camp. Three leagues from
the Ouma's landing, I had a canister shot fired to notify them of
my coming, so that I would avoid surprising them. Today we
have kept going for thirteen hours; my men are very tired and,

---

[96]Étampes is a town near Paris famous for engravings and woodcuts. Fr.
estampe means "print" or "engraving."
[97]Margry, 4:174: " . . . et avec des palans je les fis passer de l'autre costé et les
jeter dans la rivière." The problem here is to determine the antecedent of the
pronoun *les:* "mes chaloupes" or "bois de trente pieds de haut." Moodie
thought Iberville had the trees moved with the pulleys and cast into the
Mississippi. But working tired men in the rain, and night coming on, Iberville
would certainly have done no more than was necessary to clear a way for his
longboats. It would have been foolish for him to try to clear up the driftwood.
The pronoun *les* stands for longboats.

having only sagamité to eat, are swearing and storming at the writers of forged narratives,[98] who may be given the blame for my going so far.

The 20th. I got to the landing for the Ouma's village at ten-thirty in the morning, 3 leagues from the place where I spent the night. There I found five men, three Ouma and two Quynypyssa, who were awaiting me with the calumet of peace. They had come from the village upon hearing the shot from the swivel-gun. Far off as they were when they saw us, they started singing, and the Bayogoula with me sang as my representative. When we got on shore, we all embraced one another and rubbed one another in their fashion and smoked together. About eleven o'clock I went to the village, the Bayogoula and his men escorting us all along the way.[99] The Ouma's deputies marched in front, singing all the way, even though we had to go by a rather bad road full of hills or small mountains, quite steep, for almost the entire way. At one o'clock in the afternoon we came in sight of the village. When 400 yards from it, I was met by three men appointed to bear the calumet of peace to me. I had to smoke ceremoniously, seated on the mat, which I find very unpleasant [as I have never been a smoker].[100] These three new singers led me to high ground, where there were three huts, 300 yards from the village. Here they made me stop

---

[98]Father Paul du Ru refers to a book of doubtful authorship, which is sometimes attributed to Henri Tonty and often called a forgery; it is *Dernières découvertes dans l'Amérique Septentrionale de M. De la Sale, Mises au jour par M. le Chevalier Tonti, Gouvernour du Fort Saint Louis, aux Yslinois* (Paris, 1699). Louis Hennepin's *Nouvelle découverte d'un très grand Pays, situé dans l'Amérique, entre le Nouveau Mexique et la Mer Glaciale* (Utrecht, 1697) was inaccurate and generally considered untruthful. It gave the Recollect Father Hennepin a very bad reputation. Iberville carried with him, at times in his longboat, vol. 2 of Chrestien Le Clercq's *Premier établissement de la Foy dans la Nouvelle France*, 2 vols. (Paris, 1691). This book Iberville himself said he had with him. Presumably he had read the others.

[99]Margry, 4:175: " . . . les Bayogoulas et ces hommes nous escortant tout le long du chemin." But the context, the MS. spelling *ses* instead of Margry's *ces*, and facts yet to be given all indicate that the proper reading should be "le Bayogoula et ses hommes."

[100]Deleted in the MS., but still legible.

and sent a messenger to notify the chief that I had arrived; we waited for instructions about what we were to do. A man came and told us to enter the village. As we were entering, the three singers marched in front, singing, presenting to the village the calumet of peace, held as high as their arms would reach. The chief and two of the most distinguished men came to meet me at the entrance to the village, each carrying a white cross in his hand. They greeted me in their fashion, held me under the arms, and conducted me on to some mats in the middle of their village square, where the whole village was assembled. Here we smoked again, and they bestowed on me many marks of friendship. I gave them a small present in advance of what I intended to give them at my longboats. About four o'clock in the afternoon we were given a formal ball in the middle of the square, where the whole village had assembled.

To the middle of the assembly were brought some drums, *chychycoucy,* which are gourds containing dry seeds, with sticks for handles. They make a little noise and help to mark the beat. A number of singers made their way there. Shortly afterwards came twenty young men, between twenty and thirty years old, and fifteen of the prettiest young girls, splendidly adorned in their style, all of them naked, wearing nothing except their *braguets,* over which they wore a kind of sash a foot wide, which was made of feathers or fur or hair, painted red, yellow, and white, their faces and bodies tattooed or painted various colors, and they carried in their hands feathers that they used as fans or to mark the beat, some tufts of feathers being neatly braided into their hair. The young men went naked, wearing only a girdle like the girls, which partly concealed them. They were prominently tattooed and their hair was well arranged with tufts of feathers. Several had kettles shaped like flattened plates, two or three together, tied to their girdles and hanging down to their knees, which made noise and helped to mark the beat. They danced in this way for three hours, appearing very merry and frolicsome. When it got dark the chief lodged us in his hut or house, which he had had vacated.[101] After we had eaten a supper of Indian-corn sagamité, a flambeau of canes 15 feet long, bound together, as big around as 2 feet, was fetched, lighted, and set up in the middle. It burned at the top and gave sufficient light. All the young men of the village made their way there with their bows and arrows and headbreakers and war equipment along with a few women and girls. Here they began all over, and sang war dances up until midnight, which I found very pretty; then all withdrew except the chief, who stayed and spent the night in his hut with us and all the Bayogoula, on whom the Indians bestowed the same honor as on us, looking upon them as Frenchmen, because they had brought us into their homes.[102] The two chiefs made speeches to each other, the Bayogoula speaking as my proxy to the Ouma. This village is located on a hill, on which there are 140 huts. There are possibly 350 men at most and many children. All the huts are on the slope of the hill, in two rows in certain places and in a circle. In the middle, there is a village square 200 yards wide kept in good order. The corn fields are in little valleys and on hills in the vicinity. This whole region is chiefly hills of fairly good black soil. There are no rocks whatsoever; I have not yet seen any at all since I left the sea. The village is 2½ leagues north of the river. The woods are hardwood trees, mixed with all sorts of oaks, and particularly a great many canes in the bottoms.[103] I saw no fruit tree there. They gave me nuts of two kinds: one kind being hard nuts like the ones of Canada, the other kind small ones shaped like olives and no bigger. So far

---

[101]Margry, 4:176: "La nuit venue, le chef nous fit loger dans sa cabane ou maison qu'il avoit faite." This sentence loses all of its special sense because Margry dropped the word *vider*, "to empty" or "to vacate." The MS. has, "La nuit venue, le chef nous fit loger dans sa cabanne ou maison qu'il avoit fait vuider [*or* viuder]."

[102]MS.: " . . . nous ayant amené chez eux."

[103]McDermott's *Glossary of Mississippi Valley French* gives *fonds* as meaning the village woods (p. 77), but in a French village rather than an Indian village. I take *les fonds* here to mean "low places" or "bottoms."

they have cultivated nothing except some melons, but have sowed tobacco.

The 21st. At ten o'clock in the morning I left the village to go back with my men. The Bayogoula went along with me, singing the while. When leaving, I gave this village two salutes of musket fire, and at noon I arrived at my longboats. At two o'clock the chief of the Ouma arrived with more than 150 of his men and women and children, who brought us some bread, made of Indian corn, and some pounded meal. I gave them a present of axes, knives, kettles, mirrors, scissors, awls, needles, shirts, blankets, and jackets made of red cloth. When I asked them for Indian corn, they sent messengers throughout the night to the village to tell them to bring it the next day. They spoke at length about Tonty, who had spent five days at their village, having left his canoes with one of his men at the place where my longboats are. I could not get any information about the fork. I saw some Quynypyssa, who tell me that their village is seven days from here and that neither Tonty nor any Frenchmen have been to it. That truly disappoints me and puts me in a great difficulty. Believing that these men could have the same reasons as the others to conceal the truth from me, although they seem to me to be quite sincere,[104] I made up my mind to go as far as the Coroa.[105] The Recollect Father's narrative says that the fork is 15 leagues this side of the Coroa.

The 22nd. At eight o'clock in the morning they brought me three barrels of Indian corn from the village. I set out in a canoe in which there were six Ouma and one Taensa,[106] whom

---

[104]MS.: " . . . quoique ils ne me paroissent pas de bonne foy." Margry removed the negative from this clause, as both logic and context demanded (4:178).

[105]The Coroa or Koroa (sometimes Coloa) lived on the west side of the Mississippi below the Natchez; other parts of the tribe lived on the Yazoo River and in areas close by. Finally all of the Coroas lived on the Yazoo. These were belligerent, treacherous, and cruel Indians. Typical of Coroa behavior was the murder of the Abbé Nicolas Foucault and his three companions by some paddlers the priest had employed because he and his party were sick. The paddlers had coveted Father Foucault's baggage and other possessions. *DCB,* s.v. "Foucault, Nicolas," and Richebourg Gaillard McWilliams, trans. and ed., *Fleur de Lys and Calumet: Being the Pénicaut Narrative of French Adventure in Louisiana* (Baton Rouge, 1953), pp. 98–100.

[106]This map-making Taensa was from a tribe that lived on an oxbow lake, Lake

I took into my longboat to have him make a map of the country[107] and to see whether he will not talk differently when he is away from the others. Once that he had seen us on our way to go there, he assured me that the Malbanchya—that is the name of the Myssysypy—does not fork between here and the Acansa,[108] where he has been. He made a map for me on which he shows me that on the third day of our journey we shall come to a river on the left side that is named Tas[s]enocogoula,[109] in which he shows two branches: On the west one are eight villages, which he calls Yaché, Nacthytos, Yezito, Natao, Cachaymoüa, Cadodaquio, Nataho, Natsytos.[110] The fifth and the sixth of these villages M. Cavelie[r][111] visited on his

St. Joseph, in northeast Louisiana, not far from the Mississippi River. Their general culture shows that they were related to the Natchez Indians. On his second voyage to the Mississippi Iberville visited the tribe. Hodge, *Handbook*, 2:668–69.

[107]In several places in this journal, Iberville gives evidence of the Indian's understanding of maps and map-drawing. Map-making was particularly important to the plains Indians who followed the buffalo herds for great distances, as they needed maps to guide them back to their home villages.

[108]The Quapa or Kapa Indians, a Siouan tribe that came downriver before De Soto's time. They lived mainly near the juncture of the Arkansas and the Mississippi. In writings of the seventeenth and early eighteenth centuries, the name of these Indians is spelled without the letter *r*. One sees such forms as Acansa and Akansea. Hodge, *Handbook*, 2:333–35.

[109]The Red River of Louisiana was called by several names: Tassenocogoula, Seignelay, Sablonnière, Marne. See the unsigned *mémoire* in Margry, 4:313: "Mémoire de la Coste de la Floride et d'une partie du Mexique."

[110]Within the conditions of the way the questioner and the informer were communicating, Iberville's list of Caddo tribes is fully 50 per cent accurate. The Yataché, the Natao, the Cadodaquio, and the Natsytos seem to be the Yatasi, the Adai (if Swanton is correct), the Kadohadacho, and the Natchitoches in Mooney's list of Caddo tribes in 1886. I have no idea how Swanton (*Indians*, p. 83) determined that Iberville's Natao and, I judge, the Nataho (a duplication) were the Adai. Nacthytos and Natsytos both appear to be the Natchitoches. The Cachaymoua in Iberville's list, as I read the MS., appear in Margry as Cachaymons and were accepted as such by Hodge. Cf. Margry, 4:178, and Hodge, *Handbook*, 1:178. In the literature of the Caddos there are so many unidentified names of villages and tribes that Hodge made four lists of names: those (1) undoubtedly Caddoan, (2) probably Caddoan, (3) possibly Caddoan, and (4) tribes just living in Caddo country (1:178–83). See also Swanton, *Indians*, pp. 98–100.

[111]In this year Robert Cavelier de La Salle reached the Cenis (Senis or Senys)

way back overland from the Senys[112] to the Acansa. From the Senys to the Cadodaquio they found to be a distance of 53 leagues, according to their calculation. This Taensa informs me that from the Ouma to those villages could be a distance of eight days by canoe, which is 60 leagues. On that branch that they call Tassenocogoula, they mention one nation that they call the Nyhatta.[113] They speak of it as of a very important nation, three days' journey from the Ouma. Going up the Malbanchya for one day above this Tassenocogoula River, we shall find ourselves again at the Ouma's landing, where the canoes are and where the chief should be and should regale us with a feast when we go by. From that landing to the village it is possibly 1½ leagues. The river makes a big bend to the west at that place. From that landing to the village of the Théloël three days' travel. These eight villages together make only one, of which the Nachés are one; the others are named Pochougoula, Ousagoucoula, Cogoucoula, Yatanocha, Ymacacha, Thou-coue, Tougoula, Achougoucoula.[114] All these villages together

---

before he was slain; but so did his older brother, the Abbé Jean Cavelier, who survived the dissention in the group of La Salle's followers trying to reach Canada. Although I cannot be sure about which brother is meant, I think it is the Abbé. *DCB* s.v. "Cavelier de La Salle, René-Robert," and "Cavelier, Jean."

[112]The names Cenis and Senys seem to be short forms taken from Hasinai, which was the Caddos' own name for their confederacy. Acansa—without the r sound—was the form of the name of a division of Quapaws. Such observers as La Salle, Joutel, Gravier, and St. Cosme wrote the name without r. Dumont *dit* Montigny spelled the name Arcancas. From 1750 on, one rarely sees the word written without r. See Quapaw in Hodge, *Handbook*, 2:335–36.

[113]I cannot find anything about the Nyhatta other than what Iberville has written here.

[114]I count nine villages without including the Théloël, which apparently is just another name for the Natchez nation. Later observers, seeing more of the Natchez than Iberville had an opportunity to see, give the village names as Corn, Gray, Jenzenaque, White Apple Village, and White Earth Village; the Grigras and Tioux are two other nations under Natchez protection. The Tioux had migrated from the Yazoo River to the west side of the Mississippi; the Grigra (often just Gris) are listed by Swanton as being "probably of Tunican stock." This little village of some sixty warriors in the 1720s maintained their hostility toward the French till the end of their identity as a tribe. See Swanton, *Indians*, p. 134.

make only one nation, which is named the Théloël. He describes this village for me as having three or four hundred huts, crowded with people. From the Théloël, going upriver for one day, there is, on the right side, the river of the Chycacha,[115] of which I shall speak later; a day and a half above this river is the village of the Taensa. The village is on the right side, going upstream,[116] being seven villages together, making only one, to which they give the names Taensa, Ohytoucoula, Nyhougoula, Couthaougoula, Couchayon,[117] Talaspa, Chaoucoula. The Indian I have with me is a Taensa. [The village] has many men and many huts, like Théloël, but is not quite so big.

Three days upstream from this village are the Coloa, on the left side, and the Yachou, who make only one village. In the narratives they are given the name Coroa. From the Coroa to the Ymahan,[118] which is a village of the Acansa, they count 10½ days, on a scale of 7 leagues, which I take to be the equivalent, at most, of one of their day's travel by canoe. On the river of the Chycacha, which I referred to above, he shows seven villages, which are the Tonyca, Vyspe, Opocoula, Taposa, Chaquesauma, Outapa, Thysia.[119] From the Théloël to the Tonyca, four days; from the former to the most distant of the others, two days; and from the Ouma they go overland to it

---

[115]The Yazoo River, whose upper branches drained the land close to an area in north Mississippi drained by the Tombigbee. This was the home of the warlike Chickasaws.

[116]An obvious error. The Taensa were domiciled, not on the east side but on the west side of the Mississippi, on Lake St. Joseph in present-day Tensas Parish (Hodge, *Handbook*, 2:668). I cannot account for this error. The Taensas' huts were scattered along the lake in the villages that Iberville names immediately below.

[117]"Couchayon" is my reading of the MS.; Hodge (*Handbook*, 2:669) has "Conchayon."

[118]MS.: "Ymahan"; Margry, 4:179, has "Imaho." This was a Quapaw village usually given the name Imaha (Hodge, *Handbook*, 2:336). Bénard de la Harpe visited this tribe.

[119]The Tunica Indians (MS.: "Tonyca"), a distinct linguistic stock able to pronounce *r*, occupied some two hundred cabins on the Yazoo River toward the end of the seventeenth century—until 1706, when conflicts with the Chickasaws and Alibamu Indians drove them downriver as far south as the Huma, with whom they were allied (Hodge, *Handbook*, 2:858, drawing on

in six days. These Chycacha and Napyssa are joined together; their villages are near one another. South of the Chy[c]acha all the nations are at peace with one another. These Indians and the others I have questioned locate the nations that are on the Myssysypy quite differently from what the Christian Father reports in his second volume of *L'Establissement de la Foy*,[120] following the account of Father Senoble,[121] the Sieur de Lassale's[122] traveling companion, who says that, on their way down to the sea, they found:

From the Acansa to the Taensa	80	Leagues
From the Taensa to the Naché	12	"
From the Naché to the Coroa	10	"

Bénard de la Harpe). The Ofogoula (MS.: "Opocoula") occupied ten to twenty cabins on the Yazoo when André Pénicaut passed by with the Le Sueur expedition to the Upper River. The able-bodied men of this tribe were away on the hunt when the Natchez massacred the French in 1729. Instead of siding with the Yazoo and Coroas against the French, the Ofogoula moved downriver to reside with the Tunica (Hodge, *Handbook*, 2:108). The Taposa occupied some twenty-five cabins near the Chakchiuma, either just above or just below them on the Yazoo (Swanton, *Indians*, p. 190). They probably merged with the Chakchiuma (MS.: "Chaquesauma"), who with the Taposa had some seventy cabins on the Yazoo, according to Father Montigny. Pressure drove them east, and they occupied a site between the Choctaws and the Chickasaws (Swanton, *Indians*, p. 106). The Ibitoupa (MS.: "Outapa") was a small tribe high on the Yazoo. They joined the Taposa and Chakchiuma and then perhaps merged with the Chickasaws (Hodge, *Handbook*, 1:593). The Tiou (MS.: "Thysia") or a part of them moved to a site a few miles below the Natchez landing (Hodge, *Handbook*, 1:758). I cannot find in the literature any references to the tribe Iberville recorded as the Vyspe.

[120]By Chrestien Le Clercq.

[121]Father Zénobe Membré, a Recollect missionary in Canada and a friend of La Salle's, went with La Salle on the 1682 journey to the mouth of the Mississippi and sailed with him in 1684 for the Mississippi with the colonists and soldiers entrusted to the discoverer. As chaplain he blessed the cross planted by La Salle when he took possession of "La Louisianne" for France on April 6, 1682. This Recollect was given the honor of bearing the news to France that La Salle had discovered the mouth of the Mississippi and had taken possession for France (*DCB*, s.v. "Membré, Zénobe").

[122]Robert Cavelier de La Salle was born at Rouen in 1643 and was slain in

From the Coroa, or Coloa, to the
branching of the river or fork   6   "
From the fork to the Quynypyssa   40   "
From the Quynypyssa to the Tangibao   2   "
From the Tangibao to the sea   40   "
Which would be, from the Acansa
to the sea   190   "

In the statements of Indians whom I have examined thoroughly, and at a rate of 7 leagues to one day's travel upstream, they calculate:

From the Acansa to the Coroa	73½ Leagues
From the Coloa to the Taensa	21 "
From the Taensa to the Naché	17½ "
From the Naché or Théloël to the Ouma	53½ "
	164½ [sic] "

By my estimation and the estimation of the two pilots I have with me:

From the Ouma to the Bayogoula,
following the river   35   Leagues
From the Bayogoula to the sea   64   "

Making from the Acansa to the sea   263½ [sic] "

America by some of his own men in 1687. He was well reared and was educated by the Jesuits; but he turned from the life of a priest to the more exciting life of a promoter and discoverer. He had been in Canada and near the Great Lakes fifteen years before he made his historic voyage down the Mississippi to its mouth in 1682. At a point near Venice, La., slightly above the river passes, La Salle donned a scarlet garment trimmed with gold and took possession of the middle third of the present area of the United States for his king, Louis XIV, on April 9, 1682, creating by the act of seizin the potential for a French colonial empire in the heart of North America. But when he was given a colony by the crown to plant at the mouth of the Mississippi—320 souls, including 100 soldiers—he failed utterly because of flaws in his character. From the debacle at Matagorda Bay, Tex., only a few people saved themselves (*DCB*, s.v. "Cavelier de La Salle, René-Robert").

Which would make a difference of 73½ leagues. Moreover, I could not think it possible that so many different Indians whom I persuaded to make maps in private could be lying about the question of the fork: They were, I could see, giving me too many pieces of evidence that it was by this river that the Sieur de Lassale and Tonty had gone down to the sea. The Bayogoula, seeing me persistent in my desire to go find the fork and persistent in my belief that Tonty had not come that way, gave me to understand that Tonty had left with the chief of the Mogoulascha a piece of writing that, like the one I was leaving with them, was closed—to be given to a man who was to come from the sea. That led me to conclude that it was a letter from Tonty for M. de Lassale and that, if it was true that there was a branch, it could not flow east of the one that I was on or, at all events, it was not the one Tonty had taken on his way down, considering that there was no river between the Apalascha[123] and Pensacola. It could not be Pensacola,[124] which is a bay into which empties a river of clear water; and the country there is not subject to inundation. La Mobille appeared to me to be a river indeed big enough to be the Myssysypy, its waters roiled and muddy, with strong currents; but it cannot be the one our Frenchmen took on the way down, for the mouth of it is more than a league wide and it forms a bay close to where it empties into the sea, more than 4 leagues wide, in which fresh and salt water are mixed by the reflux of the sea for more than 6 leagues up the bay. The soil along the shore is sandy and covered with pines, like the islands there. The mainland is not a country subject to overflow, but is covered with all sorts of hardwood

---

[123]It is difficult to say whether "Apalascha" means an Indian village of Apalachees or the Spanish settlement about a fort slightly inland from Apalachee Bay. The word in question may refer to the bay itself or to the Apalachicola River or settlement. Iberville had never been to this area. More will be said about the Spanish settlements in Florida, in the Port St. Joe and Apalachee Bay areas.

[124]The MS. reading, dropped from Margry, 4:180, is "que ce n'estoit point Pensacola."

trees and so flat that, in heading for the shore, a longboat cannot get closer than a fourth of a league on the west side of the river. This has no resemblance to what the narrative of the Recollect Father reports about the lower part of the fork of the Myssysypy by which they went down, but does indeed resemble the lower part of the stream I am on, although he specified in his narrative that he went down by the west branch. I know that when he was at St. Louis Bay with M. de Beaujeu,[125] he was telling, like M. de Lassale, that it might indeed be the west branch of the Myssysypy that emptied into St. Louis Bay, for he was not acquainted with it, having come down to the sea by the east branch. He is a liar that has disguised everything, so that I cannot determine the resemblances of this river to the one they descended.

Seeing that time was pressing for me to go back and that my longboats would require time to return to the ships from the lower part of the river if they did not find a fair wind, I went back to the Ouma's landing from 3 leagues above it, and got there about six-thirty in the evening, finding no one there. I immediately sent my brother and two Canadians to the village to try to fetch the Bayogoula and his men,[126] in order to start at daybreak the next day. He found them in a debauch with some women at the village. He urged them to come to me, but they put him off till the next day. After my brother had entreated them several times and they were unwilling to come, he left them and, seeming to be displeased with them, came on as fast as he could and got back at nine o'clock at night after great

[125]Taneguy Le Gallois de Beaujeu, the irascible officer commanding the vessels of La Salle on the expedition through the Gulf of Mexico to Matagorda Bay in 1684. The French called that bay St. Louis Bay. By the time Iberville returned from his successful journey to the Mississippi in 1698–99, Beaujeu was ready to belittle his accomplishments and damage his reputation in any way he could (*DCB*, s.v. "Cavelier de La Salle, René-Robert").
[126]The MS. has ambiguous grammar: "les Bayogoula et ses gens." "Bayogoula" can be and is plural, but the possessive adjective, *ses*, refers to one possessor. The Journal has already provided the information that there was a Bayogoula chief who had Bayogoulas with him.

effort, for he could not see at all among the canes. At ten
o'clock at night, three Bayogoula and six Ouma came back
bearing the calumet of peace to us all over again, believing us to
be angry. After I had made them come close and had given
them something to eat, they told me that my brother's hasty
departure from the village had thrown all the people into a
turmoil as they thought him to be angry, and that they had been
sent to pacify us. The chief was sending me eight fowls and
some pumpkins and would come himself the next day, in the
morning. I gave a few trifles to these Indians and immediately
sent five of them back, lighted by dry-cane flambeaux, to tell the
village that I needed some Indian corn and was to be brought
some, which I would pay for. Two leagues above the Ouma's
landing, there is a small island half a league in circumference.
That is the third island I have seen in this river between the
Bayogoula and the Ouma.

The 23rd. Toward eight o'clock in the morning the chief of
the Ouma came along with eighty of his men and women in a
group, laden with corn, pumpkins, and fowls;[127] and the chief of
the Bayogoula and the rest of his men told me that they had
believed I would be angry because they had not come the night
before with my brother, but that it was too late to come. I gave
them a few glass beads, awls, knives, and needles in exchange
for their corn. After we had shown affection to one another
and said goodby, I embarked. The chief of the Ouma and one of
his distinguished men escorted me to my longboat, holding me
under the arm to help me walk, lest some accident should

---

[127]Chickens were plentiful at the Humas' villages because the Indians kept
them, not as poultry to be eaten but as curiosities. The Indians would not even
eat chickens killed by the dogs (Du Ru, *Journal*, p. 20). The cocks, possibly
because they saluted the break of day, may have been objects of reverence, for
many southern Indians worshipped the sun. Shea attributed the presence of
chickens at the Humas to a ship wrecked off the mouth of the Mississippi, from
which the Humas acquired their first birds (Ibid., p. 20 and p. 28 [n. 36]). The
Aztecs had chickens when Cortés conquered Mexico, but I do not know what
kind. See Hernando Cortés, *Five Letters of Cortés to the Emperor, 1519–1526*,
trans. J. Bayard Morris (New York, 1962), pp. 50, 79, and 96.

happen to me on their land. The chief of the Bayogoula got into the boat with me. He is a forty-year-old man who is intelligent and cunning. After we got clear of the bank, I had three salutes of musket-shot fired and "Vive le Roy" shouted three times, to which they responded by giving three shouts of joy, resembling my shouts of "Vive le Roy!"

The Ouma, Bayogoula, Théloël, Taensa, the Coloa, the Chycacha, the Napyssa, the Ouacha, Choutymacha,[128] Yageneschyto speak the same language, and they and the Bylocchy and the Pascoboula understand each other.

The chief of the Ouma is a man five feet ten inches tall and proportionately big. He has a flat forehead, although the other men of his nation do not have it; at any rate, just a few of the old men do. This vogue changes among them. The chief is about seventy[129] years old, and has one son twenty-five to thirty years old, well built, who will succeed his father as chief. These chiefs have no more power over their people than do the chiefs of other nations on the confines of Canada. I have noticed solely among them a little more politeness. This same day we came 12[130] leagues below the village and spent the night. This river has a very swift current, and my men are rowing willingly in order to go back and get bread and wine in place of water and the Indian corn.

The 24th. At three o'clock in the afternoon, we got down to the stream that goes to the Bylocchy and to the bay where the ships are. I have seen no possibility of getting the longboats

---

[128]The Chitimachas (here Choutymacha) belonged to a distinct linguistic family. Their early home was Grand Lake, La., and they became notorious when they murdered the missionary Jean-François Buisson de Saint-Cosme, the successor to Father Montigny at the Natchez. The French got revenge by killing some Chitimachas and taking a good many slaves, whose presence at La Mobile shows in baptismal records over a period of years. Hodge, *Handbook*,1:286, and *DCB*, s.v. "Buisson de Saint-Cosme, Jean-François."

[129]The MS. seems to have either "10" or "60" for the age of the chief. Margry (4:184) gives 70 years, which seems acceptable; I cannot be sure that 60 is correct.

[130]MS.: "12." Margry, 4:184: "deux."

through it. M. de Sauvole has gone on in the longboats. I ordered him to take soundings of the river mouth and the middle pass; and my brother went on in my longboat, in which was the chief of the Bayogoula. He gave me a Mougoulascha to guide me to the sea by way of this little stream, which I entered about four o'clock in the afternoon with the two bark canoes and four of my men and the Mougoulascha. I went 2 leagues down it and there spent the night. This river or creek is no more than 8 or 10 yards wide, being full of uprooted trees, which obstruct it. During low water there are 3 to 4 feet of water; during high water 2 to 3 fathoms. Within these 2 leagues I have made ten portages, some being 10 yards long, others 300 or 400 yards, more or less.

The 25th. I ran mostly east, like yesterday afternoon; I must have made today 7 leagues and 50 portages over trees and log rafts; and we came on and spent the night at a landing, where we found six pirogues. Here two small streams unite with this one, one from the north-northwest and the other from the southeast, making it half again bigger and twice as wide.

The Mougoulascha, whom I had in my canoe and who got out 3 leagues from here, leading us to believe that he would catch up with us at these forks, failed to make his way here and apparently returned to his village, which cannot be more than 6 to 7 leagues from here in a straight line. There is a well-trodden road leading to within a league of his village. The place where I am is one of the prettiest spots I have seen, fine level ground, beautiful woods, clear and bare of canes; but the whole country becomes inundated to a depth of 5 to 6 feet during high water. We are hearing many turkeys gobble but have been unable to kill any. In these streams are many fish and crocodiles. It would be easy to clear out this stream[131] during low water and make it navigable all the way to the Myssysypy. Those portages have worn us out today, me in particular, as I had to carry the

---

[131]For speculation about clearing the rafts of uprooted trees choking the waters of Bayou Manchac, see the material drawn from the letter Capt. James Campbell wrote to the Earl of Loudon, Mobile, December 15, 1763. See *The Alabama Review* 22 (July 1969): 235.

front end of my canoe and guide it for fear of having it split, because Deschyers, one of my Canadians, was sick. Three leagues from here I took the elevation of the sun and found 31°3′.

The 26th. Although I am without a guide, I have gone on nevertheless, even though it is a rather venturesome undertaking with four men; but if I turn back and go by way of the Myssysypy I shall not catch up with my longboats, and I prefer to follow this stream and show the Indians that, without a guide, I go wherever I want to go. In any event, I shall still come out at the ships, even though I have to go overland, abandon my canoes, and make some more wherever I shall find at the seashore tree bark that peels easily at this season.[132]

Four leagues east-southeast of the place where I stopped for the night I found a river on my left, coming from the north, twice as big as the one I am on; it has a slight current and is no more than 50 yards wide and 5 feet deep. The two unite, and below the junction of them I found 2½ fathoms of water, a width of 80 yards; the country is very fine, becoming inundated to a depth of 1 foot during high water. A great many places do not become inundated. A league and a half from this river, going on east-southeast, I came to still another, flowing east, as far as I can judge, with so little current that I had difficulty in telling which way it was running, and as wide as the one I was following, in which I found a slight current and 3 fathoms of water; for these reasons I took it, leaving the other on the left. Four leagues and a half from the former, to the southeast, I came to a river on the right that flows south with so little current that I was hardly aware of it, as wide as the good one, and having 3 fathoms of water. I left this one on the right and came on and spent the night 1½ leagues from it, on the right

---

[132]MS.: " . . . quelque chose qui arrive, je gagneray tousjours les navires, quand je devrois aler par terre et abandonner mes canots et en faire d'autres où je me trouveray à la mer d'escorce d'arbre qui pesle bien à présent." Margry's text (4:186) makes no sense because of two petty errors: he gave *ou* where *où* was demanded and changed *me* to *ne*: " . . . ou, je ne trouveray à la mer d'escorce d'arbre." Margry's corrupt text led Moodie astray.

side of the river. On the left side I found four or five small streams about which I have nothing to say. The land becomes inundated a foot deep in many places during high water, and the high water does not rise more than 2 feet above the present level. This country seems to me much finer than the area close to the Malbanchia. Today I made fully 11 leagues; I might indeed say 12. There are many bends on this river. We are seeing a great number of crocodiles.[133] I killed a small one 8 feet long, which is very good to eat, the flesh being very white and delicate but smelling of musk, which is a scent that the flesh must be rid of before one can eat it.

The 27th. At six o'clock in the morning we continued on down the river, in which I do not find bottom with 23 feet of line. Five leagues southeast of the place where I spent the night, I came upon a herd of more than two hundred cows and bulls on a point of land. Although we shot at them, we did not stop any. This point marked the way out of the river, which emptied into a lake 4 leagues wide, 6 long, oval in shape. I cut straight east, to where I could see the entrance to a river 2½ leagues from the one I have just been following, which has been named for me.[134] While crossing this lake[135] I found 8 and 10 feet of water time and again and made my way to the river through which this lake empties,[136] which is one-sixth of a league wide. I followed it for 2½ leagues, going east-southeast. Here, on the left, I found a branch river 150 yards wide. From there I proceeded on my way for 1¼ leagues and came out on a

---

[133]Father Du Ru reported in his *Journal* that Indians, far from being afraid of alligators while in swimming, played with them instead. Father Gravier saw an alligator 3 fathoms long.

[134]Rivière d'Iberville was later called Bayou Manchac or the Manchac, which is a Choctaw word meaning "rear entrance," according to William A. Read (*Louisiana-French*, in Louisiana State University Studies No. 5 [Baton Rouge, 1931], p. 157). Fred B. Kniffen states that the Manchac as a distributary was "officially severed" from the Mississippi in 1826 (*Louisiana* [Baton Rouge, 1968], p. 48).

[135]Lake Maurepas, named for Jérôme de Phélypeaux, Comte de Maurepas, who was presently to assume the title of his father, Comte de Pontchartrain, and his father's position as Minister of Marine.

[136]This stream is called Pass Manchac.

Leaving the Mississippi, Iberville proceeded down the Iberville River (the Manchac), through Lakes Maurepas and Pontchartrain, and on to his anchorage at Isle aux Vaisseaux off Biloxi. (Section of a map from the Rucker Agee Map Collection, Birmingham Public Library, with placement of the cartouche altered. Photograph of modified map by Dr. Douglas F. Munch)

lake whose shoreline runs west-southwest. We named it De Pon[t]chartrain.[137] I spent the night on the left point of the river mouth. The land in the vicinity of Lake de Pon[t]chartrain did not seem to me to have been inundated. I do not believe that it is a greater distance than a musket shot from the south shore of the lake I first came to, to the shore of De Pon[t]chartrain; for, from the mouth of D'Hibervile River onward, I was watching sparkling light, which I took to be the sea, but which was this lake crossing in front of the first one. I noticed some columns of smoke 2 leagues inland, to the north. I estimate that from the west end of Lake de Pontchartrain to the Malbanchya should not be more than half a league, where one would be 10 leagues[138] below the Bayogoula. The southwest end of the lake is about 30 leagues up the Malbanchya.

The 28th. We went on along the shore of this lake for about 10 leagues east by south, the wind being northeast. The water in the lake is too brackish to drink, and I came on and camped on a grass-covered point, without trees, rather uncomfortably, as we had no drinking water, and there were many mosquitoes, which are dreadful little beasts to men who need rest. For 4 leagues prairies extend along the lake, being deep enough to extend to the great forest, about a league away. I cannot make out the other side of this lake. Half a league out from shore I found 5 and 6 feet of water. The lake seems to me to be rather deep.

The 29th. We broke camp early in the morning, and 4 leagues east-southeast of the place where we had spent the night I came to the way out of the lake, which is a pass one-eighth of a league wide, between islands of grass and

---

[137]Named for Louis Phélypeaux, Comte de Pontchartrain and Minister of Marine when the first Iberville expedition was being prepared for the first voyage to the Mississippi. His son, Jérôme Phélypeaux, assistant to his father, was more immediately concerned with the details of preparation. The MS. spells it "Ponchartrain."

[138]The MS. has a figure for the distance, almost illegible—10 or 20. And after "Malbanchya," which is the last word in this paragraph, are some words omitted by Margry (4:188) as well as by Moodie. They appear to be "26 L³ louest du Nord a 48 L³," which makes no sense to me.

meadows. I could not touch bottom with 23 feet of line. The wind being in the southeast, I left the main pass and proceeded between islands, where I found a freshwater river 300 yards wide and 3 fathoms deep, which branches into two streams, one flowing into the main pass and the other running among islands. I followed it for 5 leagues, and there stopped for the night. All these areas near the river seemed to me very fine country, filled with beautiful meadows and a few islands, suitable for habitation. I did not put myself to the trouble to follow the channel of outflow from this lake, which I estimate to be 8 or 10 leagues from the ships, for Surgère will have sent someone to explore it.

The 30th. I proceeded on my course, east by north, along the coast, [the water] being very salty. I made 7 leagues and got to a point that I recognized as the one at which I landed the first time I went ashore north of the ships. The sky overcast and a slight wind blowing. I spent the night there and made a big fire to be sighted from the ships, which are 4 leagues from me, so that I could get the longboats tomorrow for the run to the ships if there is a blow. I have found by my corrected course that the direction from the embouchure of the D'Hibervile River at the Malbanchya on to the ships should be east-south[139] and the distance 48 leagues, the ships being at 30°9' and the river at 31°3'.

March 31st. Calm. I set out with my two canoes to cross over and go aboard my ship. Half way across I met the two feluccas, which were coming to investigate the fire I had made on shore. I got to my ship toward noon and found all of my men enjoying good health except my petty officer, dead, and two sailors, [one] from disease and the other from drowning.[140] About two

---

[139]MS.: "Le romb de vent estre Lest suds et la distance de 48 L." "Lest suds" is not a point of the compass. The direction from the Malbanchya or Mississippi beginning of Iberville River, or Bayou Manchac, to the anchorage at Ship Island is between east by south and due east. Moodie failed in her attempt to clarify this line. The best guess I can make is that "Lest suds" should be "Lest ¼ sordest" or "east by south." But it isn't given that way.

[140]MS.: " . . . je me suis rendu à bord sur le midy où j'ey trouvé tous mes gens en bonne sante seulement mon contremaistre de mort et 2 matelots de maladie

o'clock in the afternoon the two Biscayans arrived from the Myssysypy. Sauvole told me that he had not been able to sound the middle channel because of wind and that he had not remained there to wait for fine weather for that purpose, as he had little food. He had failed to get any at the Bayogoula because of a little dispute that the Recollect Father caused. Having lost his breviary, he went off to the village weeping and appealing to the chief of the Bayogoula, giving him to understand that his men had stolen it. This offended the Bayogoula, who came to the camp rather angry with the father, who was still making such a big fuss that he had to be silenced and made to leave, as he had no sense. The Bayogoula, being truly angered that his men should be accused while there were several Indians present from different nations who could have done it just as readily as his men, gave the Sieur de Sauvol[e] to understand that he should go away. The disturbance finally calmed down. As a mark of friendship, the chief of the Bayogoula gave my brother an Indian boy he had adopted, and my brother gave him a gun and some ammunition.[141] Our men noticed that some women carried back the bread they had brought, and they came away without it. The wind was favor-

---

et L'autre neyé [noyé]." Margry (4:189) changed "de maladie" to "de malades." Another translation besides the one I gave is possible: " . . . my petty officer dead—drowned—and two sailors dead of disease." Moodie accepted Margry's alteration and translated " . . . except that my boatswain's mate was dead, two sailors ill, and another drowned."

[141]In this, the entry in his Journal for March 31, Iberville says that his brother (Bienville), who had gone downriver when Iberville entered Bayou Manchac, acquired a Bayogoula boy, either as a gift from the chief to put an end to friction with the French or as a slave sold to Bienville to be taken to France and trained as an interpreter. That is my speculation. The Journal of the *Marin,* entry dated March 25, 1699, reports that Iberville himself bought the boy for a gun, a powder horn, a wad-extractor, and some bullets. But to say Iberville bought the boy is to give the impossible, because on the 25th, Iberville was fighting his way through the entanglements of trees in Bayou Manchac. The *Marin* account, however, does give valid information about the boy: He was twelve to thirteen years old and was probably a slave boy, captured, and adopted by the Bayogoula chief. "Ce pauvre enfant avoit si grand regret de quitter ces Sauvages, qu'il pleuroit incessamment sans pouvoir l'empescher" (Margry, 4:274). This young boy will appear again in these journals after his residence in France.

able to make them come this way, which does not occur often, as the prevailing winds are usually east-northeast. My brother brought me a letter that the chief of the Mougoulascha had been keeping.[142] Tonty, on his way upriver, had left it with the chief for M. de Lassale.

Village of the Quynypyssa
April 20, 1685

Dear Sir:

When I found that the post on which you set up the arms of the King had been knocked down by driftwood, I had others erected on this side, about 7 leagues above the sea;[143] and I left a letter in a tree close by, in a hole on the back side, with a notice above it. The Quynypyssa having danced the calumet for me,[144] I left this letter with them, to assure you of my very humble respects and to let you know that, acting on information I received at the fort—that you had lost a vessel and that Indians had looted your goods and you were fighting with them—upon this information I came downriver with twenty-five Frenchmen, five Chaouenois[145] and five Illynoys.[146] All the nations have

---

[142]The Journal of the *Marin* (Margry, 4:274–75) gives some details about the acquisition of Tonty's letter to La Salle: Sauvole gave some axes and knives for it. The chief wanted powder, and Sauvole gave it. According to French understanding, the chief had kept quiet about the letter when the French first came by his village on their way upstream because he feared that they were Spaniards. Iberville reported to the minister that Bienville bought the Tonty letter from the chief of the Mugulasha with one ax. D'Iberville au Ministre de la Marine, June 29, 1699, in Margry, 4:124.

[143]MS.: "7," but this figure is difficult to read; it appears to have been superimposed upon another figure, possibly an 8, which is the distance above the sea that Iberville gives when he is discussing the way he might have recovered the other Tonty letter, left in a hole in a tree.

[144]Near the phrase, "The Quynypyssa having danced the calumet for me," there is a marginal note in the MS. of the Journal of the *Badine:* "Le 1er avr. Un gros sud est."

[145]Although I suspect that Chaouenois is another of the many French spellings for Shawnee, I cannot find in Hodge's *Handbook* any spelling of Shawnee closer to it than Shaonois, which Hodge attributes to Evans (1707). See 2:537.

[146]A confederacy of Algonquin tribes having their homes in southern Wisconsin, northern Illinois, and west of the Mississippi River. The tribes in question

danced the calumet for me. These are people that have feared us in the extreme since you destroyed this village. I shall end by telling you that I am greatly grieved that we are going back, having suffered the misfortune of failing to find you after two canoes skirted the coast for 30 leagues toward Mexico and 25 toward the Florida Cape. For want of fresh water the canoes were forced to turn back. Although we have heard no news of you and have seen no signs of you, I am not without hope that God will give you marked success in your business and your undertaking. This I wish with all my heart. You do not have a more faithful servant than I, and I am giving up everything to look for you.[147]

The remainder of the letter, which is just as long, contains news of the nations of the Illynoys, Chaouenoys, Outaouas,[148] and of the war that people intended to wage against the Yroquoys,[149] and about the deaths of several persons in Canada, and about the arrival of M. Perrot[150] with twenty-five soldiers

---

here were the Cahokia, the Kaskaskia, the Peoria, and the Tamaroas. They later occupied village sites along the Illinois River and rivers close to it. Their position was a perilous one because the Iroquois on the east were dangerous enemies, and on the west the Sioux were both numerous and hostile. For many years the Illinois Indians were loyal to the French who had settled in the so-called Illinois Country. See Hodge, *Handbook*, 1:597–98.

[147]The Journal of the *Marin* does not carry a copy of Tonty's famous letter to La Salle but gives a summary of it (Margry, 4:274–75).

[148]Outaouas were Ottawas (from *adawe*, "to trade"). They lived in various places as Iroquois hostility put pressure on them. The Ottawas were Algonquin Indians, whose most famous man was probably Pontiac. Hodge, *Handbook*, 2:167–72.

[149]The Iroquois were called by an Algonquin name meaning "real adders." They indeed were adders in their treatment of many tribes west of them and in their hostilities to the French in Canada and at various posts near the Great Lakes. They were made up of five tribes, whose population in the late seventeenth century was put at 16 thousand. In the early eighteenth century the population had been reduced by war and new diseases to 10–12 thousand. Being brave, even fierce, warriors whom the English and the Dutch provided with guns, the Iroquois may have been the most feared of the tribes north of the Río Grande. See Hodge, *Handbook*, 1:617–19.

[150]François-Marie Perrot, Seigneur de Sainte-Geneviève, was governor of Montreal in 1669–84 and of Acadia in 1684–87. See *DCB*, s.v. "Perrot, François-Marie."

to be governor of Acadie.[151] The letter was addressed to M. de Lassale, Governor-General of Lousiana. This letter removes all doubt that the Malbanchia is the Myssysypy and that the Bayogoula and Mogoulascha are the Indians he calls Quynypyssa. The Mogoulascha displayed a book, *l'Imitation de Nostre Seigneur*, on which was the name of a Canadian. They have forgotten the name. They had some bottles that they say Tonty gave them. They call him Le Bras Coupé or La Main de Fer. The two Breton sailors who got lost on the way upriver were found again at this village, to which they had been brought by Indians who had found them straying off. I am sorry that I was not with the longboats, for I would have located the tree where the letter was, in the hole on the back side, which Tonty mentions. There are so few trees 8 leagues from the sea that it would have been easy to examine all of them, and there are no trees except on the left, going upriver.

That same day, the 31st, I sent the two feluccas to take soundings in the mouth of the river of the Bilocchy to see whether the smacks could come in, with a view to establishing a settlement there, acting on what I have been told, which is that there was insufficient water at the mouth of the river of the Pascoboula. Because the little provisions I had left would not permit me to stay longer on the coast—at least the *Marain* was running quite short of provisions—it was necessary to establish a post quickly, and as near to the ships as would be possible, so that we could draw from them a part of our crews for the work on the fort we had to build to provide a safe place for the men I would leave behind. While waiting for our ships to return from France, a part of the men at the fort will be employed in thoroughly exploring the country and the most suitable places to establish a colony if people want to send one there. This bay of the Bylocchy appears to us to be the most suitable, being only

---

[151]Acadia, Fr. *Acadie*, a name once used for Nova Scotia and New Brunswick in east Canada. When the British, who had gained sovereignty over the area, deported the French residents out of fear that they would prove treacherous during the war between the English masters and the Canadian French, great numbers of the deported farmers settled in the Evangeline country of Louisiana. A vulgar and debased form of the name *Acadien* is Cajun.

5 leagues from our ships, at a place where the winds are favorable, going and coming back, and our longboats can go back and forth in one day; and from there to the village of the Bylocchy, Pascoboula, and Moctoby is only 2½ days, according to what has been told us by the Indians, from whom we shall easily get help.

April 1st. A heavy wind blew from the southeast. The 2nd, the feluccas returned to the ships. The officers that were in them report that they found only 4 and 5 feet of water, which is not sufficient for the smacks to be brought in loaded. I set out at noon with the two feluccas to go sound the mouth of the river by which I came from the Malbanchya, and to take soundings all the way from here to the mouth, which is only 8 leagues west of here. [During the month the ships have stayed here, a little curiosity surely must have urged the individuals remaining on board to have soundings made in the vicinity of this anchorage, for they had two smacks and two longboats.][152] In a head wind I got from the ships to the river mouth by rowing, about eight o'clock in the morning of the 3rd, in foggy weather, wind west-northwest. At ten o'clock I took soundings of the mouth of the river and up the river and found 36 feet of water everywhere. On my way back to my ship, being 1½ leagues out from the river, I found only 8, 9, and 10 feet of water. I continued to take soundings on the way back to my ship, in a heavy wind from the north-northwest. Rain and mist. I found it difficult to follow the channel. I found shoals on which there were depths of 25 and 30 feet. When I missed the island lying 2 leagues west of the ships, I became aware that wind and current were driving me out to sea. I had the men row with her head to the wind and located the island, in the lee of which I ran on and, at ten o'clock at night, got to the ships with great difficulty, having run the risk of being driven out to sea. While I was crossing from the island to the ships, the wind and the current had driven me seaward in the dark.

---

[152]The passage in brackets was deleted in the MS. but is still legible. The MS. has "ayant deux traversiers et 2 [3?] chaloupes" where Margry (4:193) has changed the MS. reading to "ayant des traversiers et des chaloupes."

The 4th. All day a heavy wind has blown from the north, the seas being rather heavy. I got ready to establish the post at the Pascoboula River, acting on information given me by an officer on the *Marain:* that at the mouth there was sufficient water for the smacks. That river is 9 leagues from here, east-northeast. We go to it easily from where our ships are, and the ships can go and anchor 1½ leagues out from the mouth. Inside, the river is 5 and 6 fathoms deep everywhere, free of reefs, and 500 yards wide.

The 5th. I left at eight o'clock in the morning in the felucca with Surgère; Lescalète in the Biscayan with forty-five men; Vilautré in the other one from the *Marain,* with thirty men; and my brother with the two bark canoes. The two smacks are to follow us when the wind is favorable, bringing everything required for the post. At six o'clock in the evening we reached the river, on which I took soundings for more than two hours trying to locate a channel and follow it through the reefs, but I failed to find one. This entrance is obstructed by oyster banks, and I found but one channel, in which there is only 3 feet of water.

The 6th. In the morning I sent my Biscayan back to the ship and sent the other one 1 league up the river for fresh water for the run to the ship,[153] to which I too shall return in order to go and establish the post on the shore of Lake de Ponczartrain, to which the smacks will be able to sail. When passing by, I went and took soundings within the entrance of the bay of the Bylocchy. We located a channel there with 7 feet of water. I sent Surgère's felucca to notify the smacks, which were on their way back to the ships, and the *Marain*'s Biscayan to come on and anchor at the entrance to this bay. Surgère and I went inside to spend the night and look for a place suitable for a post. We all thought it advisable to establish the post on this bay,

---

[153]MS.: "Le 6. au matin j'ey renvoyé ma biscayenne a Bord et l'autre a une lieue en haut dans la rivière chercher de l'eau douce pour s'en aler de là a Bord où je m'en retourneray aussy pour faire L'établissement sur le bord du Lacq de Ponczartrain . . . " Moodie gives, "for some fresh water for the journey from there to the ship . . . "

which is only 3 leagues[154] from the Pascoboula River, on which
are located the three villages of the Bylocchy, Pascoboula, and
Moctoby, for we would finish it sooner, because we could call
on a part of our crews to do the work there, whereas if we had
gone on Lake Pon[t]chartrain we would have been able to send
only the men assigned to the colony; and the time I would
spend in going and coming to take them there would be sufficient to erect a good fort, which will suffice while we are
waiting to see where it will be judged most advantageous to
locate a good establishment.

The 7th. I went out to the smacks to take them in. The small
one came to within a cannon's shot of the place chosen for the
post and the big one nearly as far. I had two longboat loads of
goods removed to lighten it. I sent the felucca to the ship to tell
Lescalète to bring back the Biscayan and the men to do the
work; toward evening they arrived.

The 8th. The smacks have arrived in a breeze. I have started
men to clear ground for the fort and to sink a well.

The 9th, 10th, and 11th. We continued to clear the trees
away. I put ten men to squaring timber for the bastions, to be
made of beams a foot and a half thick, laid one upon another
and dovetailed at the corners.[155] I had thirty men transported
from the ship in my longboat. The work goes along slowly: I
have no men who can use an ax; most of them take a day to fell
one tree; but the trees are truly big ones, oak and hickory. I
have had a forge set up to repair the axes. All of them break.

The 12th. My longboat brought from the ship the cows that
belong to Surgère and me. We brought them from France. All
those I got in St. Domingue died, three on board the *François*,
one on the *Marain*, and four on the island where they had been

---

[154]It is impossible to tell whether this number, 3, is correct, as the MS. has two
figures, one superimposed upon the other, seemingly a 3 upon a 4.

[155]So the architect Samuel Wilson, Jr., defines the construction called "pièce
sur pièce" ("Colonial Fortifications and Military Architecture in the Mississippi Valley," in *The French in the Mississippi Valley*, ed. John Francis McDermott [Urbana, 1965], p. 107). Wilson attributes the design of Fort Maurepas to
Iberville's draftsman, Remy Reno.

placed. Most people say it is owing to the cold weather, although it has not been cold.[156]

The 13th. My longboat brought the hogs and a bull. I had the woods burned and the site for the fort cleared.

The 14th. My longboat brought from the ship two pieces of cannon—eight pounders—and the gun-carriages and cannon balls. I sent men half a league from here to cut the stakes for the palisade. Every day the longboat brings eighty to a hundred of them. I am having an oven made and trenches dug for the palisade. The bastions are coming along. For two days I have kept twenty-five men busy sowing peas, corn, and beans.

The 15th and the 16th. It rained all day, and we got no work done. The rain has refilled our trenches.

The 17th. My longboat brought two cannon and Surgère's brought the same number.

The 18th. My longboat again brought two—in all, six from the *Marain,* and the equipment for them. Our smacks are filled, serving as warehouses.

The 19th, 20th, and 21st. I had some pales squared and dressed down to 3 inches thick to floor the bastions, which I have built to a height of 9 feet. In them I put the cannon, with a parapet 4 feet high. The Recollect Father[157] came from the *Marain* and asked me to let him go back to his monastery, which he does not want to leave again. In his place I have given the chaplain on the *Badine*[158] the assignment of remaining at the fort. He is a very upright man. Now that I see that the Recollect does not want to stay here, I deeply regret that I do not have a Jesuit missionary, who in a short time would know the native language of this country.

The 22nd. Five Spaniards reached the fort, having deserted from Pensacola on foot to go to New Spain. They came upon some Indians from La Mobile, who brought them here. These

---

[156]What seemed like cold weather to some men might not have seemed cold to a Canadian like Iberville, who had explored on land in the Hudson Bay area and had fought on both land and sea in very cold weather.
[157]Father Anastasius Douay.
[158]Father Bordenave.

men tell us that they sailed from Vera Cruz in October to establish a post at the Myssyssypy, where they knew that we were to come and that we meant to locate a fine harbor. Because they knew no other on this coast, they had come straight to Pensacola, where they had found a boat from Havana, which had been sent there in haste to take possession and which had been waiting for them for twenty-nine days. They had orders, if we got there first, to say nothing to us and to go back. I have my doubts about that. When we did get there, they were three hundred men,[159] of whom forty were there under duress and others were men condemned to serve there a number of years. They had all decided to desert if we should come into the port and to ask us for passage to get away from there, where they had only Indian corn to eat, very little bread, and a little meat. They had sent several ships to Havana and Vera Cruz before we got there, and the commandant himself had gone, more than three months earlier, to ask for help. They were short of everything when they deserted. Some had deserted to go to the Apalasche. Others, not daring to undertake such a long journey and having no knowledge of our being so close by, are dying like wretches. Of the three hundred there were when we came by, not fifty could keep going any longer and the remainder were dead or dying. They do not doubt that the Spaniards will abandon Pensacola. They had settled there only to force us to go back when we found no harbor; for they did not believe that there might be other harbors where big vessels can anchor other than there.

The Spaniards in New Mexico and Havana did what they could to induce families to settle at Pensacola. They could not find any. Some are to come from the Canary Islands for that purpose, according to what they had been told. They say that the river that empties into Pensacola Bay is a fine place to live and that the place where they are located was selected solely to prevent people from entering the harbor. From these men I learned that there was at Pensacola a soldier and maker of

---

[159]The MS. has the figure 300 or 200. Margry, 4:197, has "trois cents hommes."

edge-tools who had been in the group that went to drive M. de
Lassale out and seize the rest of his people; that he had been
chosen to live at a fort they had built in an Indian nation. Here
he had remained for three years; but, failing to get along with
these Indians, they had been compelled to abandon the fort, in
which they had two cannons. They claim that from there to
Mexico there is a fine beaten trail over which these Spaniards
hoped to go, for they thought themselves to be close to that
Indian nation, whose name they could not tell us. To all the
Indians in Florida they give the name Chychymèque.[160] They
say there are two Frenchmen who have married among these
Indians and are living as the Indians do. I am of the opinion
that the fort they abandoned was among the Senys. Three of
these Spaniards are half-breeds who were sent to Pensacola
under duress; one is from the mining camps of St. Louys de
Potasy.[161] He readily gives information about his country and
would like for us to go there. He talks a great deal about the
weakness of the Spaniards in that country. It would be a fine
thing to go there and get silver if we should go to war with them.
Five hundred good Canadians would make that whole country
tremble. It is heavily covered with woods and by no means
what people in France think it is. With little expenditure, many
millions could be taken out of that country. In the capital of
New Mexico, there are not more than 250 Spaniards. The
caravans that come from there are easy to capture. It is also

---

[160]*Chichimecs* is a word of opprobrium meaning, loosely, "wild men, heathen,
numerous, and aggressive." The word comes from the name of an Amerind
culture of Mexico between the Toltecs and the Aztecs. The Chichimecs are
said to have introduced the bow and arrow from the north. The word has, in a
derogatory sense, been applied to people and spotted or brindle bulls, probably
for the bulls' wild and dangerous demeanor in the streets and the bull ring. Cf.
the use of *Huns* for German troops during World War I and the early use of the
word *barbarian*. See William H. Prescott, *History of the Conquest of Mexico*, 2
vols. (Philadelphia, 1873), 1:15–16 ff., and Gordon Randolph Willey, *Introduction to American Archaeology*, 2 vols. (Englewood Cliffs, N.J., 1966–71), 1:153.
[161]San Luis Potosí, a city west of Tampico and in the state of San Luis Potosí,
Mexico. The Spanish noun *potosí* is a colloquial word meaning "a mint," where
money is coined.

easy to capture the town of St. Louys de Potasy. I am going to
take these Spaniards to France with me, two on the *Marain*
and three on the *Badine*.

The 23rd. I sent my brother and two Canadians 5 leagues
from the fort, to the far end of this bay, to inspect it and the land
in the vicinity. He found it perfectly fine for a settlement. I went
and examined the back side of the little bay and, with one man,
I penetrated 4 leagues inland to examine the country. I found it
very beautiful with pine woods, mixed with trees of other kinds
in spots, many prairies, light, sandy soil everywhere; I saw a
good many deer. Deer are killed everywhere in the vicinity of
the fort.

The 24th. I had the guns mounted on the bastions and
completed the fort.

The 25th. I had the warehouses erected and had the quarters
for the garrison finished.

The 26th. M. de Surgère came to the fort. I had men unloading the smacks and took an inventory of everything and fully
inspected all provisions and chose the garrison, of eighty persons, all told.

The 27th. Surgère went back to his ship with twenty-three
men belonging to his crew.

The inventory of provisions showed:

4 barrels of peas entirely rotted
2 kegs of bacon spoiled for lack of brine
6 barrels of flour like dust and turned sour, which had to be
    jettisoned
The equivalent of 1½ barrels of brandy lost from leakage out of
    one cask
2 barrels of wine gone bad, turned sour, taken aboard at Roche-
    fort
Nearly all the olive oil lost from leakage.
(Olive oil should not be shipped in kegs to hot countries.)[162]

Being unable to leave at the post fewer than eighty persons to

---

[162]Margry's inventory, 4:199–200, has several items differing in amount from
the MS. inventory, which I have translated.

do all that I am ordering them to do, I decided to send the big smack to St. Domingue with ten men to ask M. Ducasse[163] for some provisions to keep the men at the post from running short, although I do not doubt that some provisions will be sent from France as soon as I arrive; but it can happen that that won't be done. I am in no condition to provide provisions out of what I have, as I believed when I sailed from France, as I took only twelve months' provisions for the crew of the *Badine,* from which I have issued 13,220 rations to the passengers left in the colony.

The *Marain* has twelve months' provisions for her crew, out of which about 2,500 rations have been issued. I have had an inventory taken of my provisions on my ship. I have, calculating from May 1st, the dinner issues of wine and brandy that have been withheld from the crew since March 1st, being seventy-five days.

The 28th. I sent back a part of my men.

The 29th. My longboat returned.

The 30th. There was a southerly wind, and I could not send my longboat. All day I had men sowing peas.

May 1st. I sent back the rest of my men.

The 2nd. I had the Sieur de Sauvole, naval sublieutenant, proclaimed commandant—he is a well-behaved young man of ability—and my brother De Bienville proclaimed deputy commandant and Le Vasseur Russouelle major. I am leaving in all seventy men[164] and six cabin boys,[165] which includes the crews of the smacks. About noon I got back to my ship with the Sieur de Sauvole.

---

[163]Jean-Baptiste Ducasse, a famous corsair, was "gouverneur de l'île". When the Iberville expedition arrived off Cap Haitien, the governor was away at La Paix, having suffered a stroke. See Frégault, *Iberville,* p. 282, and Ducasse au Ministre de la Marine, January 13, 1699, in Margry, 4:92–95.

[164]For the rolls of the men left by Iberville at Fort Maurepas in 1699 and 1700, see the convenient lists of names—Christian names and *dit* names, too—in Jay Higginbotham's *Fort Maurepas: The Birth of Louisiana* (Mobile, 1968), pp. 81–86 and 87–93.

[165]Higginbotham gives the names of the *mousses,* or cabin boys, left in Louisiana as St. Michel, Pierre Huet, Gabriel Marcal, Jean Joly, Jacques Charon, and Pierre Le Vasseur. See Appendix 2, *Fort Maurepas,* p. 85.

The 3rd. About eight o'clock, wind in the southwest, the Sieur de Sauvole returned to the fort, and we got underway and tacked to go out. At four o'clock in the afternoon we anchored off the island in 4 fathoms, and there spent the night, the wind southeast.[166]

The 4th. At five o'clock in the morning we raised anchor, the wind being in the south-southeast, which is a trade-wind that has been blowing for a week. We tacked at noon; the west end of the island, where the roadstead is, is 1½ leagues north-northwest of us. We are in 29 feet of water, the bottom muddy, at latitude 30°6'.

The 6th.[167] At noon I am in latitude 30° and am 30' east of my point of departure. The wind has been southeast by east, light enough for us to let out the two reefs we had taken in the topsails[168] in order to tack. I anchored yesterday evening at six o'clock in 7 fathoms of water, northeast of the island in the offing, 3 leagues out in order to tack. From one island to the other, one finds 40 feet of water, diminishing, the distance from one island to the other being 4 leagues.[169] I am 4 leagues out from the middle of Lescalète Island.[170]

The 7th. At noon, I am in latitude 29°45' and am 50' east of my point of departure, in 13 fathoms of water. The wind has been southeast. On La Mobile we see columns of smoke, which are north of us.

From the 7th at noon till the 10th. My corrected course gives me, by dead reckoning, a latitude of 28°55' and a longitude of 2°40' east of my meridian; I am in 120 fathoms of water, the bottom black mud. I calculate that I am 10 or 12 leagues

---

[166]Between this line and the next one, beginning, "The 4th. At five o'clock . . . " there is a break in the Margry text (4:201), filled with a four-line heading: "*II* / *R*ETOUR DE D'*I*BERVILLE EN *F*RANCE / Journal du Voyage de la *Badine* / Jusqu'au Débouquement de Bahama." This break and the heading are not in the MS., which shows no interruption at all at this point.

[167]Margry, 4:201, has "Le 26ᵉ." The next date in Margry is the 7th, and the date before the 26th is the 4th. MS.: "6th" instead of 26th.

[168]From "light enough . . . " as rendered in the Burton MS by Moodie.

[169]From "diminishing . . . " as Moodie translates it.

[170]Now Horn Island.

southwest of Apalachycoly Cape.[171] Since the 8th, the wind has been south and south-southwest, southwest in fine weather, the wind light enough for us to set our topgallants. I have steered a southeast course as much as I could.

The 11th. At noon I am at 28°45′ north and 3°48′ east of my meridian. These twenty-four hours I have run east-southeast, taking soundings every two hours, the first being 120 fathoms; 6 leagues from my position at noon yesterday, 75 fathoms; 1 league farther on, 40 fathoms; and the depth then fell off to 36, 35, 34, 28 fathoms, the bottom being sandy at 28 fathoms.

The 12th. I am at 28°15′ north and 4°8′ east of my meridian. Since the 28 fathoms of noon yesterday, when I was running southeast, sounding every hour, I have found all along 28, 25, 24, and down to 18 fathoms, bottom of shell, sand, and seaweeds. The wind has been south-southwest, light wind, fine weather.

The 13th. At noon I am at 27°30′ north and longitude 4°58′. These twenty-four hours I have sailed southeast in 19 fathoms, 17, and 15. When I steered south, the depth increased; and when I steered southeast, it diminished; when I ran south by

---

[171]Not a rare spelling for "Apalachicola." I do not believe that the spelling "Apalachicoly" has yet fallen into complete disuse in Florida. This is not the Apalachicola River or the name given to the Southern Creeks in the eighteenth and nineteenth centuries, but a place name. But where was the place if it was not present-day Apalachicola? According to Ross Morrell, archaeologist of the State of Florida, Apalachicola was located in 1701 at the north end of St. Joseph Spit, some 200–300 yards back from the line where the sand ends and the trees begin. Supporting this belief is G. Delisle's "Carte du Mexique et de la Floride," 1703, which shows three words on the west side of the spit and close to it: "St. Joseph—Habitation Espagnole," the words written each one below the preceding one. There is a noticeable dot near the end of the spit or hook. Mr. Morrell cited Joseph Frederick Walsh Des Barres's 1779 map as showing a legend that places the ruins of St. Joseph near the end of the spit. Dr. Hale Smith, of Florida State University, who excavated a spot of the spit in 1965, found only some nails and some pieces of European pottery. Although the precise location of Apalachicola remains in some doubt, the able scholars cited have located it on the spit west of Port St. Joe. See the map of Joseph Frederick Walsh Des Barres, "The North East Shore of the Gulph of Mexico," London, January 1, 1779, owned by Florida State University Library.

east, it remained the same. The bottom was of shell. Wind in the south, southwest and west, and the weather fine, light wind. We were sounding every half hour and finding a very level bottom. We did not observe any current.

The 14th. At noon I am at 26°13' north and 5° east of my meridian of departure. These twenty-four hours I have run south, sounding every half hour and finding all along 15, 16, 18, 20, and 22 fathoms of water, the bottom a mixture of mud and sand and shell. I have not yet seen any seafowl since I sailed. About nine o'clock in the morning I fell in with an English brigantine of thirty tons' burden, out of Tabasque[172] with a cargo of Campeachy[173] wood and bound for New York. I sent a letter to Canada by her, addressed to the owner, a Frenchman from Bordeaux who is settled there,[174] named Menvieille.[175] The wind has been northwest, light breeze.

May 15th. At noon I am at latitude 25°35' north and 5°12' [east of my meridian], and these twenty-four hours I have run south-southeast in 22 fathoms of water all along. I am beginning to notice seagulls and seaweed. I find no evidence at all that there are currents, judging by the altitudes I take, and I take an altitude every day. The wind has been north to east-southeast, light breeze.

The 16th. At noon I am in latitude 24°50' north and 5°12' east of my meridian of departure. The wind has been east, a light breeze. I take a sounding each hour, finding from 22 to 27 fathoms, the bottom fairly level. Running southwest, the depth increases. We are seeing pelicans and sea-swallows.

The 17th. At noon I am in latitude 24°35' and 5°12' east of my meridian of departure, in 29 fathoms. About four o'clock

---

[172]Moodie changed "Tabasque" to "Tobago," which is an island off the northeast coast of Venezuela. "Tabasque," the MS. spelling, is just French for the town of Tabasco in the State of Tabasco, on the Bay de Campeche. Margry (4:203) erroneously gives the port as Tabaque.

[173]Campeche and the State of Campeche are on the west side of the Yucatán Peninsula.

[174]MS.: "habité là." Margry, 4:203: "habitué là."

[175]Both Moodie and Margry (4:203) give this name as Mainvieille. The MS. has "m'envieille."

yesterday afternoon, the wind having freshened out of the northeast and east, I sailed southeast by south for 2 leagues; and from the masthead I sighted the Dry Tortugas Islands to the southeast and south-southeast and south of me, 3½ leagues away. I approached to a depth of 20 fathoms, till I could see them from the deck, 1½ leagues away, and ran by them in 17, 18, and 19 fathoms. They are of white sand, very low. I think that in foul weather, when the sea is rough, it passes over them. I counted seven of them. They extend southwest by west for 4 leagues. The one I saw farthest to the southwest is the smallest. I ran within 1¼ leagues of it, in 16 fathoms; but, as night was coming on, I did not dare go closer. I ran south-southwest, southwest, and west-southwest, the depth of water diminishing all along. I decided not to go to find the end of these islands by night, for fear of shoals. I ran 1½ leagues north-northwest, as far out as a depth of 25 fathoms, and hove to at nine-thirty at night, to drift west, as I wished to go and reconnoiter them in the morning. These islands are a league and a half-league distant from one another, some lying farther to the south and others more to the east and southeast. I found the latitude of them by an observation, a very good one, taken in the daytime: The one farthest northeast is in latitude 24°35′ north and 5°15′ [east][176] of my point of departure; the one farthest south is in 24°20′ and 5°10′ east of my point of departure. All the charts, new and old, mark them at 24°50′ and at 25°. When coming from northwest of it and you are in 25 fathoms, you are no more than 4 leagues west of it. It is almost the same thing if you double them and get farther south of the islands in 25 fathoms of water, after going through 18, 19, and 20 fathoms. When you come from the north and find a depth of 27 fathoms, you must be at 24°17′. Going 1 league south from there, you get to 55 fathoms; half a league farther, to 70 fathoms; and another half league, to 120 fathoms. When you draw near these islands, where the depth is 30 fathoms, you see many birds, kelp, and

---

[176]MS.: "ouest," which Margry (4:204) does not question, even though Iberville's point of departure, his temporary meridian, was Ship Island, from which he was sailing east for France.

sea grapes on the surface of the water, like what is called Flemish cap, big as an egg. I estimate that I passed 3 leagues to the west of the last island in 20 fathoms, 6 feet to the fathom. For four days we have had nothing but calms day and night, with a light wind from the east-southeast.

The 18th. At noon I am, by dead reckoning, at latitude 23°40′ north and 5°15′ east of my point of departure. The wind has varied from east to southeast. Light wind and clouds.

The 19th. At noon I am, by dead reckoning, at latitude 23°30′ north and 5°48′ east of my point of departure. The wind has varied from east-northeast to southeast, the sky overcast with clouds, and there has been such a brisk gale that the ship can carry no more than her topsails.

The 20th. At noon I am at latitude 23°30′ and longitude 7° from my point of departure. At noon I am about 7 leagues north of the Pan de Matanzas,[177] which appears to me like a cape or round mountain rising above all the lands in the vicinity. West of it is a flat one, which is a little lower and is very rough terrain. When you have the Pan de Matanzas to the south-southeast and south of you, it appears to be long and saddle-shaped with some breaks.[178] If you have it to the south-southwest, it looks quite round, shaped like a slightly pointed hat. East of it the land is low for 2 leagues, where the entrance to the harbor lies. Ten or 12 leagues east, I see a fairly high mountain and then some low lands. I notice that the currents have carried me 12 leagues farther east than I had expected.

---

[177]This word *pan*, Spanish for "loaf" or for "bread," appears plainly in the MS. several times. Not once does *pan* resemble the word *port*. Either Pierre Margry or some assistant making the transcription for him, not knowing the word *pan*, deliberately changed this word to a word he knew: He wrote "au nord du port de Matanse" (Margry, 4:205). The Pan de Matanzas is a bread-loaf hill or mountain on the north coast of Cuba; it was a prominent landmark to navigators some distance out from the port of Matanzas, useful on their way through the Old Bahama Channel, also known as the Bahama Passage (Straits of Florida).

[178]As rendered by Moodie from the MS., "long en scellé, avec quelque coupe" or from Margry, 4:205, "long et scellé avec quelque coupe." My own translation was first "long, in the shape of a saddle, showing some ruptures."

The 21st. At noon I took an elevation, and I am at 23°50′ north and 7°31′ east of my point of departure. At noon I see the Pan de Matanzas 15 leagues south-southwest of me. I see it from the deck and see no other land. Fourteen leagues out one can sight other land to the west of it. From the deck one loses sight of the Pan de Matanzas when 16 leagues out from it. I notice that 15 leagues north-northeast of Matanzas the currents set to the northeast at half a league per hour. I steered a north-northwesterly course for 10 or 11 leagues.

At seven o'clock on the morning of the 22nd, I was 1½ leagues off some sandy islands. Certain ones appeared to be covered with small trees. One is visible to the west, lying south of the others; it appears to be quite scarped and small. The wind has varied from northeast to east and southeast. All day I have been tacking, toward the open sea and toward land, where I observe several islands lying east and west, rather low as I view them from the deck, 3 leagues away, at least. I proceeded to within 1¼ leagues of them. I am not observing many currents. At seven o'clock in the evening I hailed three English ships out of Jamaica, which sailed up to the north of Cuba after having gone east to get to the open sea. We are sailing in company.

The 22nd. At noon I am at approximately 24°22′ north, by dead reckoning. At midnight I hove to and drifted west for four hours. At seven o'clock in the morning I sighted land and beat to windward all day.

The 23rd. At noon I am, by dead reckoning, at latitude 25° and 8° east of my meridian. I have beat to windward these twenty-four hours, the wind holding in the east-northeast and southeast, with mist, rain, wind, thunder, and lightning. The land of the Florida Cape lies west by south of me. When one is 1½ leagues out, coming from the west, the land lies northeast and northeast by north. For 6 or 7 leagues I have been observing, at about 1 league off the islands, some rocks on which the seas are breaking. I am getting fairly close to them. No bottom at a quarter of a league from them. When seen from the deck 3 leagues away, the lands are low, and there are some on which you see trees. The wind is northeast, and we are beating to windward. As we are coming away from the Florida Cape, I am observing what appears to be a big island lying north by east or even still farther east. At the north end, a rather large bight is visible to the west. This island is possibly 15 or 17 leagues long; trees are visible on it. I notice that the currents, fairly strong ones, set to the northeast.

The 24th. At noon I am at latitude approximately 27° and 8°10′ east of my meridian. Every hour during the past twenty-four hours I have tacked, as the wind is a moderate gale out of the north-northeast, the sea heavy. I notice that the currents set to the north-northeast, at 1 league per hour. I tacked about, 2 leagues from land, close to some islands that came into sight; and at the back of the mainland, 10 leagues to the north, I see fires. About seven o'clock at night I sight a point at which the shore recedes to the northwest, forming a bight. Two leagues west and south of this point, I sight an island 2 leagues long and, 1 league south of that one, another one, round. Trees are visible on these islands.

The 25th. At noon I am at latitude 27°45′ north and 8°20′ [east of my meridian]. In the north and northeast the wind has blown up a storm. All along we have been under short sail and hove to, the sea being very rough. Toward six o'clock in the evening, as we could sight no land at all from the tops, we sounded over the bank, which on charts is marked at the lower part of the passage, along the Florida coast; on it we found 18 fathoms of water and a muddy bottom. We ran 1½ leagues south-southeast and found 25 fathoms; 1 league southeast, 28 and 30 fathoms; 2 leagues east-southeast, 30, 35, 40, 50, and 60 fathoms, the bottom mud. We noticed that the sea was not as rough on this bank of 18 fathoms of water. Half a league to the northwest of us was a white shoal, on which, apparently, there was not much water, for the sea there looked very white. Elsewhere it is quite blue. I notice that the currents have caused me to drift at a rate of 1¼ leagues per hour; without wind they would at most have carried me at a rate of half a league an hour. They set approximately north-northeast if a ship is 4 leagues out or closer to land, within 1½ leagues. The point that I mention above may be some 25 leagues south of this bank.

The 26th. For the past twenty-four hours the wind has been east-northeast with mist and rain. I am at latitude 28°27′ north and longitude 294°37′ as marked on corrected maps.[179] I have beat to windward, running on many tacks.

From the 26th till May 31st. My corrected course has given me a latitude taken by observation . . .[180] and a corrected longitude: 303°21′. Since the 26th the wind has varied from east-southeast to south, with mist and rain. I have run into currents that have carried me to the northeast 80 leagues beyond my reckoning.

I am not putting here a copy of my logbook from the end of the Bahama Passage[181] to the Island of Aix,[182] for that is a well-known part of the navigation. You will discover many errors throughout this journal, which has been copied from my day-by-day journal of the voyage. Before I sent it to you, it needed to be corrected. But I have been utterly unable to correct it, for I have been in no condition to work since I returned. Believing that you would think it fitting for me to send it to you as it is, I have done so.

On board the *Badine*.   D'IBERVILLE

---

[179]Here Iberville abandons the use of Ship Island as his temporary meridian and gives his longitude as his distance east around the earth from Tenerife in the Canary Islands.

[180]The latitude has been dropped from the MS.

[181]MS.: "le débouquement de baama."

[182]The small island of Aix is about 5 miles northwest of Rochefort. The Iberville MS. gives the Island of Aix as "Lisle d'e."

The Second Voyage to the Mississippi

THE JOURNAL OF THE *RENOMMÉE*

JOURNAL OF THE VOYAGE OF THE
CHEVALIER D'IBERVILLE ON THE
KING'S SHIP THE *RENOMMÉE,* IN 1699,
FROM CAPE FRANÇOIS TO THE SHORE OF
THE MISSISSIPPI AND HIS RETURN

DECEMBER 22ND. AT SEVEN O'CLOCK IN THE MORNING, I sailed from Havre Français[1] in company with the *Gironde* and set the course for Cape San Antonio, which we doubled on the 30th at eight o'clock in the morning, having observed nothing unusual on that part of the voyage.

From Cape San Antonio I steered for the Biloxy Bay anchorage, at which we arrived on January 8, 1700, and moored with two anchors in 21 feet of water.

The 9th. In the morning, M. de Sauvolle came aboard. I learned from him that the garrison was in good health, although four men had died, among them two Canadians, one buccaneer, and one enlisted man from La Rochelle.

---

[1] Now Cap Haitien, which, as Cap François, was the most important port on the north coast of French St. Domingue.

He told me that an English corvette of ten guns, commanded by Captain Louis Banc,[2] had entered the Mississipi and gone 25 leagues upstream, where my brother, De Bienville, with five men in two bark canoes, had come across the corvette at anchor, awaiting favorable winds to go higher upstream. My brother sent two men to tell him to immediately leave the country, which was the possession of the king, and that, if he did not leave, he would force him to. With this he complied after talking with my brother, whom he knew from having seen him with me at Hudson Bay,[3] where I captured this captain.

He told my brother that three ships had departed from London in October [1698] to come and establish a settlement on the Mississipi, acting on information they had received that I had put back into Brest, being unable to continue my voyage. He had gone by way of Carolina, where the majority of their men and women intended for the colony had remained, as they found it to be a fine country. One of their ships returned to London; the other two, of twenty-six twelve-pounders, set out again from Carolina in May 1699 to carry out their plans, not having dared to do so during winter because of the foul weather. He said that he had gone looking for the Mississipi 30 and 40 leagues [east][4] of where the relations about Louisiana written by the Recollect Father and Tonty locate it; there he found nothing but poor harbors and a Spanish post about 90 leagues west of this river. They believe, as I do, that it is St. Louis Bay.[5] From there they returned along the coast, taking

---

[2]The captain of the English corvette that went up the Mississippi during the interval between Iberville's first two voyages to the Mississippi was William Lewis Bond, not Banc or Barr, as he is sometimes called. (Verner W. Crane, *The Southern Frontier, 1670–1732*, [Ann Arbor, 1956], pp. 56–57.) The *Dictionary of Canadian Biography*, hereafter cited as the *DCB*, lists a certain William Bond, sea captain, who seems to be the captain in question. See also Jay Higginbotham, *Fort Maurepas: The Birth of Louisiana* (Mobile, 1968), p. 45.

[3]MS.: "la baie au [*or* du] d'Heson." Notice how close the sound of *Heson* in French is to English *Hudson*.

[4]Recovered from the Burton MS.

[5]Not the St. Louis Bay on the Mississippi coast, but the bay associated with La Salle's landing on the Texas coast in 1684—now called Matagorda Bay.

soundings with some big pirogues. They say they found no good harbor except about 40 leagues west from here, among some sandy islands, in a bay into which no river empties. And the country is a sandy coast. Chancing to be at the mouth of the river, he had sounded the three passes, finding only the East Pass[6] to have 11 to 12 feet of water. Through it he went in, as he had no doubt that this was the Mississipi, for it was the biggest river he had come to along this coast.

The other ship had gone on, following the coast to the west, to explore it as far as Pánuco.[7] From there, they were to meet at the Indios River, at Cape Blanc,[8] where they had arranged to rendezvous. This captain questioned my brother at length about whether he had got any information about the English that were in the direction of the Chicachas and were to come and join him. On his ship he had several kinds of goods, which he offered to sell for peltry or bills of exchange.

Those ships were sent out on behalf of a company formed at London by some Englishmen and French refugees. On this ship was a man representing the interests of those two groups; the Frenchman was greatly distrusted by the English; he told my brother about it and testified that he wished with all his heart, as did every single one of the French refugees,[9] that the king would permit them to settle in this country, under his rule, with liberty of conscience. He guaranteed that many would soon be here who were unhappy under English rule, which could not be sympathetic to the French temperament, and he

---

[6]Now named North Pass.

[7]An important river in Mexico whose outfall is close to Tampico. The portion of the stream near its origin has the name Cuautitlán, and another name for an upper part is Moctezuma. In the colonial period the Pánuco River was an important landmark. An administrative division of Nueva España carried the name. *Columbia Lippincott Gazetteer of the World*, ed. Leon E. Seltzer (New York, 1962), p. 1425.

[8]The Santa Rosa Inlet probably slightly east of the present-day East Pass at Destin, Florida, where Iberville made his landfall on January 23, 1699, on his first voyage. The fact that the two English captains chose Cap Blanc, or Indios River, as a place to rendezvous shows how well known the Santa Rosa Inlet was at the end of the seventeenth century.

[9]Huguenots.

begged my brother to ask me to bear their petition to the king;
and he left for me his address in Carolina and in London, so
that I can write them the king's will about it. This Frenchman
showed great disappointment over our forestalling them, saying
that they were losing this country, which his associates would
not wish to contest with the French. This English captain, on
parting company with my brother on the lower part of the
river, where they spoke with each other for the third time,
threatened to come back and settle this river with ships having
bottoms better constructed for the purpose; there was land for
them and land for us, one on one side, and the other on the
other side; they had discovered this river several years before,
and it was as much theirs as ours. Here is a threat that can
have no important consequences; it will always be easy to keep
them from carrying it out.

The Sieur de Sa[u]volle tells me also that two missionary
priests from Quebec, one of them named Montigny,[10] descended the Mississipi and came to the fort on July 4th with
fourteen men; they set out again to establish their missions at
the Taensas, who are 150 leagues from the sea, and at the
Tonicas, who are 170 leagues. One of these missionaries,
named Davion,[11] had gone overland from the Tonicas to the

---

[10]François Jolliet de Montigny, a priest of the Foreign Missions, Paris, was at
one time vicar-general of the Bishop of Quebec. He came to the Lower
Mississippi with Antoine Davion and Jean-François Buisson de St. Cosme.
Father de Montigny began his missionary work among the Taensa Indians
and, being not far away, made an effort to serve the Natchez. Owing to the
jurisdictional dispute between the missionary priests and the Jesuits in the
Mississippi Valley, he left Louisiana for France in 1700 and from France went
to China. Jean Delanglez, S.J., *The French Jesuits in Lower Louisiana (1700–
1763)* (Washington, 1935), pp. 22–25.
[11]Albert (usually Antoine) Davion, a member of the Seminary of Quebec, was
chosen to go along with the Abbé Jean-François Buisson de Saint-Cosme to
Louisiana and serve as a missionary under the supervision of Father François
de Montigny. Father Davion was called a "very good priest" but in poor health.
When he was sent to the Tunicas, on the Yazoo River, he served faithfully,
making an occasional lengthy visit to the French on the Mobile River or on the
present site of Mobile. His cramped autograph "davion" can be seen in Mobile
Baptismal Records. In 1722 he retired to New Orleans; in 1726, when he died,
he was back in France with his family. *DCB*, s.v. "Davion, Albert," the article
having been written by the Abbé Noël Baillargeon.

Chicachas on horseback, along with an Englishman, who had come from the Chicachas to the Tonicas to see whether the French would not carry on a trade in beaver with them. I later learned that this Englishman tried to make the Indians kill this missionary,[12] but they would not do so. For several years this Englishman has been among the Chicachas, where he does a business in Indian slaves, putting himself at the head of Chicacha war parties to make raids on their enemies and friends and forcing them to take prisoners, whom he buys and sends to the islands to be sold.

I have learned that the king's smack, the *Précieuse,* arrived at the fort, returning from St. Domingue on August 22, 1699.[13] The Spaniards were still at Pensacola; my brother De Bienville went there on June 15th with eight men and saw no evidence that the Spaniards had enlarged their fortifications since we came by. He saw a small ship, of about 120 tons, anchored before the fort.

Having to take soundings along the coast, which had not been done after I left, I dispatched the two masters of the smacks in the longboats to sound the pass southwest of Ile-aux-Chats, so that, if possible, I could have the ships brought in through it, and take them and the other boats into Lake Pon[t]chartrain.[14]

Toward evening I went to the fort with the Sieur de Sauvolle.

---

[12]The Jesuit Paul du Ru wrote in his journal for February 28, 1700 (?) that the two Englishmen at the Chickasaws had caused the death of a missionary upriver. If this report refers to Father Antoine Davion, Iberville is certainly correct in quashing a false rumor. Paul du Ru, *Journal of Paul du Ru,* trans. and ed. Ruth Lapham Butler (Chicago, 1934), p. 22.

[13]Pierre Margry, *Découvertes et Établissements des Français dans l'Ouest et dans le Sud de l'Amérique Septentrionale (1614–1754),* 6 vols. (Paris, 1879–1888), 4:398, gives this date as August 26, 1699. I read it in the MS. as the 22nd. Higginbotham (*Fort Maurepas,* p. 45) gives Le Voyageur with François Guyon master as the name of the *traversier* that brought supplies from St. Domingue on August 21. Here Iberville says the *Précieuse* arrived on the 22nd from St. Domingue.

[14]There is ambiguity here in the words "les autres." Margry, 4:398: " . . . l'isle aux Chats, pour faire passer par là, s'il est possible, les vaisseaux, et les autres dans le lac de Pontchartrain."

Upon arrival, we found that the small smack was on fire.[15] We could not put out the fire because of the powder aboard; it burned up a quantity of goods. For all our investigations, it could not be ascertained who had started the fire.

The 13th. The masters of the smacks returned, having found enough water for the ships everywhere except on a bar a cable's-length long, on which there was only 6 feet of water.

The 14th. I went back to my ship.

The 15th. I set out in the two feluccas and three bark canoes with my brother De Bienville to go to the portage from Lake Pontchartrain to the Mississipi, to see whether the barques could get in there. As the wind was in the north, I could go no farther than 5 leagues from the ships.

The 16th. I reached the entrance to the lake and spent the night, 11 leagues west of the ships.

The 17th. I got to the mouth of the stream that leads to the portage.[16] This stream is at the far end of the lake, towards the south; it is 20 yards wide, 10 feet deep, and 1 league long. Where it flows into the lake, I found only 1 foot and 2 feet of water; 3 feet during high water.

The 18th. I went to the portage, which I found to be 1 league long, about half the distance being full of water and mud up to the knee, the other half fairly good, part of it being a country of canes and fine woods, suitable to live in. I had three canoes carried over the portage. I went and looked at a spot where the Quinipissas once had a village, 1½ leagues above this portage;

---

[15]In Sauvole's letter report of events that occurred at Ft. Maurepas and in the Biloxi area, he too wrote an account of this fire in the small smack. [Sauvole], "Recueil que j'ai pris sur mon journal de ce qui s'est passé le plus remarquable depuis le départ de M. d'Iberville du 3 mai 1699 jusqu'en 1700," in Margry, 4:460–61. Jay Higginbotham has translated and edited *The Journal of Sauvole,* (Mobile, 1969.) See p. 41.

[16]Bayou St. John. This bayou was successively called *Choupicatcha,* "grindle river"; Rivière d'Orléans; and Bayou St. Jean, its final name bestowed in honor of Jean-Baptiste Le Moyne de Bienville, according to Marcel Giraud. Richebourg Gaillard McWilliams, *Fleur de Lys and Calumet: Being the Pénicaut Narrative of French Adventure in Louisiana* (Baton Rouge, 1953), p. 13, n. 40; and Marcel Giraud, *Histoire de la Louisiane Française,* vol. 1, *Le Règne de Louis XIV* (1698–1715), p. 35.

here I found that the land did not become inundated, or did so
very little. Trees have grown back in the fields as big as 2 feet
around. It has rained a great deal. Today I had a small field
cleared in which I had some sugar cane planted that I brought
from St. Domingue. I do not know whether the cane will take
root: it smells very sour, and the inside is yellow.[17]

The 19th. I sent my brother with three canoes and eleven
men to the village of the Bayogoulas to let them know of the
arrival of the ships and to learn what is happening among them,
to get the news they have from upriver and ask them about
places on the lower part of the river that are [not][18] subject to
overflow. I could not send with my brother the Bayogoula
Indian I had taken to France and brought back, as he had
fallen ill.[19]

I came back and joined my feluccas. It rained hard most of
the day.

The 20th. I set out with my two feluccas and crossed Lake
Pontchartrain, which I find to be 11 leagues long from east to
west, 4 and 5 leagues wide, and 15, 16, 17, and 18 feet deep.
The little stream to the portage runs north and south with the
one by which I came down from the Mississipi last year, the
two being 4 leagues apart.[20] The south side of the lake is
bordered by a prairie half a league to one league wide, after
which one comes to the tall trees. This looks like a fine country
to live in. I came on and spent the night 3 leagues from the
outlet of the lake. The islands here are covered with meadows;
from among them issues a freshwater stream, flowing from the
north.

[17]In an entry for April 12, 1700, Father du Ru reported that the "sugar canes"
died or dried up. "They were dead before they were planted" (*Journal*, p. 57).
[18]Supplied from the Burton MS. Obviously the topic of discussion and inquiry is
places along the river that are *not* subject to flooding.
[19]This Indian was the young slave boy mentioned in the first Journal.
[20]Bayou St. John, which runs north. The other small river referred to is Bayou
Manchac, which had been given Iberville's name after he had gone by bark
canoe from the Mississippi to Lake Maurepas. The trip necessitated back-
breaking portages because of rafts choking this small stream.

Beyond the outlet of the lake for 4½ leagues of country there are grass-covered islands; certain ones become inundated. They would make excellent pasture lands. The mainland north of these islands is a country of pine trees mixed with hardwood. The soil is sandy, and many tracks of buffalo and deer can be seen.

The 21st. A rather heavy wind has blown out of the north. I could make no more than 3½ leagues and came to the mainland and spent the night 1½ leagues from St. Louis Bay.[21]

The 22nd. Wind in the southeast. I could make no more than 1½ leagues and came to the east point of St. Louis Bay and spent the night. A part of my men, whom I sent hunting, killed seven deer and saw a few buffalo, but could not shoot them.

The 23rd. In the morning the Bayogoula boy died of a throat ailment, without getting to talk to any of his people.[22] Toward noon I reached my ship.

The 25th. I sent a Biscayan to sound the pass north of Ile-aux-Chats. In it only a small channel was found, a musket-shot wide and 8 or 9 feet deep.

The 30th. My brother sent a canoe and four men back to me, informing me that he is going down to the lower part of the Mississipi, where the chief of the Bayogoulas is to show them some places that are not subject to overflow, 15 leagues from the sea.

The 31st. I ordered M. de Sauvolle to go and examine a river that empties 10 leagues west of the ships, to see whether it is suitable for a settlement.

February 1st. I set out from the ships in the smack to go and

---

[21]On the north side of Mississippi Sound and not to be confused with St. Louis Bay on the Texas coast, now called Matagorda Bay.

[22]There is some evidence that the Bayogoula boy had been nicknamed Mousquet, "musket," by the French: In late April 1700 Father Paul du Ru was starting off on a search for pearls with De Sauvole. Here are two entries from Du Ru's *Journal*, p. 63, the first on April 26, 1700. "We are now in camp at a point of land which is named after the little savage who died some time ago."

"April 27, 1700. We left Pointe à Mousquet early in the morning. We said Mass at the head of the Bay of St. Louis."

establish a post on the Mississipi,[23] in order to take possession of it, for fear the English might come and put a post on it, having noticed that we had no posts closer than 30 leagues from the river, and might use that as a pretext for holding on there. With me I am carrying along at the same time enough supplies to make a journey inland and look over the country as well as the River Marnes,[24] near the upper part of which the Senis live and, on my way, to make peace between the Bayogoulas and the Oumas and force the Nadezés to sue for peace and hand over to me the murderers of M. de Montigny. All the Indians assure me that he was killed by that nation. I have thought it important, at the beginning of a settlement, not to permit the Indians to kill any Frenchman without making a show of preparation to avenge his death, in order to avoid making ourselves contemptible to every nation in the area; moreover, it seemed to me of the utmost importance to go among that nation, which is the strongest of all the nations that are on the bank of the river, but not strong enough to resist eighty men whom I am taking with me, they being enough for me to compel that nation to disown the men who did it and to make them unwilling to side with them. They will be in hiding, and I shall not be hampered by having to make a search; I shall be satisfied with showing them that we are not men that are to be given an affront; thereby I shall make safe all Frenchmen who may come and go in small groups from one nation to another, wherever we shall need to send them.

The 3rd. At nine o'clock in the morning I reached the mouth of the river, having followed the coast from the ships along the

---

[23]In his *Journal* Father du Ru wrote in the entry for February 1, 1700, that Iberville, having coasted rather close to an island, decided that the island should have the name Isle de la Chandeleur. No reason is given for the choice, but one can easily be inferred: They passed by on Candlemas Eve, February 1 (*Journal*, pp. 2–3).

[24]MS.: "la rivière des Marnes." An early French name for the Red River. There were to be several others.

islands,[25] three-quarters of a league to seaward, in 13 and 14 feet of water, without finding any shoal. I find that from the ship anchorage to the mouth of the river is, north and south, about 26 leagues. I entered the river at nine o'clock in the morning through the East Pass,[26] the same one through which I went in last year, in which I found 11 feet of water. This is the only good pass, for I have had my two feluccas take soundings everywhere. In the good pass between rocks,[27] three of them level with the water, on which one can see waves breaking, there is a width of only 30 yards; then the river widens out to more than 200 fathoms. At noon I was as high as the three forks. The wind very strong in the southeast, with rain and mist, I came about midnight to a point on the right, 17 or 18 leagues from the sea, where I found my brother, coming from the lower river with one canoe, having overtaken the other at this point. Here he was awaiting me, where the Indian in-

----

[25]In or near the Chandeleur chain. In Mississippi Valley French, *chat sauvage* means raccoon. *Chat* alone meant "raccoon skin" in the fur trade. At least two islands in Mississippi Sound are called Cat Island because of the number of raccoons living on them in the early years. On February 2, 1700, Father Du Ru recorded in his journal that the islands in the Chandeleur group were overrun by raccoons and that the sailors clubbed many to death. Even though they killed fat ones, Father Du Ru recorded, they proved to be tasteless (*Journal*, p. 3).

[26]After Father Du Ru entered the Mississippi through the East Pass, he wrote on February 3, 1700, that "the Spaniards were correct in calling it the river of palisades; the mouth is entirely fenced in with trunks of trees, petrified and hard as rock" (*Journal*, p. 4). This intelligent Jesuit was tricked as badly by the unique geological formations at the mouth of the Mississippi as Spanish explorers and Iberville had been.

[27]Here Iberville shows that his opinion about the palisade has not changed since he went into the river through the East Pass the year before. This time when he entered the river with Father Du Ru they were traveling in a smack or transport. When they come out of the river later, through the same pass, Iberville's disillusionment over his first and second observations about the headland and the palisade at the East Pass will be complete. There were no petrified trees or black rocks.

sisted[28] that, in several places, over a distance of 6 leagues, the land does not become inundated.

The 4th. It has rained all day and a very stiff gale has blown from the south. If I had not come in yesterday morning, I would have had a hard time at sea. Last night there was a heavy blow from the south, dangerous on this coast.

The 5th. I examined the land in the neighborhood of the point [and had a clearing begun around the point],[29] which is the best spot in the locality. For 3 leagues upstream and 3 downstream, there is along the river a border of hardwood trees 600 yards wide and, behind it, prairies and clumps of trees. Everywhere near here are blackberry bushes in abundance, especially where we are located.[30]

The 6th and 7th. I carried on the work of clearing land and squaring logs to make the house and working on a powder magazine 8 feet square, of wood, raised 5 feet high, roofed, and contained by a mud wall 1½ feet thick.

The 8th. I went 2 leagues above the fort to select some cedar trees, called cedars of Lebanon, to make some pirogues; here I left the Sieur de la Ronde, a naval cadet, and six men.

The 10th. The wind from the south is favorable for going up the river. I have sent my big felucca loaded with provisions to the portage, 22 leagues from here, to meet M. du Guay,[31] who is to come there with the two Biscayans, bringing ten naval

---

[28]At this point in his experience Father Du Ru shows in his *Journal* the Jesuit's compulsion to learn. The priest wrote that for two days he had been "going to school to the old savage to learn to speak the Bayogoula language." Indeed, he reports that in two days he learned fifty of the most essential words. *Journal*, p. 8.

[29]These words, dropped from the Margry text, 4:403, have been recovered from the Burton MS.

[30]Father Du Ru reports that tents were set up on the cleared land and that he shared a mattress with M. d'Iberville. They were so hungry that the pumpkins they dined on, given by the Bayogoulas, seemed to Father Du Ru to be better than French pumpkins. *Journal*, pp. 7–8.

[31]The name of this officer is written Pierre du Gué or du Guay de Boisbriand. Occasionally it appears as Boisbrillant and often as Boisbriant. More will be given about this prominent officer.

cadets and eight Canadians and the Sieur Le Sueur[32] and his men and all his belongings, in order to send him on safely to the Nadchés. I instructed the Sieur du Guay to take the felucca and go to the Bayogoulas and await me there. I have found the fort to be at 29°45′ north.

The 11th and 12th. It has rained so much that I have been unable to have any work done.

The 15th. A bark canoe arrived from the portage, bringing me a letter from M. du Guay, notifying me of his arrival. M. de Sa[u]volle writes me that he went and examined the river I told him to look at: it is suitable only for the location of a fort—not for a colony.

The 16th. M. de Tonty arrived toward evening[33] in a boat with eight men, having left fourteen at the Bayogoulas along with their baggage and canoes. The men with him are *habitans,* most of them from the Illinois and Tamarouas,[34] who came on their own initiative to see what there might be to do here, in

---

[32]Pierre-Charles Le Sueur (1657–1704) came to the Mississippi on Iberville's second voyage, bringing some hired men (one being the writer André Pénicaut) to go to the Upper Mississippi with him and help him exploit copper mines and deposits of other minerals, about which Le Sueur was supposed to have special knowledge and experience, gained from his residence in Canada and on the Upper Mississippi. He had skill in the use of Indian languages and good connections, being married to Iberville's cousin. Iberville seems to have been a silent partner in the Company of the Sioux, formed by Le Sueur. Whatever ore he brought downriver the following year, presumably copper ore, did not amount to anything. He returned to France with the third Iberville expedition, in 1702, and died aboard the *Pélican,* in 1704, on his way back to the French colony. *DCB,* s.v. "Le Sueur, Pierre-Charles."

[33]Father Du Ru records the popularity of Henri Tonty: The entry is for February 16, 1700. "A great uproar, lots of shouting, great rejoicing, M. de Tonty has come!" (*Journal,* p. 12).

[34]An Illinois tribe living on both sides of the Mississippi River, near the mouths of the Illinois and Missouri rivers. Their principal town was on the site of East St. Louis, Illinois. A French missionary was sent there in 1700 even though the tribe had lost its tribal status before 1700. Frederick Webb Hodge, *Handbook of American Indians North of Mexico,* 2 vols., Bulletin 30 of the Bureau of American Ethnology (Washington, 1907 and 1910), 2:682.

response to the letter M. de Sauvolle sent up there, [saying][35] that if men came from upriver they would find work and would be welcomed here. Two of these men have been employed by M. de Tonty for the round trip. They tell me that it is not true that the Indians have killed M. de Montigny and that they are quite friendly to us and delighted to learn that we are on this river.

The 17th. I sent off a canoe and four men with an order to M. du Guay not to cross the portage but to wait for me there, as I wish to send them back to the ships, for I have no need to take naval cadets into the woods or a good many of the others, who are not at all suited for such; I brought them along only to go to the Nadchés. All day it has been sleeting, and the weather has been quite bad, very cold.

The 18th. It has continued to sleet and to freeze. I sent the smack off to take soundings 30 leagues west of the river and to return from there to the ships. I sent back several men whom I do not need; too, I sent my brother off in the felucca with two pirogues in command of the Sieurs La Ronde and my brother Chât[e]auguay[36] to go to the Bayogoulas.

The 19th. The cold continues. Toward evening I set out in the company of M. de Tonty. I went on and spent the night 2 leagues from the fort, at which I left the Sieur de Maltot in command, with fourteen men, half of them well, half sick.

The 24th. I got to the portage,[37] where I found Le Sueur,

---

[35]A necessary word supplied by Moodie.

[36]Antoine Le Moyne de Châteauguay, born in 1683, was given the name of his father's fief, Châteauguay, which had been given first to Louis Le Moyne de Châteauguay. When Louis died in 1694, the fief was given to Antoine. Thus there are two Châteauguays as well as two Bienvilles in the Le Moyne family. The first De Bienville was named François and the second Jean-Baptiste. Châteauguay II and Bienville II are the ones that came to the French posts on the Gulf Coast.

[37]Father Du Ru reported parrakeets by the thousands near the portage. Pierre-Charles Le Sueur, the explorer, gave his party some parrakeets, which Du Ru found to have beautiful plumage but flesh that was not very good to eat (Journal, pp. 17–18). On the Atlantic seaboard droves of these bright birds were destructive of apple harvests, for they liked to eat, not the apples, but the seeds, and they came in great flocks, as Father Du Ru reports here.

who is having [all] his belongings carried to the bank of the
Mississipi. M. du Guay has gone on to the Bayogoulas. [My
canoe did not catch him.][38] I sent one Biscayan back to the
ships and had the other go downstream to wait for the men I
wish to send back.

The 25th. I caught up with my brother 2 leagues from the
Bayogoulas.

The 26th. I reached the village about eleven o'clock. I sent a
felucca back to the portage to take the naval cadets and other
persons I do not need. They will join the Biscayan there and
will let Le Sueur have the felucca to use in transporting[39] his
belongings to the Bayogoulas. From there I wrote the Chevalier de Surgère to sail for France and to leave me a month's
supply of his provisions, as I do not know what I shall do on the
coast. By that vessel I reported[40] to the minister what I have
done and what I shall do. At noon I took the altitude and got
30°40′ north latitude.[41]

The 28th. When I learned that the two Englishmen at the
Chicachas were continuing to lead Chicachas parties and were
going among all the other nations to make war on them and to
carry off as many slaves as they could, whom they buy and use
in extensive trading, to the distress of all these Indian nations, I
instructed M. de Tonty to go by the Tonicas on his way back to
the Illinois with his two men and try to lure those Englishmen
there under pretext of trading for beaver, and arrest them and

---

[38]"All" and "My canoe did not catch him" are supplied from the Burton MS.

[39]MS.: "charoyer" in which the *y* resembles *g*. Modern French *charroyer* means
"to carry in a cart." Margry (4:405) misread this word, I believe, and gave it as
charger. Either word makes some sense.

[40]This report has been printed as Lettre de d'Iberville au Ministre de la Marine,
February 26, 1700. Margry, 4:360–67.

[41]On February 27, 1700, a day on which Iberville made no entry in his journal,
some interesting comments are supplied from Father Du Ru's journal. The
priest called the painting or tattooing of Bayogoulas' faces "one thing prettier
than anything I ever saw before . . . the bizarre colors with which they paint
their faces" (*Journal*, p. 22). In the same entry, Father Du Ru described
Bayogoula customs, clothes, and games. He compared the fringe attached to
the hem of women's *braguets* to the nets that Frenchmen put on horses in
summer to protect them from flies.

deliver them to the Sieur de La Ronde, whom I am sending with him, as well as five of my Canadians. They are going down to the fort,[42] where there is something the Sieur de Tonty needs; he is to go back upriver at once.

I have hired the other Canadians who came in company with M. de Tonty to go with me, as I do not have thirty of my Canadians to take with me, having left some at Fort Mississipi and more than twenty, sick, at the fort on the bay of the Biloxys.

I have sent M. de St. Denis[43] on with two pirogues and two bark canoes to take the lead and to hunt if they find game within 15 leagues from here. I am having repaired two pirogues that I bought from the Indians and am having a field sowed to wheat. I bought the field from the Mougoulachas.

March 1st. I sent my brother off with one bark canoe and two pirogues and one pirogue of Bayogoulas, who are coming along to seek their men who are prisoners at the Oumas. I want to persuade the Bayogoulas to make peace with them and want to make the Oumas give up their prisoners to the Bayogoulas.

In the felucca I have sent, too, my pilot, Richard, with a sailor and four Indians with a bark canoe I bought from those Canadians, to go together to the fort and leave the felucca there and come back upstream with these Indians 2 leagues above

---

[42]This fort is the one on the bank of the Mississippi, called La Boulaye and also called Fort Mississippi; Father Du Ru's *Journal*, p. 22, in the entry for February 26, 1700, identifies the fort in question.

[43]Louis Juchereau de St. Denis (1676–1744) was one of the most talented Canadians that founded, or helped to found, France's colony in Louisiana. He is called St. Denis or M. Juchereau or Juchereau de St. Denis. He had courage as an explorer and trader, skill as an Indian diplomat and leader, and a sophisticated social style of life that made him attractive to all people except those—e.g., Bienville—whom his manners and sensitivity offended. St. Denis is the father of Natchitoches on the Red River, a town older than New Orleans, where St. Denis lived in some splendor as keeper of the marches between France in Louisiana and Spain in Texas. He engaged in the first illicit trade with the Spaniards in Mexico, was arrested on the Río Grande, and made love to and later married the granddaughter of the Spanish commandant who arrested him. Ross Phares, *Cavalier in the Wilderness: the Story of the Explorer and Trader Louis Juchereau de St. Denis* (Baton Rouge, 1952), p. 12 ff.

the fort and make a portage to get into a river that empties near the ships, in order to explore it and find out whether it is navigable. On this river the Indians formerly had five villages, which were destroyed by war. They believe that it is a good place for a settlement.

About noon I set out with two canoes of those Canadians from the upper river, leaving M. du Guay to wait for six of those men, who went to the fort to take one of their men whose left arm had been shot off by a gun. My surgeon amputated it for him with a saw made from a knife,[44] as gangrene had developed in it. I came on and spent the night 4 leagues from the village.

The 2nd. I made 9 leagues and spent the night opposite the first islands one finds going up the Mississipi, coming from the sea.

The 3rd. I caught up with my brother and all the other boats, numbering [four][45] pirogues, in which I have thirty men; and two bark canoes, eight [men]; and the two I have with me, fifteen; and M. du Guay's five—which makes fifty-eight men all told.

The 4th. At ten o'clock in the morning, I got to the Oumas' landing, which I found out was 27 leagues from the Bayogoulas by way of the portage and 35 leagues following the river. My brother, to whom I had assigned the lead, was at their village. Two Oumas had come to pay respects to me on behalf of the nation, that is, to bring us tobacco to smoke. It has rained all afternoon. The landing is at 31°46'.

The 5th. I sent part of my men to the other landing for this village, which is 11[46] leagues above this one; and I went on to the village, arriving toward noon with six men and six Bayogoulas. The Oumas sent two singers to meet me and bring me

---

[44]The Canadian who was about to become an amputee in this fashion confessed before submitting to the surgeon and his jerry-built saw (Du Ru, *Journal*, p. 16).

[45]The MS. as well as Margry, 4:407, has *trente:* "au nombre de trente pirogues," far more pirogues and other boats than needed to transport fifty-eight men. The number four is supplied from the Burton MS.

[46]MS.: "onze." Margry, 4:408, has "vingt."

the calumet. In the interview with the old men, talking to them in their manner, I expressed to them the distress I felt upon learning that they were at war with the Bayogoulas, after the alliance we had formed together last year. They defended themselves on the grounds that it was not they who had started the war, but the Bayogoulas; in spite of that, [they said], they were forgetting everything and were making me master of the peace. I demanded the Bayogoula prisoners they held—to deliver them to the Bayogoulas—for which I gave them a present. They told me that their custom was that the Bayogoulas, who had started the war, should come and sing the calumet of peace to them and give them presents to get back their prisoners. I made them understand that I was doing that on behalf of the Bayogoulas and that I was giving them my word that the chiefs would come and sing the peace to them. After several objections, they gave me their prisoners, seeing that I was getting angry because they were refusing to give them to me. I turned them over to the Bayogoulas, who led them away. It rained during the 6th and 7th.

The disease diarrhea, which had been in this village for five months, had killed more than half the people.[47] In this village were about forty Little Taensas,[48] who had come to see them and to offer their services against the Bayogoulas. These Taensas are rovers; usually they dwell three days west of this village. They are well-built men that live on the deer, the bear, and the game they hunt; in their district they have few buffalo. My intention was to obtain guides in this village and go up the

[47]Father Du Ru saw the village in mourning: "The women bewail their dead night and day. I was in the Great Chief's cabin where his body has been lying for more than two months. After the flesh drops from the bones, they will take them to the temple, where they will be served as he was served in his lifetime; he is given a part of the presents which we gave to the tribe" (*Journal*, pp. 26–27).

[48]This small branch of the Natchez tribe was identified by Hodge (*Handbook*, 2:669) as the Avoyelles. Margry, 4:408, "Il y avoit chez eux près de quarante petits Taensas" was translated in the Burton MS. without regard to the context. These were well-built men, hardy enough to wish to offer their help against the Bayogoulas. But Moodie, a very good scholar, thought these forty visitors were young Taensas—possibly children.

River Marne, or Sablonnière River.[49] These Indians spoke to me about it last year, leading me to believe that it was fine, and told me about the nations that live on it, saying that they had been there; but today they assured me that it is not navigable, being obstructed by logs. No matter what I did, they would not consent to guide me up it to the Cadodaquios. They told me that the only route they knew to get there was by way of the Big Taensas, who are above the Chéloëlles,[50] or Nadchés, which is the route they commonly take, making the trip overland. Although this river seems fine to me, I did not dare undertake to go up it without a guide, since it makes several forks, and I thought it better to go to the Taensas and from there by land to the Nadchitoes[51] and the Cadodaquios, by whose village this river flows. There I shall get some canoes, or shall have some made, to go down the river and explore it well.

The 8th. I came to the upper landing of the Oumas, where some of my boats are. I had the others notified, as the men in them had stopped to hunt at the mouth of the River Marne. The chief of the village and a group of their men came and brought me some meal.

The 9th. I sent one of my pirogues with ten men back to the fort, with several things that are of no use to me on land. All my boats joined me, coming from the River Marne, which is 2 leagues below this landing. The landing is only 1 league or 1¼ leagues from the village, hill after hill all the way. I gave this village half a bushel of wheat to sow and some peas, a few orange seed, apple seed, and cotton seed. This landing is 10½ leagues from the other one. I went on and spent the night 8 leagues from there. On the way up to the Nadchés, 5 leagues from the Oumas' landing, I found an island about 4 leagues in circumference. I took the small channel on the right, going

---

[49]Another French name for the Red River.

[50]Margry, 4:409, gives Théloelles, which is the expected spelling. But the MS. plainly gives Cheloelles. What I read as an initial *C* could possibly be *T*, and ought to be *T*, but I believe that the penman wrote *C*. I cannot explain this odd spelling.

[51]In the MS. this tribal name looks like Nadchitocs as well as Nadchitoes. With either spelling, the Natchitoches, or Natchitochs, are meant.

upstream. Three-quarters of a league below this small channel is a little river, on the right side. Two and a half leagues from this big island there is a little one on the left. All the country I have passed through today becomes inundated 5 and 6 feet in many places. The land is no better than downriver—I mean the banks of the river. The land appears quite elevated 1 and 2 leagues back from the river.

The 10th. I proceeded onward. About noon I came to two islands half a league long; this is to all appearances the three channels mentioned in the narratives of this country, which they locate at 60 leagues from the sea and I[52] at 125. I came on and spent the night 15 leagues from the Oumas' landing. The river has many bends in it and runs north.

The 11th. I reached the Nadchés' landing, which I find to be 18 leagues from the Oumas. One league below the landing is an island three-quarters of a league long. Between this island and the landing I found several Indians who fish with nets from a little platform that extends 7 to 8 feet out over the water.[53] They sold me some white fish,[54] very small, and some very good

---

[52]MS.: "mois," which seems to be a penman's slip for *moi*. Margry, 4:410, has "et nous."

[53]The Margry text is inexcusably corrupt in this sentence, because Margry, upon encountering a word he didn't know, would sometimes change it to a word he did know. For this sentence, the MS. gives "de cette île jusqu'au débarquement j'ai trouvé plusieurs sauvages qui pêchent avec des carles dans le fleuve, sur un petit échafaud qui avance dans l'eau de sept à huit pieds." The word causing the difficulty is *carles,* which is a telescoped form of *carrelets,* "small square nets" or "traps." I did not know this word, nor did the average educated Frenchman to whom I showed the word. But I found several Frenchmen who did know it. One young Frenchman told me that he thought it was a trap made of a basket, and he may be right. The Margry text changes the important words "pêchent avec des carles" to "peschent des carpes." Margry, 4:410: "De cette isle jusqu'au desbarquement, j'ay trouvé plusieurs Sauvages, qui peschent des carpes dans le fleuve . . . "

[54]Not knowing what could be the identity of small fish caught just below Natchez and called in Canadian French "poisson blanc," I got the opinion of Dr. Dan Holliman, the zoologist at Birmingham-Southern College: He thought these "poisson blanc" might be weakfish, the smallest of the three kinds, known along the Gulf Coast as white trout. I am aware that many different kinds of fish on this continent are called white fish, for example "white perch," a common name for one of the crappies.

buffalo, 1½ feet long. When I got to the landing, I sent a man to notify the chief of my arrival. The chief's brother with about twenty men came and brought me the calumet of peace and invited me to the village. About two o'clock in the afternoon I went to this village, which is 1 league from the edge of the water. Halfway there, I met the chief coming to meet me, accompanied by a score of men of good stature. The chief was suffering from diarrhea,[55] which is an illness fatal to almost all Indians. As we met, this chief handed me a little white cross and a pearl that was not a fine one at all; and he gave similar presents to the Jesuit father, to my brother, and to the Sieur du Guay.[56]

We proceeded to his hut,[57] which is erected on a 10-foot mound of dirt carried there, 25 feet wide and 45 long. Close by it are eight huts. Facing the chief's is the temple. These form a ring somewhat oval-shaped and enclose a public square about 250 yards wide and 300 long. Close by flows a little creek,[58] from which they get their water. I found there a letter from M. de Montigny, a missionary at the Taensas, who left three days ago with a Canadian to return to the Taensas. He states that he has visited most of the huts of this nation, which he estimates at 400, within an area of 8 leagues along the bank of a small creek that waters this country. He says that he has baptized 185 children between one and four years old. From the river landing[59] one climbs a hill, about 150 fathoms high, a sheer bluff covered with hardwood trees. Once on top of the hill one discovers a country of plains, prairies, full of little hills, with

---

[55]Father Du Ru says in his entry for March 12 that the chief of the Natchez had been ill for two months (*Journal*, p. 34).

[56]This name is also spelled Dugué. Pierre Dugué de Boisbriant, already mentioned, became governor of Louisiana after the recall of Bienville in 1724. See McWilliams, *Fleur de Lys and Calumet*, p. 21, n.3.

[57]Father Du Ru reported that the grand chief had a bed of state in his cabin, "very broad, about three feet from the floor and supported by four large columns which are all painted in different colors. It is said that the chief never mounts that bed except to die" (*Journal*, p. 35).

[58]St. Catherine's or St. Catherine, and sometimes written St. Catharine's.

[59]At Natchez-under-the-Hill, which became a notorious place during the nineteenth century. The Mississippi River has purged it away.

clumps of trees in some spots, many oak trees, and many roads criss-crossing, leading from one hamlet to another or to huts. Those who have rambled around for 3 or 4 leagues say they have found the same country everywhere, from the edge of the hill to the chief's village. According to what I have seen, it is a country of yellowish soil mixed with a little gravel as far out from his hut as the distance of a cannon's shot, where the gray soil begins, which appears to me to be better. This countryside is very much like France. This chief is a man 5 feet 3 or 4 inches tall, rather thin, of intelligent countenance. To me he seemed the most tyrannical Indian I have beheld,[60] as beggarly as the others, just like his subjects—all tall men, well made, quite idle, showing us many marks of friendship. I gave them a present of a gun, some powder and shot, a blanket, a hooded coat, a few axes, knives, and glass beads, and a calumet, according to the usual practice of those that visit others. This language is different from the Oumas'. There happened to be a man of this nation who spoke it. We made ourselves understood through my brother, who is beginning to make himself understood in Bayogoula, Ouma, Chicacha, Colapissa,[61] and in [the languages] of the three nations up the branch of the river, which are just the same language, with little difference.

I found the Nadchés' landing at 32°15' north, and the distance from the Oumas' upper landing to the Natchés', following the bends in the river, to be 18½ leagues; and, in a straight line, I find the direction to be north by west and the distance 11

[60]On March 12 Du Ru wrote: "The chief's manner impresses me; he has the air of an ancient emperor, a long face, sharp eyes, an imperious, aquiline nose, a chestnut complexion, and manners somewhat Spanish. For two months he has been ill of a flux of blood which makes him very thin and weak." Du Ru gives the title of the Grand Chief as "Great Chief Ouachilla" and calls the sky "Ouachi" (*Journal*, p. 34). Ouachilla was perhaps his name.

[61]The same as Acolapissa, both derived from Choctaw *okla pisa*, "those who listen and see"—i.e., watchers, spies. The Colapissas lived first on headwaters of the Pearl River (William A. Read, *Louisiana Place-Names of Indian Origin*, in Louisiana State University and Agricultural and Mechanical College Bulletin, 19, n.s., no. 2 [February 1927], p. 26). Then they moved to the north side of Lake Pontchartrain and various lagoons in the area. The name sometimes was used to include other tribes of Choctaw lineage. Hodge, *Handbook*, 1:9.

leagues, and the distance from the cleared land of one village to the other, by way of the hills, about 5 to 6 leagues.

The 12th. At six o'clock in the morning, I set out in a bark canoe with six men to go to the Taensas and to get everything ready to go overland to the Senis, leaving my brother with the rest of [my][62] men at the Nadchés to prepare meal for the journey, where it is more easily done than at the Taensas. Today I have gone about 8¾ leagues and have passed by two islands about half a league long. The country is like that which I have already passed through, quite fine, becoming inundated almost everywhere, according to what I notice on the river-bank in passing by.[63] There is less cane than between the Oumas and the Nadchés.

The 13th. I went on upriver, finding country like that of yesterday, but the river straighter. At noon I reached the Taensas' landing, 6¾ leagues from my camp for the night. Here I left my canoe and baggage and two men to guard them and went on with four men to get to a small lake 1 league away, where one gets boats to go to the village. My guides lost their way, and we could not reach this lake. We had to sleep in the open, without supper, as we had brought nothing except our guns. I have found that, from the Nadchés' landing to the Taensas', following the river, it is about 15½ leagues; and the direction, in a straight line from one landing to the other, I have found to be north by east, north 1°15′, and the distance to be 11¼ leagues. I found the Taensas' landing to be at 32°47′ north.

The 14th. In the morning we reached the shore of the lake, where we came upon four Indians, who were bringing us some canoes, having heard our musket-shots. On the lake we made

---

[62]Margry, 4:412: "laissant mon frère avec le reste de ses gens aux Nadchés." These being Iberville's men even though it is no error to speak of them as Bienville's, as he is in charge of the detachment, the reading "ses gens" appears to be an error for "mes gens." Some two pages below, in the entry for the 15th, Iberville alludes to the same detachment thus: "Le 15ᵉ, je m'en suis retourné avec M. de Montigny au desbarquement, où j'avois laissé mon canot pour y attendre mon frère et tous mes gens" (Margry, 4:414).

[63]Here Iberville discloses how he estimates the depth of flooding to which various places are subject: by means of trash that floated into an entanglement on low limbs of trees and by mud marks left on trees as the water receded.

about 2 leagues and reached the village at noon. Here I found
M. de Montigny, a missionary, who had two Frenchmen with
him. He has had a house built there for himself and is preparing
to build a church. In this nation there are about 120 huts
stretched out over a distance of 2 leagues along the lake shore.
In this place there is a rather fine temple. Once this was a large
nation, but now they are no more than three hundred men.
They have very big fields and a very fine location along the
shore of this lake, which is not at all subject to inundation. The
lake may be a fourth of a league wide and 4½ leagues [long],[64]
coming from the northeast and making a bend to the west.[65]
The main part of this village is about 2 leagues from the end, as
one comes from the Mississipi River, and facing a small river,
100 yards wide, along the bank of which are a few Indian huts.

I interrogated these Indians about the nations west of them
and along the River Marne,[66] questioning particularly a Ouatchita[67] Indian who had been to the Cadodaquios and to some
Spanish posts. He reports the roads as being very difficult, the
whole route being overland. I asked him whether he would
guide us there, and he agreed to do so after I had promised to
pay him well. M. de Montigny, acting as my interpreter, induced them to do what I wanted them to do.

[64]A correction of "de large," an error in the MS. caused by reduplication of the
preceding *de large*, "wide."
[65]This is Lake St. Joseph, an oxbow lake cut off from the Mississippi River, in
Tensas Parish, La.
[66]Here is ambiguity: "Je resonnai avec ces sauvages des nations qui sont a
l'ouest d'eux et de la rivière Marne." Are the tribes in question west of the
Taensa Indians and west, too, of the River Marne or just "de ["along"] la
rivière Marne"?
[67]The Washita, who belonged to the Caddo confederacy, gave their name to the
Ouachita River, in Louisiana. Many of the members of this tribe moved from
the present location of Columbia on the Ouachita River and settled near the
Natchitoches on the Red River. See John R. Swanton, *The Indians of the
Southeastern United States,* Bureau of American Ethnology Bulletin 137
(Washington, D.C., 1946), p. 204. The choice of this Ouatchita Indian as a
source of information about tribes to the west was a good one, because there
were many kindred tribes to the west, all of whose languages he probably
understood.

The 15th. I went with M. de Montigny back to the landing, where I had left my canoe, to wait for my brother and all my men.

The 16th and 17th. It rained and thundered a great deal. The night of the 16th–17th lightning struck the Taensas' temple, set it on fire, and burned it up. To appease the Spirit, who they say is angry, these Indians threw five[68] little infants-in-arms into the temple fire. They would have thrown several others into it had it not been for three Frenchmen, who rushed up and prevented them from doing so. An old man, about sixty-five years old, who played the role of a chief priest, took his stand close to the fire, shouting in a loud voice, "Women, bring your children and offer them to the Spirit as a sacrifice to appease him." Five of those women did so, bringing him their infants, whom he seized and hurled into the middle of the flames. The act of those women was considered by the Indians as one of the noblest that could be performed; accordingly, the Indian women followed that old man, who led them ceremoniously to the hut of the Indian who was to be made chief of the nation, for the chief had died a short time before. At the death of their chief, they observed the custom of killing fifteen or twenty men or women to accompany him, they say, into the other world and serve him. According to what they say, many are enraptured to be of that number. I have strong doubts about that. That old man whom I mentioned above was saying that the Spirit had become angry because, at the death of the last chief, no one had been killed to accompany him and that the chief himself was angry and had had the temple burned. The old man accused the French of being the ones that had caused this calamity, because M. de Montigny, who happened to be in the village when the chief died, had prevented any one from being killed—with which everybody in the nation seemed highly

---

[68]Father Du Ru, who was not present when the children were hurled into the flames, puts the number at "four or five." André Pénicaut's account of this sacrifice of the innocents gives the number as seventeen, which seems to be a gross exaggeration. (Du Ru, *Journal*, p. 41, and McWilliams, *Fleur de Lys and Calumet*, p. 29.)

pleased except this high priest. When these women, sanctified and consecrated[69] to the Spirit by the deed they had just done (that is how several of these Indians speak of them), were brought to the house of the claimant to the throne, they were caressed and highly praised by the old men; and each of them was clothed in a white robe made from mulberry bark, and a big white feather was put on the head of each. All day they showed themselves at the door of the chief's hut, seated on cane mats, where many brought presents to them. Everybody in the village kept busy that day, surrounding the dead chief's hut with a palisade of cane mats, reserving the hut to be used as a temple. In it the fire was lighted, in keeping with their custom.

From the 18th to the 19th and 20th. These women and this old man spent the whole night singing in the new chief's hut, and during the day they stayed beside the door, in view of all passersby.

The 18th. It rained during a part of the day; toward evening my brother arrived and all my men.

The 19th. My brother and the Sieur de St. Denis got ready to set out with twenty men to go by land to the Senis.[70] I could not make this journey because of an aching in the knees, which prevents me from walking.

The 20th. I went to the village with my brother and the twenty men. I sent M. du Guay off in a canoe to the fort and thence to the ships to give notice that I was on my way back.

About six o'clock in the evening the Indian high priest continued to hold, in front of the new temple, a ceremony that he has held every day since the other one burned; it has lasted eight days without letup.[71] Three young men, twenty years old, brought each a bundle of dry tree limbs, which they put down

---

[69]"Ces femmes sanctifiaient et consacraient" in the MS. is faulty spelling of two past participles, which has been corrected in Margry, 4:415.

[70]The Senis or Cenis, who belonged to the Caddoan group, were called by various names: Assinnis, Iscanis, Hasinai. Du Ru, *Journal,* p. 41, n. 43.

[71]Margry, 4:416: "laquelle cérémonie a duré huit jours de suite." The question here is whether "eight days," a week, is not an error for "eight hours." The women were sanctified the night that lightning struck the temple and started the fire—that is, on March 16, only four days before Iberville wrote the entry in

in front of the temple door, 10 steps away. A man about fifty years old, who was custodian of this temple, came with a cane flambeau and stacked the wood stick on stick to make it burn easily. Next he went into the temple and lit his flambeau at the eternal fire and came on up to the stack of wood. Seeing him there, the chief priest, who was 30 steps away, at the door of the chief's hut, came forward with a solemn step, bearing in this left hand a feather pillow, rather big, covered with skin, and in his right hand a little stick, with which he was striking on the pillow as if to mark the beat of a song he was singing. He was followed by the five women who had cast their infants into the temple fire. They were carrying in both hands a bundle of wet moss, which in that country is like tow. When they came near the stack of wood, the Indian who was there lighted it; and the old man, along with the women, marched around it three times, singing the while. Then they attacked the fire, striking it with their wet moss to extinguish it. After they had done this, the old man went back, and the women went off and bathed themselves in the lake, in view of everybody that wanted to watch them. Then they returned to the chief's hut, where, united with the old man, they sang throughout the nights for a week.[72] Certain of these women, when marching around the fire, had the impulse to laugh and to say something, for which the old man rebuked them severely.

The 21st. It rained during part of the day, and my brother could not start. I went to my boats, to which I had all M. de Montigny's belongings carried; he is to take up residence at the Nadchés without deserting the Taensas, among whom he is going to locate a missionary he has been expecting from Canada.

---

question on March 20, 1700. Eight hours is a more logical reading. Even so, Iberville may have let several days pass before he wrote the entry containing "huit jours." Here and below in the text may be evidence that Iberville could not find time on a given day to write about all the events of that particular day.
[72]This passage supports my idea that possibly several days passed before Iberville wrote the entry about the temple fire and is consistent with my retention of "eight days without letup" for the ceremony. Moodie changed eight days to eight hours, and she may have the correct sense.

The 22nd. M. de Montigny joined me about noon, having seen my brother set out around eight o'clock in the morning with one Chaouenon,[73] one Ouachita, who is his guide, and six Taensas, whom M. de Montigny persuaded them to give to my brother to help him carry his baggage.

Toward noon I set out and came on to the Nadchés' landing about nine o'clock in the evening and spent the night. Here I found my three pirogues, which I sent off yesterday.

The 23rd. I went to the village with M. de Montigny, for I wished to talk with the chief about the war they have with the Chicachas. I found the chief dying and all his people grief-stricken. They seemed quite pleased to see M. de Montigny take up residence with them. There I left him with his two servants and set out around two o'clock, my pirogues having been gone since morning.

The 24th. Six leagues above the Oumas I met M. Le Sueur with my felucca loaded with all his belongings. I let him keep it, for without it he could not go upriver this year without great difficulty. I also had him given a big bark canoe belonging to those Canadians that came from the upper river, and I promised them a light pirogue to replace it. I let him have the master of my felucca and gave an order for him to take a Canadian with a pirogue that he is to meet, as he missed one pirogue that is to pass the night at a place where there were three pirogues that I notified him to take. With him he is taking only five of my men. Toward evening I got to the Oumas' upper landing, where I found M. de Tonty and the Sieur de la Ronde.

Seeing no likelihood that I can seize those Englishmen who are at the Chicachas, as there are several, according to the report of some Taensas that have come from there, I sent the Sieur de la Ronde off at once to go to the ships with four men and tell them not to send me the cattle I had asked to be sent through Lake Pontchartrain into the Mississipi, as I foresee too many difficulties in taking them from there to the fort.

The 25th. In the morning I started for the Bayogoulas. The Jesuit Father [is] leaving his servant at the Oumas to build a

---

[73]One of the many French spellings of Shawnee. Hodge, *Handbook*, 2:536–37.

church. M. de Tonty is going back to the Illinois. I entrusted to him several presents to give to the Tonicas and to the chief of the Chicachas who are to come to the Tonicas,[74] as I want him to talk to them there through M. Davion, a missionary. I instructed M. de Tonty to tell them that we have settled on the Mississipi—friends of all the nations nearby, with whom we are doing business in everything; that it rested entirely with them to do as much and become friends of ours by ceasing to make war on the Nadchés and the Colapissas and the Chaquitas;[75] that, if they did not make peace with them, I would arm those nations with guns like the ones they had, because of which they would be unable to hold out against so many Indians equipped to fight them; whereas, if they made peace with those nations, we would all be friends, making one nation. This would be advantageous to them on account of the trade they would have with us, who would give them merchandise at one-fourth less than the English were giving, who take from them only deer skins,[76] whereas we would take buffalo skins, which they have in great quantity without doing anything with them.

---

[74]Margry, 4:418: "Je l'ay chargé de quelques présents pour faire aux Tonicas et au chef des Chicachas qui y doivent venir." The adverb *y* is ambiguous, meaning "aux Illinois" or "aux Tonicas." I chose "aux Tonicas" because M. Davion, who was to be the interpreter, was located as a missionary at the Tonicas. Moodie, usually right, is according to my reading incorrect in taking *y* as "aux Illinois."

[75]The French used the forms *Chaquitas* and *Chaquetas* for the great Choctaw tribe, whose name was finally stabilized as Chactas in French. It is very easy to confuse these early spellings with the various spellings of the small Chatot tribe that settled on a hook near the mouth of the Mobile River, now named for the Chatots, but incorrectly spelled Choctaw Point. When the French moved to the present site of Mobile, they objected to the proximity of the Chatots and moved them to a site on Dog River. When I once lived on Dog River, several people wanted to tell me about the Choctaws that had occupied a site there. Of course, none had. Swanton, *Indians*, pp. 107–08.

[76]To make money or gain a profit, the people of Carolina trafficked in Indian slaves, raised rice and indigo, bought the few available beaver skins. In 1747–48 the value of deerskins shipped to England, which were inferior pelts or skins, amounted to £252,000 (Carolina currency); and the sale of beaver, considered a superior pelt, amounted to only £300. Putting guns in the hands of Indian hunters reduced the deer population. See Verner W. Crane, *The Southern Frontier, 1670–1732* (Ann Arbor, 1956), p. 111, n. 9.

The 26th. I reached the Bayogoulas at ten o'clock in the morning, where I found two of those *voyageurs* that had remained there to guard their baggage. Four of those men are with my brother and the others with me, having the intention of descending the river to the fort and of proceeding to the ships to sell a few beaver pelts they have, which I take to be very few.

I set out from the village at noon with my brother De Chât[e]augay and one man to go to the fort in a bark canoe. I arrived there at nine o'clock at night, on the 27th, having made 42 leagues in 34 hours' journey. There I found the Sieur du Guay, who had arrived 8 hours earlier. I am going to make ready to set out for the ships, to which I am proceeding in order to go and sail west along the coast up until May 15th, as my brother is not to be back sooner, for I set a time for him even as late as the 25th.

The 28th. I went and examined a river a fourth of a league behind the fort and found it to be fresh water, 20 yards wide, 12 feet deep, bordered by prairies on both banks, which become inundated during high water. They appeared to me to be rather dry for a season like this one, when it has rained frequently. Work on the fort has not advanced much; the majority of the men I left there have been ill. The wheat they planted is very fine, and so are the peas.

The 29th. I sent the Sieur du Guay with a bark canoe and three men to go to the ships by way of this river, as it is bound to empty into the sea fairly close to the anchorage; and I, too, set out in a canoe with two men to go to the ships by way of the portage, which is 2 leagues above the fort. I found the portage so bad that I was forced to come back, as I have a fever that is quite high.

The 30th. My fever has not broken. I have been in no condition to go to the ships. I had to send the Sieur de Maltot there in my bark canoe to inform MM. de Sauvolle and de Ricoüart[77] about my indisposition and to tell them to send by

<hr/>

[77]After giving Iberville instructions about the food to be put on the *Renommée*, the minister wrote him from Fontainebleau, September 22, 1699 (Margry, 4:349) that the king had chosen the Sieur de Raucoüart as "escrivain principal

the smack, when it returns from Pensacola, the cattle I want
and the other things.

The 31st. The smack and the felucca have arrived at the fort,
coming from the ship, which they left thirty-six hours ago.
They brought me five cows, one bull, one calf, twelve pigs,
some turkeys, and a great many other things I had requested.
They inform me that the commandant of Pensacola[78] came to
the anchorage on March 23rd with one ship of 24 guns and 140
men, one bilander of 6 guns and 40 men, and one longboat with
6 swivel guns and 20 men. He sailed back on the 27th. They
inform me that the commandant said he had come to drive us
away, having an order from the viceroy to do so, assuming that
we represented some company; but, if we represented crowned
heads, he had been ordered to do nothing.

The smack that I had sent to Pensacola and Apalache he
had met out from La Mobile. They delivered my letters to him,
and he told them that they did not need to go to Apalache, as
the commandant staying there was subordinate to him, and
that their errand was completed and they should go back. This
commandant left for me a written injunction against the posts I
am establishing, saying that to come and seize a country that
belongs to the King of Spain and is within the jurisdiction of the
Viceroy of Mexico is to go against the good understanding
existing between the two crowns. He said he must report it at
once and asked that I refrain from establishing any other posts
whatsoever in these regions until his king is informed about the
matter. This is the whole of it so far as we can decipher a very
poorly written copy that M. de Surgère left for me; he carried
off the original as well as the commandant's answer to the
letters I sent him by the smack, without leaving me a copy of it.

The commandant came to our ships, where he was sump-

---

de marine" to be in charge of munitions, food, and wearing apparel. The
escrivain was to perform the functions of commissary; and he was to take part
in decisions, holding the position of second in authority. This lieutenant
commander, le Sieur de Raucoüart or Ricoüart, is listed just beneath Iberville
among the officers to be aboard the *Renommée* on the second voyage. Margry,
4:335.

[78]The governor, or commandant, of Pensacola was Don Andrés de Arriola.

tuously entertained and much honor was shown him. They plainly disclosed that they[79] were keeping Pensacola solely because we were on this coast, where they do not think that we can remain, as there is no harbor other than Pensacola, which is worthless and which they would abandon if we would withdraw, they say. I have no doubt that their purpose was to drive us from this coast and destroy our post. They had made preparation to do so; they had no idea our ships were here, or they would have come in greater strength. The smack went 28 leagues west-southwest of the river and took soundings, finding only a flat coast.

April 1st. The Sieur du Guay returned, having failed to get to the sea, as he had taken a branch [leading] into a lake, which took him inland.

The 2nd. I sent him back to my ship along with my brother De Chât[e]auguay and six of my sailors in the felucca. I still have fever.

The 5th and 6th. The wind has been in the south, quite strong. With the heavy seas, the water has risen and covered the ground to a depth of two fingers in several places. That happens during the three hours when the tide is rising, as we notice every day. Ordinarily it rises and falls one foot. Several of those Canadians from the Illinois have come to the post.[80]

The 7th. The Jesuit father arrived from the Bayogoulas, where he had remained to build a church with one of his servants and one man I had let him have to help him. The Sieur de la Ronde also arrived in a bark canoe, coming from the ship, from which he set out 3½ days ago. The high water has stopped the work for 4 days; the ground is so wet that it is nothing but mud. The water has not risen enough to reach the site [of the fort], which is 300 yards from the river.

The 9th. There was a heavy southerly gale and heavy rain. The water has risen to three fingers over the ground in many

---

[79]The Spaniards.

[80]In his *Journal*, p. 56, Father Du Ru wrote on April 7 that he found all sorts of people at Fort Mississippi: "voyageurs, soldiers, French, Canadians, sailors, filibusters, and others like them."

places. Those Canadians went back to the Illinois, all but four. I gave each of them forty-five pounds of powder as payment for the time they worked and for their canoes that have been damaged. I sent with them a cabin boy to the Nadchés to learn the language of that nation.

The 13th. I set out at nine o'clock at night in the smack, leaving the Sieur la Ronde, naval cadet, to assume command at the fort during the absence of the Sieur de Maltot. I also sent two bark canoes to the river running behind the fort, to follow two ways to the sea and discover whether they empty far from the ships. I have waited in vain for some Indians to whom I gave two muskets to hunt for buffalo and to catch some young calves. I hired twenty men to catch them, promising them a musket each. I believe that the high water must have made those animals withdraw to high regions, which are some distance away. I have left fifteen men to work at this fort.

The 14th. After nine o'clock I drifted throughout the night. Calm. I came at noon to the mouth of the river. I came out by the same pass through which I had entered, it being the best. All those rocks that are above water are nothing but mud hard enough to withstand the sea; those that are level with the water

GÉOLOGIE PRATIQUE DE LA LOUISIANE, PAR R. THOMASSY.

MUD LUMP en voie de destruction
haut de 8 pieds à marée basse (D'après la carte du Capt. Talcott)

Mud lumps, erroneously thought to be a natural barricade of petrified trees, had kept the Spanish out of the mouth of the Mississippi for many years and had served as the origin of the name "Río de la Palizada." ("Mud Lump en voie de destruction" from *Géologie Pratique de la Louisiane,* by R. Thomassy, Paris, 1859.)

are of somewhat softer mud. In drifting out, I grounded cross-wise on one; the vessel bumped the side and passed without drag, carrying away the mud. The lead sinks a foot in it. I had a pole pushed more than 3 feet into it without finding the hard part. From the river mouth I steered north-northwest for 8 leagues and came to St. Pierre Island, close to which I found 30 feet of water to the southwest, south, east, northeast, and north; but 1¼ leagues from the island there is no more than 13 and 14 feet of water. From this island I steered an east-south-easterly course to pass the point of the islands lying south of Chandeleur Island, which is 2½ leagues from St. Pierre Island, and I find no more than 14 feet of water.

The 15th. At ten o'clock in the morning I reached the ship, having followed the Chandeleur Islands all the way in water 15 feet deep. From M. de Ricoüart I have learned that the *Gironde* sailed on April 3rd, that the Spanish ship was wrecked on Chandeleur Island the night of the 30th. The commandant and 140 members of the crew made their escape to the island in their longboat; in it the commandant made his way to the ships, from which men were sent at once for all the Spaniards on the island; and a longboat was sent to Pensacola to notify the Spaniards to come with their bilander and their other longboats for a part of the men. On the 10th the commandant left for Pensacola with all his men in the felucca and the Biscayan and his bilander and pinnace. Messieurs Desjourdis and de la Haute-Maison took them and got back to the ships on the 17th. At that fort they observed no more than 250 men, 40 to 50 of them being convicts. Several had deserted after the commandant had left. They lack provisions there and seem quite destitute. As for the way they live, they have no fresh food at all.[81] Their fort is a trifling thing. This shipwreck has not enriched us, for it was necessary to help these Spanish gentlemen with clothes and other things, as they had lost everything.

---

[81]Haute-Maison reported that the Pensacola Spaniards killed a steer upon the arrival of the French. But who can tell from the translation "steer" whether this slaughtered animal was of the domestic cattle or a *boeuf sauvage*, a buffalo? After some years had passed, buffalo were still being killed in Florida. Father Du Ru, *Journal*, pp. 60–61.

The 18th. My two bark canoes arrived from the Mississipi, having been stopped for two days along the way by contrary winds. They came out at the sea 12 leagues from the ships. That river loses its identity among the lakes and salt-water bays, in which there is no more than 2 and 3 feet of water.

The 20th. I set out from my ship in the felucca with M. de Ricoüart to go to the fort and from it to the Pascoboula River. I sent the smack to take soundings in the pass between Massacre Island and the island[82] east of the one at the anchorage[83] as well as between the mainland and those islands and to see whether some anchorage better than this one could not be located.

The 25th. In the morning the southeast wind, which has held me at the fort, died down, and I left about seven o'clock in the felucca with one bark canoe to take soundings inside the Pascoboula River, and examine it and see whether it would be easy to cut a pass across the bar at the river mouth. I left orders for M. de Sauvolle to go to the Colapissas and oversee the pearl-fishing.

Toward six o'clock in the evening I was 2 leagues up the river; here I made camp on a very high hill covered with pines. I could not examine the river mouth on account of a very heavy wind that is blowing from the south.

The 26th. The south wind continues. I went up the river about 4½ leagues and got to the village of the Biloxys. Here I spent the night. This village is deserted, this nation having been destroyed two years ago by diseases. Two leagues below this village one comes to many cleared fields, quite close together, on both banks of the river. The Indians report that this nation was formerly quite numerous. It did not appear to me that in this village there were more than thirty to forty huts, built oblong and roofed with tree bark, as we make ours. They were all of one story, about 8 feet high, made of mud daub. Only three are left; the others were burned. The village was enclosed with pales 8 feet high and about 18 inches thick. There still remain three square lookout boxes, each side being 10 feet

[82]Now named Horn Island.
[83]Ship Island.

wide; they are raised 8 feet high, on posts; the sides are made of clay daub mixed with grass, 8 inches thick, well covered. There were several loopholes for them to shoot their arrows through. It appears to me that there was a lookout box at each angle, and one in the middle of the curtains. It was strong enough for them to defend themselves against enemies that have nothing more than arrows.

For 4 leagues from the seashore the river flows through prairies that become flooded during high water. The high grounds are in places half a league from it and farther away on the east or the west, depending on the way the river bends, for it goes north. Two leagues below this village the trees begin to get tall. There are a great many oaks, poplars, and cedars. The land here and at the village is subject to overflow for a few days in the spring when the streams are swollen.

The 27th. I went on up the river, in which there are many currents. It winds from north to east and from north to west. It is about 200 yards wide and 15 feet deep. I came to several small streams that flow into it. Nearly all the way there are abandoned fields in which the canes have grown back. The soil here appears gray, mixed with a little sand. The country is covered with very fine woods of oaks, poplars, copal trees, maples, cedars. I possibly made 4½ leagues today. At six in the evening I made camp on the left side of the river. A heavy rain has fallen here tonight.

The 28th. I went on up the river, finding it of the same width all along—several branch streams on both sides and many deserted fields. Today I made about 5 leagues and came, at seven o'clock in the evening, to a hut on the left going up-stream, where I found two Indian men and three women planting corn and beans. No more than a week ago the water fell and withdrew from the land. This year the water has risen very high. The Indians tell us that it does not rise like this every year. These Indians went off to their village of Pascoboula, which is no more than 2 leagues upstream.

The 29th. At about seven o'clock in the morning I reached the village, in which there are some twenty families. This nation was destroyed by diseases, like the other. The few that were left are well-built people, especially the women, who are the best looking I have seen in this country. Having learned that I was to come to their village, they had built for me a completely new hut. People go by land from this village to the fort in one day. I discussed at length with them the country of the Chaquitas and that nation itself, which has more than fifty villages. From the way they speak of the Chaquitas, there must be more than six thousand men. They are five days' travel from this village, due north. The village of La Mobile[84] is three days from here, to the northeast. In that village there are three hundred men. The Tohomés[85] are one day from them, on the same La Mobile River, and are three hundred men.

The 30th. At eight o'clock in the morning I left this village to go back to the fort. At this village I left two of my men to go with the chief of this nation and his brother to the Chaquitas and the Tohomés and La Mobile,[86] to each of whom I am sending a present and inviting them to visit me, for I wish to be friends with them. I came on and spent the night 2 leagues above the seashore.

The 1st of the month [May]. I took soundings of all the entrances to this river, which loses its identity half a league from the sea among several islands, which form as many channels, in which one finds only 2 and 3 feet of water. It is impossible to make a pass there for boats. I brought back with me three men whom I had taken along to sow the field at the Biloccys' village, as these men had suffered a relapse of the fever they have had since they left France, where I took them

---

[84] At various times Iberville uses *La Mobile* to mean the Mobile River, the channel of the river through La Mobile Bay, and even the mouth of La Mobile Bay. Here the word cannot mean the French post on La Mobile River, which was not established till Iberville's third voyage; it has become a rather awkward name for the Mobilian Indians.

[85] The Tohomés or Tomez, who spoke a Choctaw dialect, were important to the French because they were willing to supply corn and because their location served as an advanced observation post for the French against surprise attacks from the Alibamu and Chickasaws to the north. The Tohomés' towns were on the west side of the river, 8 leagues above the French town La Mobile at Twenty-Seven-Mile Bluff. Hodge, *Handbook*, 2:771.

[86] The Mobilian Indians, the tribe.

aboard sick. I got back to my ship at two o'clock in the afternoon.

The 5th. The smack returned. In the pass between Massacre Island and the island east of here they found 25 and 30 feet of water, the island being quite free of bars; but three-quarters of a league out from this pass they found a bank on which there is no more than 15 feet.

The 9th. In the morning M. le Vasseur Russouelle arrived from the Colapissas[87] with a Biscayan, bringing the chief and his wife and twelve of his men. M. de Sauvolle went to the fort in a bark canoe. They had gone to that village by land from St. Louis Bay, where they had left their longboats and canoes. They found the route very bad; the water had overflowed, covering all the rivers and creeks.[88] M. de Sau[v]olle lost his servant there, who was drowned while swimming a river.[89] On the way, they found many buffalo and have brought back the hides of two cows they killed[90] close to the longboats. They could do no fishing for pearls, the waters being too swollen. Pearls are taken in the rivers. I sent the smack to Fort Missis-

---

[87]Father Du Ru, who had gone to the Colapissas' main village with the Sauvole detachment, held a religious ceremony there. At his suggestion (or at the suggestion perhaps of Sauvole, who was a rather pious man), the French destroyed a phallic symbol that had been raised in the middle of the village (Du Ru, *Journal*, p. 66). I do not know how many Indian tribes gave ceremonious emphasis to the male principle of life as a part of the fertility cult.

[88]MS.: "ils ont trouvé un très mauvais chemin, les eaux ayant débordé par dessus toutes les rivières et ruisseaux."

[89]Father Du Ru gives a vivid account of this drowning: "A league and a half on the way [from St. Louis Bay] we found a river as broad as the Marne. Our people tied several logs together and ferried over all their provisions first. The valet of M. de Sauvole went into a thicket, where he undressed, and next appeared in the middle of the river with his shirt packed on his head. As we watched him swim, fear seized him; he cried out, disappeared and sank to the bottom of the water before we could give him assistance. An Iroquois Indian, who guided our bark, seized him by the middle of his body but, finding him dead, let him drop back" (*Journal*, p. 63, entry for April 27, 1700).

[90]Father Du Ru wrote that men of the detachment shot down six or seven buffaloes of a herd they found. The men stopped to dine on the meat of two buffaloes, which they roasted. Watching these hungry men eat, Father Du Ru concluded that fifteen or sixteen men can eat two buffaloes at one meal. (*Journal*, in the entry for April 28, 1700.)

sipi, where I think my brother should arrive before long, so that
it can bring back twenty Canadians who are to remain at Fort
Bilocchy.[91] The wind has been in the north for two days; it is
quite cold.

The 10th. The wind has held in the north. I could not send
the Indians.

The 11th. I sent them to the fort, from which they are to go
back home.

The 16th. M. de Sauvolle came aboard, bringing with him
two Chaquitas and two Tohomés. My men went only to the
Tohomés' village, where they found some Chaquitas. From
there they moved on because of swollen streams and proceeded
to La Mobile village. There they saw eight Spanish deserters,
who are being badly mistreated among those Indians.

The 17th. I sent these Indians back, giving each a present. I
sent a present to the chief of the Chaquitas nation and invited
him to come to the fort. That nation is at war with all the other
nations to the north and east of them—allies of the English that
are armed with muskets.

The 18th. M. de Bienville arrives about noon with two bark
canoes and seven men. Upon leaving[92] the Taensas he found
the roads so bad, so filled with water, that he could not go
beyond the village of the Yatachés, from which he came back,
bringing with him one Senis and one Souchitiony.[93] At the end
of this journal I have put a copy of his journal, in which he tells
what he saw and learned from the Indians. I learn from him
that the Bayogoulas killed all the Mougoulaschas and called in
to take their place several families of Colapissas and Tious,[94]
who took possession of the Mougoulaschas' fields and huts.

---

[91] The popular name for Fort Maurepas on Biloxi Bay.

[92] Margry, 4:429: "portant des Taensas." *Portant* is a misreading of MS.
partant, "setting out from," which belongs at the head of the following sentence—not at the end of a sentence, where Margry has it.

[93] This little tribe was probably Caddo; another name for them was Doustioni.
In 1687 Joutel alluded to them as being connected with the Kadohadacho. They
had about 200 warriors in 1712. In 1714 St. Denis moved them to the
Natchitoches. Hodge, *Handbook*, 1:399.

[94] The Tioux Indians, who lived in early times on the Yazoo River, were forced
by pressure from the Chickasaws to move down the Mississippi River. Before

That will give us a clear claim to most of that village, which belonged to the Mougoulaschas, from whom I bought several pieces of land; [the chief][95] made me the owner of all his village and sold me other sites where formerly there were villages in the direction of the sea.

The 19th. M. de Montigny and Davion are arriving with a Nadchés chief and twelve of his men and two Tonicas chiefs and two of their men. I learn from M. Davion that some Acansas, having come to the Tonicas on April 20th, told him that several Englishmen had come to engage in trade at the Acansas' village during February, had given them a present of thirty guns and powder and bullets and other goods, and had engaged them to go and make war on the Choquichoumans,[96] who are a Chicacha nation, friends of the Englishmen who are at the Chicachas, 40 leagues from the Tonicas. The Englishmen were awaiting the return of the party of Acansas, who, we have learned, were defeated by the Choquichoumans. The Englishmen came by canoe to the Acansas, by way of the Ouabache River.[97] They persistently inquired where the missionaries were who had come to the Acansas to settle—they had received information about them from Canada. They were guided there by a man named Couture,[98] a French deserter

---

Iberville ascended the river and visited the Natchez, the Tioux (also called Thysia) had become attached to the Natchez as a protected tribe. Their village was 1 league below the Natchez landing and 2 leagues west of the great Natchez village. Charlevoix reported that they had been completely destroyed by the Quapaws before 1731. Swanton, *Indians*, pp. 194–95.

[95]The MS. lacks a subject in "et m'avoit fait le maître de tout son village." Margry, 4:429, has added a subject: *le chef*.

[96]Another form of the name of the Yazoo River tribe identified above as the Chakchiuma.

[97]The early French extended the name Wabash to that part of the Ohio River below its confluence with the Wabash.

[98]Jean Couture, a renegade Frenchman who brought to Tonty the news that La Salle had been murdered by his own men (*DCB*, s.v. "Tonty, Henri [de]"). On the Arkansas River, Tonty had built a stockade-protected post to serve as an intermediate station between the Illinois post and the colony Tonty thought La Salle would establish on the coast near the mouth of the Mississippi. Couture was commandant at Tonty's post in 1687 when the survivors of La Salle's detachment arrived on their way to the Mississippi River and Canada.

who had lived for several years at a post M. de Tonty had
established at the Acansas.⁹⁹ M. de Tonty writes me that, on
arriving at the Tonicas, he found the nephew of the Chicachas'
chief, whom the old men of the village of that nation had sent to
find out what we wanted to tell them in the absence of his
uncle; the uncle had gone on a war party with six hundred men
against the Chaquitas. M. de Tonty¹⁰⁰ spoke to him about the
alliance the chief had at one time made with the French, saying
that it was right to renew it, and that to do so it was necessary
for the chief to come down in the spring to the French posts,
where he would see all the chiefs of the nations of this country,
who are our friends. M. de Tonty gave him a present of several
things I had given him for that purpose.

The 21st. I sent those Indians to the fort. The smack has
arrived from the Mississipi.¹⁰¹

The 25th. I went to the fort to see about a great many things.
I gave a present to those Indians and sent them back in a
longboat with M. Davion to the portage, across which they are
to carry a canoe and from there go down to Fort Mississipi,

By 1696 Couture, who had the soul of a *coureur de bois,* had defected to the
English in Carolina, from whom he was trying to draw some men to the west
by means of his skill in Indian languages and his claim that he knew where to
find precious metals. Crane, *Frontier,* pp. 42–44.

⁹⁹The Acansas were a tribe or division of the Quapaw Indians. Quapaw means
"those going downstream," apparently a name derived from the history of a
southern branch of the Siouan-linguistic group who had descended the Mississippi River before De Soto explored the area. There was another division of
this group who ascended the Missouri River and were accordingly called
"those going upstream": the Omaha. The chronicler of the La Salle expedition
to Texas, Joutel, visited the Arkansas and considered them to be attractive
people. The population of the Arkansas may have been 5,000 people in De
Soto's time. Father Vivier estimated the tribe to have no more than 400
warriors in 1750 (Hodge, *Handbook,* 2:333–36).

¹⁰⁰The proper noun *M. de Tonty* replaces the vague pronoun *il* in "Il luy a parlé
de l'alliance" (Margry, 4:430).

¹⁰¹MS.: "Le vingt unième j'ay envoyé ces sauvages au fort, le traversier armé
[arivé?] du Mississipi." In script it can be difficult, as here, to distinguish *armé*
from *arivé.* Because *armer,* "to equip," "to fit out," does not make sense in this
context and because of the acute accent on the *e,* I am inclined to believe that
est has been omitted from the sentence: *est arrivé.*

where their canoes are. M. de Montigny is going to France with me. The eight Spaniards my men saw at the village of La Mobile have come to the fort, guided by Indians. They deserted from Pensacola at the first of March with the purpose of going to New Mexico. They assured me that the commandant had sailed from his fort to come and take possession of ours, to make us withdraw, and to establish himself in it if he found the locality good; or the post would be established elsewhere—they do not know where. They believe that it was at the Palisade River,[102] which is the Mississipi.

The 27th. I returned to my ship.

The 28th. I came out of the anchorage by warping and tacking, the wind being south, southeast, and southwest, where it has been for ten days without changing.

Copy of the Journal of M. de Bienville's
Overland Journey from the Taensas
to the Village of the Yatachés
(March 22–May 18, 1700)

March 22nd. I set out from the village about nine o'clock in the morning with twenty-two Canadians, six Taensas, and one Ouachita. I trudged all day in a flooded country through water halfway up to the knee and up to the knee. Toward evening I came to the bank of a small river 70 yards wide and very deep, 4½ leagues west of the Taensas. I found some Ouachitas there with several canoes partly loaded with salt. They are abandoning their village to go and dwell at the Taensas. They came from their village by way of some small streams that admit passage during high water.

The 23rd. In the morning I crossed this river in the Indians' canoes. Half a league west of it I found a river 30 yards wide, running north and south, with a strong current, which I had trouble in crossing, as I could not find wood to make rafts to take the baggage across. From there I made 2 leagues west

---

[102]For a study questioning the validity of the name *Palisade* as a suitable name for the Mississippi River, see my article "Iberville at the Birdfoot Subdelta," in *Frenchmen and French Ways in the Mississippi Valley*, ed. John Francis McDermott (Urbana, 1969), pp. 127–40.

through wretched, wet country. The rain forced us to make camp early. The Taensas have deserted me on account of the bad roads and the severe cold. They do not like to wade naked through water.

The 24th. We broke camp at sunup in rather cold weather. Three-quarters of a league west I found two small streams, which we passed over on trees we felled across them, obstructing them. Two leagues from there we found a fine dry prairie one-half league wide and very long, at the end of which was a river about 40 yards wide—strong current, full of crocodiles[103]—its course north and south. We crossed it on rafts. All these rivers flow into the Ouachita River.[104]

The 25th. We broke camp in the morning and walked all day on a straight course, 5° south of westward, through woods and prairies and savannas for 6 leagues, never stopping, in water up to the knee or belly and at times up to the neck. A man of medium height is at a great disadvantage when going into such country: I see some of my men in water only up to their waists, whereas I and others are almost swimming, pushing our bundles before us on logs to keep them from getting soaked. I made camp at five o'clock in the afternoon, later than we wished, as we did not find dry ground until we reached the edge of a prairie, where there seems to be good hunting. Here my men killed a buffalo, from which we prepared a good meal, as all of us had hearty appetites.

The 26th. I stayed at this hunting ground, where my men went out and killed three deer and twelve very fat turkeys. Two of my men have had a seizure of dysentery accompanied by very violent colic.

The 27th. I set out in the morning, leaving at this camp site two sick men and one of their companions to take care of them. Half a league from my camp site, I found a river 35 yards wide. The Indian guide led us to believe that farther up this river there is a Coroas village. We crossed this river on a raft. Two

---

[103]For the alligators of the southern part of North America the French used *crocodile* as well as *caiman,* the Carib word for crocodile.
[104]The north branch of the Red River.

leagues from that river we found another one 25 yards wide, which we also crossed. When we do not find wood that floats easily, we make small *cajeux*, or rafts, upon which we put our baggage, and we swim across, pushing the *cajeu* to the other bank after firing many musket shots at the crocodiles to keep them off, lest they attack us in the water, which we find to be very cold. One league from this river we found a swamp a quarter of a league wide, which we crossed in the same way we crossed the river. The water was very cold. We came on and made camp near it, on the shore of a small lake. I calculate that I have made 4 leagues west by south today, and [I am][105] very tired.

The 28th, Sunday. I arrived at the Ouachitas' village. After going west 2½ leagues, we swam across a swamp 500 yards wide and crossed several prairies separated from one another by strips of woods, with pines, ash, elms, cedars mixed. I came to the Ouachitas' village. This village is on the bank of the Marne, or Sablon[n]ière, River or, rather, on a branch of that river. There are no more than five huts and about seventy men. At this spot the river is possibly 180 yards wide, with a current as strong as that of the Mississipi. It seems to be deep. I find that the distance from the Taensas' village to this one is 21 leagues, the direction being 6 or 7 degrees south of west. From this village to the Coroas' it is 6 leagues to the north, according to what they lead me to believe.

It rained all day on the 29th. It rained until noon on the 30th, when I set out with a Nadchito to lead me to his village. We crossed a [prairie][106] 3 leagues wide, rather dry. From there I came into a country that was wet for 1½ leagues. Here we found two small, rather swift streams that we had to swim, the water being very cold. From there we went through a swamp, at the end of which we met six Nadchitos on their way to the

---

[105]MS.: "et bien fatigué."

[106]Margry, 4:434–35: "Nous avons passé une rivière de trois lieues de large, assez sèche". The MS. has the same: "une rivière." Moodie thought that *rivière* should be *prairie*, since there is no river three leagues wide in the area visited by Bienville. Other strong evidence—the phrase, "assez sèche"—supports the word *prairie* as the word that was in the writer's mind.

Coroas to sell salt. Today I have made 4½ leagues west by south. These recent rains are making our progress very difficult.

The 31st. It rained for a part of the day. I made 3 leagues west by south through a country of streams that was easy to walk through. I made camp at the edge of a swamp. My men went hunting but did not kill anything or see any signs of game. I am short of food, as I found none at the Ouachitas. Three of my men keep on walking, although they have had fever for two days.

April 1st. It poured down all night and until ten o'clock this morning, when we set out to get to some Indian huts. Our guide had us make a big detour to get around this swamp, which was half a league wide. We crossed eight small streams, which were 8, 10, and 12 yards wide and very deep. We felled trees to serve us as bridges; then we found several swamps and bogs, where the water was up to our bellies and armpits. In this wretched country we plodded on until night, as we failed to find, during all this time, one arpent of land suitable for a camp. We are seeing no signs of game and are reduced to two little thin sagamités a day. Today I have made 3 leagues northwest by west.

The 2nd. It rained all night, till two o'clock in the morning. We could not make more than 1½ leagues today on account of the bad roads through swamps, in water up to our bellies at least. We found six small streams that we had to cross on small trees lying 2 feet under water. The country was so thick with canes that we could not force our way through. This has worn us out, as we have spent the last two nights in the rain, having found no big trees from which to rip bark for a shelter. Today we found some, on a very high hillside, where there appears to be good hunting. My men went off at once and killed a buffalo and a cow and the calf, which had lain down by its mother. They caught it and killed it with blows of an ax.

The 3rd. It poured down all night and thundered. I stayed to prepare some jerky.

The 4th, Palm Sunday. I set out in the early morning and, 1½ leagues from that place, we happened upon the road to the village, which we abandoned in order to avoid a big swamp, and proceeded down a dry creek bed. I made 6 leagues southwest and camped in this creek bed.

The 5th. Half a league from our campsite, we found a swamp a third of a league wide, in which there was no bottom at 6 feet and which was partly filled with logs, from which we made rafts to support our clothes. We spent the whole day crossing it. The water was very cold. Several of my men were so seized with chills in the water that they climbed into trees to get some relief. Four stayed in trees nearly all day—until we sent a raft for them. Never in our lives have my men and I been so tired. In going through this swamp I observed some silkworm cocoons hanging on willow branches. Here you see a fine occupation to temper the fires of youth: We do not stop singing and laughing, as we wish to show our guide that fatigue does not distress us and that we are men different from Spaniards.

The 6th. We made 3½ leagues west-southwest. Here we found a big lake, which we had to go around by proceeding 2½ leagues south by east and turning back west-southwest for 2 leagues, where we came upon two huts of Natchitoches.[107] They took to flight when they saw us. Our guide reassured them, and they came back to us. We treated them well. One cannot go to their village except in a canoe (they have only two canoes) because of the overflow of water from the river.

The 7th. I took the two pirogues and departed with half of my men. I made 4 leagues southwest and arrived at the village of the Souchitionys, where I was well received. I sent the pirogues back at once for the rest of my men. I spent the night at this village. The Natchitoches[108] are about 1 league from here—all scattered in huts along the Marne River.

The 8th. All my men arrived. I have had people pounding corn.

The 9th. It rained all day. The women could not finish pounding the corn. The men came for me and carried me on their shoulders underneath a kind of sheltered market-place,

[107]MS.: "Natchitouchés," which is a poor spelling.
[108]MS.: "Natchitos."

roofed with palmetto palms, where they had assembled to sing the calumet to me. I gave a small present to them and to the chief of the Natchitoches,[109] and gave them a calumet of peace. At this village of the Soutchitionys there are fifteen huts assembled in a cluster. In front of the village the river is wide and full of uprooted trees. Now that the water is high, it is 4 fathoms deep.

The 10th. It rained all day. The chief promised to let his son guide me to the Yactachés.

The 11th, Easter Sunday. We set forth in pirogues to get across 3 leagues of wretched country north by east of the village. Quitting the river, we made camp on a hillside, where there were many deer that had withdrawn there because of the high water.

The 12th. We left our pirogues and walked overland for 1 league north, where we found a big lake 5 to 6 leagues long and an eighth of a league wide. We proceeded along it west-north-west to get by it. At the end of it we saw a great many deer.

The 13th. We crossed five small streams close together that flow into the lake. I went north-northeast for 1½ leagues and happened upon the beaten track, along which we proceeded west-northwest for a distance of 5½ leagues of hardwood forests and streams, finding creeks and good hunting for deer and turkeys.

The 14th. We are walking on. Half a league farther, we find a swamp filled with trees, very deep, and so long that our two guides lead us to believe that one has to sleep four nights before he can get around it, and that about 1 league south there used to be three huts on the bank of a stream, where there were some pirogues. I immediately set my men the task of digging out a pirogue with our hatchets. It was finished in five hours, big enough to carry the six men whom I sent to those huts for the Indians' pirogues. My men went hunting and killed six deer.

The 15th. My men returned, bringing me three pirogues, in which we set forth and, going 4 leagues north by east, reached the other side of the lake, where we spent the night.

---

[109]MS.: "Natchitouchés," the same bad spelling again.

The 16th. We left our pirogues and walked along the lake on a hillside of fine country and woods, where we killed five deer along the way, making 3½ leagues northwest and crossing over several rather high hills covered with small stones. We fired several musket shots to give notice to the Indians, who were encamped on the other side of a lake, 1 league west-southwest of us. They came in a pirogue, five men, to find out who we were. Our guides having called to them and got them to come, I embarked in their pirogue with two of my men, leaving three of the Indians in my place. I went to their hut, which was flooded with water. As the water covered the ground, these Indians had camped on platforms. Scattered there, were fifteen huts of the Nakasas[110] nation, who live on the bank of the River Marne. I sent for the pirogues belonging to the huts. Only three quite small ones were found, which I sent to my men.

The 17th. In the morning I sent the pirogues back to my men, who arrived about noon. I immediately set out in two pirogues to go to the Yatachés, striking through the woods by the shortest cut, the river having overflowed and spread inland for more than 2 leagues. Night caught us opposite a little village of Nakasas, eight huts, on the left bank of the River Marne. We went there and spent the night. The river is 160 yards wide at this spot and has as strong a current as the Mississipi.

The 18th. I sent three pirogues for the rest of my men. Around these huts there is not one arpent that is not flooded. The water is falling noticeably. I found very little corn, owing to some Yuahés[111] that came visiting here and took away all the corn their horses could carry.

The 19th. About three o'clock in the afternoon my men arrived. It was too late to go to the Yatachés, about which the Indians became badly upset; they let us know that they had no

[110]The Nakasas were the Nacisi, according to Hodge, *Handbook*, 2:6. Joutel first mentioned them. When Bienville was exploring the Red River area in 1700, he found a village of Nacisi, eight houses. Again on April 16 Bienville alludes to the Nakassas (Nacisi) and reports fifteen huts in the Nacisi village on a lake near the river.

[111]These bumptious visitors were Iowa Indians, according to Hodge, *Handbook*, 1:614.

more corn to give us. My men were busy making themselves a paddle each. All the Indians here are tattooed around the eyes and on the nose and have three stripes on the chin.

The 20th. We left in two old pirogues, the ends of which were made of clay. I followed the river, which makes a number of bends; all of this was equivalent to my having made 2 leagues north by east in a straight line. About two o'clock in the afternoon, I made my way to the Yatachés. All their huts are scattered along the river for a distance of 2 leagues. Upon our arrival, the Indians hid their pirogues and corn, because they had learned from an Indian who got there a little ahead of us that we wanted pirogues and food. I threatened to remain with them if they did not give me pirogues and corn for the journey to the Cadodaquio[s]. I immediately dispersed my men into different huts. They estimate the journey from here to the Cadodaquios by land in summer as no more than two days.

The 21st. When the Indians led me to believe that they would give me provisions and pirogues, I sent—to get quicker action— one man into each hut with glass beads and other trifles to persuade them to pound corn at once; and I took two men in one pirogue to make a search for other pirogues all along the river. I could find only three, which I bought for two axes each. Today the water has fallen 2 feet. I have gone inside forty different huts along this river.

The 22nd. I embarked for the Cadodaquios, who are north-west of here, even though these Indians tell me it takes ten nights to go there by pirogue along the river. This I do not believe, as it is only two days from this village by land; but I cannot go overland because of the high water. Even so, once we are on the way, the guides, seeing me determined to go there, will tell me the truth about how far it is, as they have already done in several places. Toward noon, after I had questioned my guides thoroughly, they assured me that it will take me at least ten nights to get there. The current being very strong, I came to the decision to break off the journey and return to the ships because I have no more than twenty days remaining of the time specified for me to get there and because I have several men weakened by diarrhea and dysentery, brought on by the cold water and the poor food. With several Cadodaquios at this village and one Naouadiche[112] and one Nadaco[113] I have discussed the neighboring areas of this country. They all tell me that they have been to a Spanish settlement, which is 5½ days by land to the west of this village. They go and come on horseback. At those establishments, they say, the Spaniards have four pieces of cannon. There are a number of men, women, and children, whites, and mulattoes and blacks, and they till the soil. The settlement is close to the village of the Nouadiches. The Nouadiche who talks to me says that he lived with them nearly a year and on several occasions went on horseback with some Spaniards, who he tells me are black, apparently Negroes, to another settlement, which he locates five days' travel west-northwest of the former one. At this settlement there were only Negroes with their families. He reports them to be rather numerous and leads us to believe that the Negroes at this settlement did not welcome any white Spaniard; and when white ones came, the blacks drove them off without speaking to them; he had not, however, seen them fight each other. He gives the name of this settlement as Connessi, that is, the Blacks;[114] and the first one, the Spanish settlement, he calls, in their language, Yayecha.[115] He reports that by land it is three days northwest by west from

---

[112]This Indian was a Nabedache. The tribe was one of the dozen or more tribes of the Hasinai, Caddos. Iberville's spelling, Naouadiche, is closer to the Indian word for salt, witish, which gave the tribe its name. Joutel recorded that Naoudiche meant "salt"; there was salt in their area, and the Naouadiche apparently engaged in the salt trade. This tribe proved to be rather stable: They maintained their chief village for over a century, a few leagues west of the Neches River, near Arroyo San Pedro. Hodge, Handbook, 2:1.

[113]The Anadarko belonged to the same tribe as the one called Nadaco as well as Nadacoc or Nadacho. The tribe belonged to the Caddo confederacy, whose dialect was spoken by the Kadohadacho, Hainai, and Adai. The tribe called themselves Nadako. Their villages were along the Trinity and Brazos rivers in Texas. Hodge, Handbook, 1:51–52.

[114]Du Ru reported that in several villages the French heard of a district where a large group of Negroes lived, mulattoes, both men and women, who had revolted and deserted the Spaniards. Journal, p. 71.

[115]The Eyeish, a tribe of the Caddo confederacy. Hodge, Handbook, 1:448.

Connessi to the Chomans,[116] and that from the Chomans to the Conoatinos[117] and to three other nations it is approximately one and two days' journey. These four nations make war on the Spaniards and on all the Indians to the south and southeast and east of them. According to all Indians of this village, the River Marne flows to the village of the C[a]dodaquios and divides into two branches one day's journey above them: One runs to the northeast and the other to the west-northwest. Along this branch are two nations: One is called Chaquantie, [118] which is four days from the C[a]dodaquios; the other nation [is named] Canchy.[119] These Indians are at peace with the Conoatinos, who are numerous. This branch comes to an end at a big mountain, which they say has a hole through it from which this river issues, coming from a tremendous lake, on which they say they never venture in a canoe because the waves on it are too strong. A day's travel beyond, to the north and northwest of the C[a]dodaquios, there are no more trees; there are just prairies, numerous buffalo on them, and a country full of hills and mountains, on most of which there are only small trees and little water in summer. On the branch going to the northeast, there is just one small Indian nation, which they do not hold in high regard; and there are numbers of buffalo. The Indians tell me that the Spaniards often ride horseback to the C[a]dodaquios, as many as thirty and forty, although they never spend the night; they go back. While asking them whether they have ever seen other white people like the Spaniards, I inquired whether these Spaniards were not digging in the ground, searching for silver, like some silver I showed them. They told

---

[116]The Chomans are identified by Hodge as the Tawehash Indians, who were a principal tribe of the Wichita confederacy. Hodge, *Handbook*, 2:705 and 1043.

[117]The Caddo name for the Red River of Louisiana and a possible name for a tribe of uncertain location. Kanohatino is the spelling that Hodge seemed to prefer. Hodge, *Handbook*, 1:653.

[118]Hodge lists Chanquantie among the tribes and villages that were "probably" Caddoan. Hodge, *Handbook*, 1:183.

[119]Hodge identifies this as Bienville's name for the Lipan Indians, an Apache tribe. Hodge, *Handbook*, 1:768–69.

me no; the Spaniards produced corn only, and they had a great deal of such silver, for they had seen them gambling with it at cards. They said there were some Spaniards that stamped their feet over losing and tore up the cards.

The 23rd. I set out with four pirogues to go down the river. About eleven o'clock I came to the Nacassas, where I stayed one hour, searching for provisions. I came on and spent the night at a hut on the right hand, which I estimate to be 10 leagues from my starting point. There have been many bends in the river. In several places I have seen a number of mulberry trees, especially at the Yatachés.

The remainder of the journal cannot be deciphered, as it got wet. I am reporting only that, proceeding down the river, he found it fine enough with the exception of certain sections he did not see, for the Indians made him cut across the land to shorten the way, the water being out in the woods. He made his way to the bank of the Mississipi on May 11th, having been delayed for 4½ days by the incessant rains and having stopped 3½ days to go hunting, as he had no provisions at all.

May 18th. He reached the ships.

The Third Voyage to the Mississippi

THE JOURNAL OF THE *RENOMMÉE*

THE SIEUR D'IBERVILLE'S JOURNAL
FROM DECEMBER 15, 1701,
TO APRIL 27, 1702

DECEMBER 15, 1701. AT THREE O'CLOCK in the afternoon, I made land 2 leagues east of Pensacola harbor, at the entrance to which I anchored in 6 fathoms. I sent an officer to the Spanish fort to pay my respects to the commandant and ask permission to enter his harbor in order to secure the ships there within reach of La Mobile River, on which I have been ordered to establish a settlement. During the morning of the 16th, the officer came back to the ship with a Spanish pilot whom the Spanish commandant sent me, the only one he had. I sent him on board the *Palmier;* and I myself went in without pilot, as I know the harbor. Here I anchored and moored the ships with two anchors. Dom Francisco Martine[z],[1] sergeant-major of

---

[1]*Dom* is a Frenchman's spelling of Sp. *don,* "master" or "lord"; both words come from Latin *dominus* (cf. Dan Cupid). Such a friendly reception on the part of the heretofore hostile Spanish was owing in part to Louis XIV's grandson's being now King of Spain. See Nellis M. Crouse, *Lemoyne d'Iberville: Soldier of New France* (Ithaca, N.Y., 1954), pp. 233–36.

the fort, who is in command during the absence of the commandant, now at Vera Cruz, came aboard to offer me his services.
In like manner I offered my services to him. From him I
learned that M. de Sauvolle died on the 22nd of August and
that a longboat from Fort Bilocchy had left this harbor only
four days ago; it had brought him five of his men, deserters,
whom M. de Bienville, deputy commandant at Fort Bilocchy,
was sending him. This longboat was leaving for the Tohomés to
buy corn.

The 17th. I sent M. Desourdis[2] in my felucca to Fort Bilocchy with orders to the Sieur de Bienville, who is in command there following the death of M. de Sauvolle, to go at once
with the smack and the longboats to Massacre Island with the
things needed to establish the post up La Mobile and to load[3] his
smack and that of M. Marigny,[4] who should be there already,

---

[2]MS.: "Mr. Desourdis." Margry, 4:504, gives this name as "M. des Jourdis."
The name is spelled in several ways.

[3]Pierre Margry, *Découvertes et Établissements des Français dans l'Ouest et dans
le Sud de l'Amérique Septentrionale (1614–1754)*, 6 vols. (Paris: 1879–1888),
4:504: "descharger son traversier et celui de M. de Marigny . . . de tous les
effets necessaires et artilleries du fort." Logic about moving the French post
from Biloxi to the new site on the Mobile River demands the verb *charger*, "to
load," instead of *décharger*, "to unload," unless the artillery pieces and other
heavy equipment are to be unloaded at Île Massacre, which served as a way
station. *Décharger* may be *de charger*, "and to load," a grammatical structure
parallel with *avec ordre . . . de se rendre*, "with the order to go . . . to Massacre
Island."

[4]François de Hautmesnil de Mandeville, here called by another of his names,
de Marigny, was born in Montreal in 1682 and died at New Orleans in 1728.
He was the object of Bienville's displeasure. He went from Canada to Louisiana, then to France for several years, and returned to the colony with the
commission of lieutenant. Bienville accused him of having obtained preferment
in France by claiming to be one of the many Le Moyne brothers. Despite
Bienville's attitude toward him, Marigny/Mandeville commanded a company
on Dauphin Island, at Mobile, and at New Orleans, where by 1727 he was
holding the position of mayor of the town. This officer and his wife set a
standard for the graciousness of social life (the *Dictionary of Canadian Biography*, or *DCB*, s.v. "Philipe[s] de Hautmesnil de Mandeville, François"). The
most splendid Creole of them all—Bernard de Marigny—was descended from
the officer and gentleman here identified.

with all necessary supplies and the artillery from the fort, leaving there M. de Boisbrillant,[5] a major, with twenty men to guard it, and to bring all the workmen with him. December 31st. M. Desourdis has returned from Fort Bilocchy. M. de Marigny has not yet got there with his smack. The Sieur de Bienville sends me word that he will go at once to La Mobile with the men of the garrison, that he is well but that more than half of his men are either sick or convalescent. January 3, 1702. I sent Pilet's[6] ketch to La Mobile loaded with provisions and the things needed for the settlement, and eighty workmen from my crew, with a Spanish launch lent me by the commandant, in which I sent M. de Sérigny[7] and

[5]Pierre Dugué de Boisbriand, a cousin of Iberville's, had had a career in military service in Canada before he came to Louisiana on Iberville's second voyage as an officer on board the *Renommée*. In Louisiana he held such important positions as adjutant of the garrison at Mobile, 1716; commandant at Mobile, the same year; first king's lieutenant, 1718, and member of the council of Louisiana; commandant of the French post at the Illinois. He built Fort Chartres, which may have been the finest fort the French built in all Louisiana. When Bienville, commandant of Louisiana, fell into disfavor and was recalled to France in 1724, the high executive position came into Boisbriand's hands, but he kept it only a short time before he, too, fell into disfavor. Although he was a hunchback, he succeeded in winning the affections of Demoiselle Françoise de Boisrenaud. But Bienville, his commanding officer, crossed the lovers, and Boisbriand never married (*DCB*, s.v. "Dugué de Boisbriand, Pierre").
[6]MS.: "pilet" or "piler" or "pilas"—it is impossible to tell the correct spelling from this entry of the word; but, as the name appears several times as Pilet or Pillet, I am using Pilet.
[7]Joseph Le Moyne de Sérigny et de Loire, who was the sixth son of Charles Le Moyne de Longueuil of Montreal. He was a successful naval officer, and, after French victories against the English in North Canada, Sérigny was made commanding officer in Hudson Bay. He did not come to Louisiana till Iberville's third voyage. When Iberville was given his greatest command to harass the British, in 1706, Sérigny commanded the *Coventry* on a raid in the West Indies. Later in his career, after long being in disfavor because of graft in his handling of the king's stores and the fashion in which he appropriated goods captured in the 1706 attacks in the West Indies, he captured Pensacola during the war with Spain and soon moved his activities to Rochefort, where he was

Châteaugué to join the Sieur de Bienville at Massacre Island, which forms the west side of the mouth of La Mobile. Here, the Spaniards tell me, there is a harbor among some islands that is rather good. The Sieur de la Salle[8] and his family are leaving on the ketch, which I have chartered at seven livres a ton to go to Massacre Island and take the king's goods, where I have ordered a warehouse to be built. I have not been able to go to La Mobile; an abscess in the side has kept me in bed since my departure from St. Domingue; it required a six-inch-long incision through my belly, which has caused me a great deal of pain.

The 12th of the same month. Pilet's ketch returned from Massacre Island, and the smack arrived, too, from Bilocchy. My brother De Bienville got to Massacre Island on the 5th of the month with forty men, and my brother De Sérigny also, with the Spanish launch and the ketch. They unloaded the boats on Massacre Island and put the effects under tents. They are building a warehouse. They could not bring the smack into this harbor owing to the stiff northwest gale, which hindered them from bringing the smacks in as well as from taking

appointed governor in 1723; and in 1734 he died as Governor of Rochefort. He probably died a rich man. *DCB*, s.v. "Le Moyne de Sérigny et de Loire, Joseph."

[8]Nicolas de La Salle sailed for Louisiana in 1701 on Iberville's third voyage to hold the position of acting commissary. He brought his wife and several young children to the new post at Twenty-Seven-Mile Bluff. There he died on December 31, 1710. According to C. E. O'Neill, who wrote a short article about Nicolas for the *DCB* ("La Salle, Nicolas de"), the acting commissary was not a relative of the explorer Cavelier de La Salle, although he did accompany the explorer on his historic voyage to the mouth of the Mississippi in 1682. Many allusions to Nicolas de La Salle identify him as a relative of the explorer. I cannot appraise Nicolas's character: I know that he appears to have been an ill-tempered man, especially in his dealings with Bienville; yet I have no doubts that Bienville engaged in graft, a way of life for officers that would nevertheless have offended any honest commissary. I judge that O'Neill found some evidence that La Salle's own account books were in questionable condition. But if he engaged in graft, he was not as skillful as the Le Moyne brothers in making personal use of the king's goods and king's ships; for after La Salle's death in 1710 his possessions had to be sold at auction to provide some support for his wife and children.

soundings on the bar of this harbor. On it they afterwards found 21 feet[9] of water.

My brothers inform me that they will leave on the 10th with the launch and two feluccas to go up La Mobile, after they have built the Massacre Island warehouse, in which they will shelter the goods; they will leave my brother De Châteaugué and ten men on the island to complete the roof.

The 17th. I sent the ketch, loaded, back to Massacre Island and sent the Sieur de Bécancour,[10] a sublieutenant, with the *Palmier*'s longboat and twenty men from my crew to help in transporting the goods from Massacre Island to the settlement, with the longboat and the two pinnaces. I wrote the Sieur de Bienville to establish the settlement at the second bluff, which is 26 leagues[11] from Massacre Island, to have the Sieur de la Salle arrange for the work by the day or by the job, and to start work on a fort with four bastions. I sent Le Roux, overseer carpenter of the port of Rochefort, and all the ships' carpenters and

---

[9]Margry, 4:505, has "où ils ont après trouvé douze pieds d'eau," but the MS. has "21 pieds d'eau."

[10]Pierre Robinau de Bécancour, a Canadian, second baron of Portneuf, may be the man in question. He lived much of the time on his fief "on the road to the great Cap Rouge." Since I cannot be sure that this is the man Iberville called a sublieutenant, I can only refer the reader to the *DCB*, s.v. "Robineau de Bécancour, René" and "Robineau de Bécancour, Pierre." Evidence that this officer was a different man appears on the map "Fort Louis de la Mobille, 1706(?)" in Peter J. Hamilton, *Colonial Mobile* (Mobile, 1952), p. 84. This map of the village up the Mobile River should be dated 1711, as it is the work of the engineer Sieur Chevillot, who came to Mobile in that year. On this map showing lots owned by the citizens of the town La Mobile, M. Beccancour's name appears on a big corner lot fronting on rue de Bois Brillant and rue de Beccancour.

[11]From Margry's text the absurd distance of 16 leagues got into secondary sources, although it is easy to catch the error if one examines the MS.: "26 lieues." Margry, 4:506 reads, "de faire l'establissement au deuxiesme écore, qui est à seize lieues de l'isle Massacre." This error is interesting: Iberville wrote "16 L dans la Rivière," which is a rather accurate estimate of the distance from Twenty-Seven-Mile Bluff to the outfall of the Mobile River into the bay. Then Iberville, or someone else, deleted "dans la Rivière", wrote "de lisle Masaquere" above the line, and changed the figure 16 to 26 by superimposing a 2 over the 1 in "16 L." Either reading would be correct. Margry made his error by using part of the first estimate and part of the second.

caulkers to build a pinnace[12] of forty-five tons, with a flat bottom, and designed so that it will navigate on the sea as well as in the rivers, and will draw no more than 4½ feet when loaded. At the entrance[13] to La Mobile River there is only 5½ feet on the bar. The smacks are too big to go in when loaded; that is my reason for having this vessel built.

Dom Francisco Martine[z], the commandant of Fort Pensacola, came aboard and asked me to lend him a smack to send to Vera Cruz to give notice that provisions should be sent to him, as he has only a week's supply. Because his provisions were to be exhausted on November 15th and because the hooker that ordinarily brings them provisions did not arrive at the beginning of December, he fears that she has sunk. He has no vessel to send for provisions. I did not think that I ought to refuse him a vessel, for I am afraid of being compelled to let him have provisions belonging to La Mobile garrison if some do not come for him. I promised him the smack *Précieuse,* which I have had careened. It had not been careened during the four years it has been here. The studding has protected it well from the worms.

The 28th of the month. I had the king's smack *Précieuse* sail for Vera Cruz with a crew of sixteen men. I put M. Dugué,[14] a sublieutenant, aboard to be in command of her. The commandant of Fort Pensacola is sending a major of infantry from his garrison by the *Précieuse* to report the destitution they are in; it could not be worse. They need provisions, clothes, money; and of the 180 men, 60 are convicts, and they are his best men. When I arrived, the commandant and the officers were up and about day and night, fearing a revolt of these men, all malcontents, who were deserting every day.

Pilet's smack[15] and the Spanish launch having come back

---

[12]Margry, 4:506: "a faire une barque longue de quarante-cinq tonneaux, à fond plat et taillé afin qu'elle puisse naviguer à la mer comme dans les rivières . . . " For *barque longue* I gave "pinnace" (the Burton reading).

[13]It is difficult to tell whether Iberville means the outfall of the Mobile River into Mobile Bay or the mouth of the bay, because Iberville repeatedly alludes to the mouth of the bay as the mouth of "Rivière de la Mobile."

[14]Pierre du Guay de Boisbriant.

[15]Usually François Pilet commands a ketch, but here the text has "traversier

from La Mobile, I sent two Canadians overland to La Mobile with orders for M. de Bienville to give ten picked men to the Chevalier de Tonty, to whom I am also sending orders to go to the Chaquetas and, from there, to the Chicacha[s], and endeavor to establish peace between them and to bring the chiefs of those two nations to La Mobile to make a lasting peace between them. [I further] ordered M. de Bienville to give M. de Tonty the goods he will require as gifts for the Indians if he is to succeed in his undertaking. If there should be no king's goods in the warehouse at La Mobile, he is to borrow some or have M. de la Salle buy some from those who have them; I shall have them paid.

February 4th. The Spaniards' launch left for the Apalaches to get provisions. I have already lent them fifteen barrels of flour. They are without provisions except for a few buffaloes[16] that they kill now and then. Also on February 4th, two men came overland from La Mobile, bringing me a letter from M. de Marigny, who has reached Bilocchy. When he was 20 leagues out of Bilocchy, bad weather forced him to put back to Havana, from which he has arrived. I am sending two other men back at once to notify M. de Marigny to take on board whatever there is at Bilocchy and bring it to Massacre Island; and when he arrives there, he will take on a load of provisions and other supplies needed for the garrison of Fort Mississipi; if it does not suit him to go to Fort Mississipi, he will give over the smack to Voyer, a coasting pilot.

The 15th. In the morning I went on board the *Palmier,* on which I have had loaded all that remained for the colony, and I left Pensacola for La Mobile. The wound that has detained me up to the present has almost healed. The wind being in the

---

de Pilet," a transport or smack, which Pilet may have been commanding only temporarily. He seemed to own the ketch.

[16]Although the French text does not have "boeufs sauvages" but "boeufs" only, I still have translated "buffaloes" because I know that buffaloes were in the vicinity of Pensacola even later, and because I cannot believe that the hungry Spaniards at Pensacola would have failed to kill and devour at an earlier date whatever domestic cattle might have been originally brought to their post on the bay.

north-northwest and northwest, I could not go closer than 4 leagues from Massacre Island. The 17th, the same thing. Northwest winds have much prevailed this year, bringing much cold weather and delaying the shipment to La Mobile of the goods now at Massacre Island.

The 18th. I beat to windward and entered the Massacre Island harbor. On the bar, which is one-eighth of a league from land, I found 21 and 22 feet of water everywhere, and I anchored in 30 feet between Massacre Island and a small island that protects this harbor from winds from the west-southwest, the south, and the southeast. Massacre Island protects it from the northwest and the north. The east point of La Mobile,[17] 2 leagues away, protects it from the northeast and east. Here one is sheltered. Ships moored in this harbor are secure from wind and sea. The pass is quite difficult[18] and [therefore] easy to defend. I would not state, however, that a stiff southerly gale would not cause this bar to shift,[19] even though it is of sand mixed with very stiff mud.

I found M. de Marigny in this harbor. His smack[20] being moored to the land for unloading, a southerly gale had dashed it against the shore; its sea-anchors had dragged, and the smack had run aground for more than 4 feet on the starboard side.

---

[17]This passage shows that Iberville still looked upon the outfall of Mobile Bay as the outfall of the Mobile River. I do not doubt that the Spanish maps he carried aboard the *Badine* on his first voyage had a lasting influence upon his conception of the waters near La Mobile.

[18]This pass was so narrow that ships entering often scraped the side of Massacre Island or the north tip of Pelican Island. The French later built a small fort whose guns certainly could have made it very difficult for an enemy ship to enter.

[19]Iberville's appraisal of the entrance to the Massacre Island harbor proved, in 1717, to be accurate: while two French ships, the *Paon* and the *Paix*, were at anchor in the port, a big blow closed the entrance to the port with sand. Although both ships escaped across the bar to the east, this destruction of the harbor endangered the future of the town of Mobile, already located near the mouth of the Mobile River, close to the present-day Bankhead Tunnel, through which traffic now passes under the Mobile River.

[20]The name of this smack or *traversier* is given in a notary's document signed by Marigny, dated Massacre Island, February 15, 1702. The name is the *Espérance,* and the document recorded the loss of goods in shipment.

The 19th. I had men working but could not get it afloat, even though I had sand dug from under it and had empty barrels put under it.

The 20th. I had the work continued; but, because I was unable to get the smack afloat and because time was pressing for me to send provisions, and other things needed, to Fort Mississipi, I had M. de la Salle strike a bargain with François Pillet, master of the ketch, to go to the Mississipi for the price and sum of 500 livres for the trip.

The 22nd. I sent the vessel off. Father Gravier, the Superior of the Jesuit missionaries at the Illinois,[21] embarked on it, on his way back, as did some *voyageurs*, who had come to talk with me about the beaver pelts they have at the Mississipi and about settling at La Mobile and on the Mississipi. I gladly permitted them to do so. They are to carry out their plans next year; the lack of provisions, which we cannot let them have this year, has compelled them to go back up the Mississipi and trade for cheap peltry[22]—buffalo hides and deer skins—and also to fetch the beaver pelts that several of them have cached there, for they did not dare bring them. Not knowing whether they would

---

[21]Father Gravier left Cahokia to journey to the sea on October 9, 1700. He was at Fort Mississippi on December 17, 1700, from which he went to Biloxi to visit Father Du Ru. Later, when he had been wounded by an Indian arrow in the Illinois Country, he went to La Mobile for surgical help, reaching Mobile on January 16, 1706. As a personal friend of Bienville's, he was appointed chaplain of the garrison at Ft. Louis de la Louisiane. He experienced conflict with the priest, Father La Vente, with whom many others had their difficulties. Father Gravier made a trip to France and returned on the ship with Martin D'Artaguiette and the newly appointed governor De Muy. Father Gravier died April 26, 1708, probably at La Mobile, at Twenty-Seven-Mile Bluff. See Jean Delanglez, S.J., "The French Jesuits in Lower Louisiana, 1700–1763" (Ph.D. diss., Catholic University of America), pp. 23–25.

[22]Inferior or cheap furs are called in French *menues pelleteries*, which is translated variously as small furs or humble furs. Usually deer skins and buffalo hides are meant, in contrast to such fine furs as beaver or marten. For the fur and hide business conducted in Charles Town in the eighteenth century, see Verner W. Crane, *The Southern Frontier, 1670–1732* (Ann Arbor, 1956), pp. 111–13. N. M. Miller Surrey, *The Commerce of Louisiana during the French Régime, 1699–1763* (New York, 1916), has two long chapters (18 and 19) on the fur trade.

be permitted to ship them to France, they had left them there with the intention of carrying them to the English in Carolina if we no longer were willing to accept them. Those Englishmen have made the *voyageurs* great promises to attract them to the English and to start a trade on the Mississipi by way of the Ouabache. This same day MM. de Bécancour and Châteaugué arrived from La Mobile with the two pinnaces and the two feluccas that are transporting the effects to Fort La Mobile.

The 23rd. The sea having risen higher than usual, which is the effect of the south wind, I had M. de Marigny's smack set afloat during the evening.

The 24th. I sent this smack to Fort Bilocchy, where there are many things to be brought here. I left, too, with all the pinnaces and longboats for La Mobile in a southerly wind, which left us becalmed 3 leagues from there; then a northerly wind came, bringing heavy rain and forcing us to put back to the ships, where the Sieur de Sérigny arrived from La Mobile.

The 25th. Upon information I have got about what was going on in the warehouse concerning the issuing of provisions and other supplies, I asked M. de la Salle not to interfere in it beyond directing the issuance according to the orders of the commandant; and, to put things in order to avoid what happened during M. de Sauvolle's time, when the purser I left there claimed the right to direct everything, saying that he had supervision and would render his account; then he would not admit the commandant's right to supervise the sailors and the workmen; and that he claimed authority over whatever he considered fitting without permission of the commandant. These were some proposals that he put in writing, on the basis of which they would be good friends. That purser is going back to France. For the good of the king's service, I have considered it essential to put a warehouse-keeper there. I thought there was no better or more capable person for me to employ than the Sieur Girard, whom M. de la Salle has put in charge of all the king's stores, with account-books in which he will keep a record of them, in accordance with the issues that M. de la Salle will establish for him each month. The warehouse-keeper will release none of the things reserved as presents for the

Indians or any other goods without an order from the commandant to the Sieur de la Salle, who will direct him to issue them,
so that nothing will be withdrawn without the knowledge of the
commandant and the Sieur de la Salle, performing the duties of
commissary.

The 29th. The weather has become favorable. I set out for
La Mobile, leaving the Sieur de la Salle a longboat to take his
family to La Mobile. I came and stopped for the night at the
little river 6 leagues from Massacre Island,[23] on the west shore
of the bay. At the mouth of this river there is 4 to 5 feet of
water. The land here is good, elevated; the woods are mixed,
pines, oaks, laurels, beeches, elms, with meadows. Up this
river I am having some stave-wood cut by three workmen I
have there. The bay is 3 leagues wide across from this river.
This river goes back only 2 leagues inland, where the land
looks good.

The first of March. The wind being northwest, I got to the
channel of the river[24] where the islands begin, 1 league from the
little river. I went 2 leagues up the river and stopped for the
night. The water is high; many spots on the mainland on the
west side seem flooded, that is, along the banks, for back from
the river the land is high. The islands are low, on a level with
the water. Owing to the wind, I did not make much of a search
for the channel, which seems to be very narrow.

The 2nd. The wind still blowing inland, I continued upriver.
The current runs half a league an hour. I made 6½ leagues. I
have found the land good all along, the banks being flooded in
some places. The greater part of the banks is covered with
cypress trees, which are very fine, tall, thick, straight. All the
islands, too, are covered with cypresses, oaks, and other trees,
being flooded in many places.

The 3rd. We reached the settlement, 1½ leagues above the
place where we stopped for the night. I found my brother De
Bienville there, busy building a fort with four bastions, laid one
upon another and dovetailed at the corners, having the trees

---

[23]Dog River.
[24]The Mobile River at the head of Mobile Bay.

cleared away, and supervising the work on the pinnace, her timbers soon to be bent. The settlement is on a ridge more than 20 feet above the water, wooded with mixed trees: white and red oak, laurel, sassafras, basswood, hickory, particularly a great many pines suitable for masts. This ridge and all the land about it are exceedingly good, extending for 8 leagues—from the lower part of the river on upstream as high as the Thomés and, in many places, coming close to the bank of the river, which in winding moves away from the ridge in certain places, for this ridge runs due north.

The 4th. I sent my brother to examine several abandoned Indian settlements on the islands in the vicinity. I have had a mainmast cut for the *Palmier* and have men working to finish it before it is sent.

My brother came back this evening. He had observed several sites formerly occupied by Indians, which war with the Conchaque[25] and the Alibamons[26] had made them abandon. Most of these settlements become flooded to a depth of half a foot during high water. These settlements are on islands, this river being full of them for 13 leagues. He got an Indian to show him the place where their gods are, about which all the neighboring nations make such a fuss and to which the Mobilians used to come and offer sacrifices. The Indians claim that a person cannot touch them without dying on the spot and that they came down from the sky. A gun had to be given the Indian who showed where they were; he did not get closer to them than 10 steps away, and with his back turned. It took a search to locate them on a little hill among the canes, near an old village that is

---

[25]Conchaque is a name that was applied to several Choctaw towns, now written Conshac. Frederick Webb Hodge, *Handbook of American Indians North of Mexico,* 2 vols., Bulletin 30 of the Bureau of American Ethnology (Washington, D.C., 1907 and 1910), 1:341.

[26]The Alibamu belonged to the Creek confederacy. They were a Muskhogean nation that, during De Soto's time, were dwelling northwest of the Chickasaws in Mississippi. When the French arrived in the Gulf, the Alibamu were living on the Alabama River just below the confluence of the Coosa and Tallapoosa rivers. Fort Toulouse was built in their country in 1713. Hodge suggests, with doubt, that the name *Alibamu* means "I clear the thicket" (*Handbook,* 1:43–44).

destroyed, on one of these islands. The gods were brought here. They are five images—a man, a woman, a child, a bear, and an owl—made of plaster in the likeness of Indians of this country. I personally think that some Spaniard in the time of Soto made the figures of these Indians in plaster. Apparently it was done a long time ago. We have them at the settlement. The Indians who see them here are amazed at our boldness and amazed that we do not die as a result. I am taking the images to France, though they are not particularly interesting.

The 6th. I went and examined several of these islands, looking for a place where there might be a creek on which I could build a sawmill and set up a tannery, but I found none. All the land is perfectly fine for settlements.

The 7th. I sent the longboats back with the mast for the *Palmier* all finished. At this place we could cut a great number of masts.

The 9th. I set out in a felucca to go to the Tohomés. I went on for 5 leagues and spent the night. Three leagues above the settlement one comes to the end of the islands. Above the settlement I have found almost everywhere, on both banks, abandoned Indian settlements, where one has only to settle farmers, who will have no more to do than cut canes or reeds or bramble before they sow. Above the islands the river has a width of half a league and a depth of 5 to 6 fathoms.

The 10th. I went on and spent the night among the Tohomés, whom I found at a distance of 8 leagues from the settlement, following the bends of the river. The first dwelling places, called Mobilian, are at a distance of 6 leagues. The two nations are established along both banks of the river and on islands and small streams, set apart into families. Sometimes there are four or five and even a dozen huts together. They are hard working, laboring much in tilling the soil. During high water, most of their dwelling places are flooded for a week to ten days. The village of the Tohomés—that is, of the Little Chief, where about eight or ten huts are grouped—is at latitude 31°22′. They have roads of communication running from village to village. The distance of that area from the settlement, which we are naming La Mobile, is approximately 6½ leagues north by east. By following these small hills one easily gets to these villages. It will be easy to make cart-roads to them; at present one can go and come on horseback. The ebb and flow of the tide comes as high up as the Tohomés when the water is low. Judging by the number of deserted dwellings I have seen, this river must have been thickly settled. These Indians speak the language of the Bayogoulas; at least, there is little difference. In these two nations there are 350 able-bodied men.[27]

The 11th. I returned to the fort, where I found M. Desourdy, who has brought M. de la Salle and his family as well as letters from Pensacola. The commandant is asking me for provisions, having none at all. We have already given him fifty barrels of flour.

The 12th. I sent M. Desourdy to the Mobilians and the Thomés with two feluccas to buy corn. During the evening MM. de Bécancour and Châteaugué arrived, loaded with provisions. On the 13th I sent them back.

The 14th. M. Desourdis returned with the two feluccas loaded with corn. Rain prevented them from returning yesterday. It has rained for three days.

The 16th. I sent one of the longboats back to buy corn.

The 17th. The two pinnaces arrived loaded. Much rain has fallen during the past six days, badly interrupting our work.

A master tanner, whom I brought to this country, got lost in the woods two weeks ago. He was found by two of our hunters on a beautiful hill, at the foot of a tree, beside a grave he had dug for himself; at the end of it he had set up a cross, on which he had written his experience. He no longer looked like a man, having gone without food for twelve days, taking only some water.

The 19th. At nine o'clock at night, Dambournes[28] arrived,

---

[27]MS.: "350 bons homes." Cf. *bons hommes* in Bégon à Villemont, June 30, 1699, BN MSS. fr. 22807:201: "J'ay trouvé Mr. D'Iberville qui a eu tout le succès qu'il pouvait désirer de son expedition ayant etabli sa Colonie composé de 80 bons hommes." At the present time natives of France who speak English are inclined to translate *bons hommes* with such slang as "guys" or "fellows."

[28]Margry gives "d'Ambournes" (4:515).

dispatched by M. de Tonty from the Chaqueta—whence he had set out on the morning of the 14th to notify me that M. de Tonty was returning, had met with success, and was bringing the chiefs of the Chaqueta and Chicacha. It has rained so hard today that a powder magazine, which was almost finished, was filled with water and the dirt caved in. We have to begin all over—twelve days' labor of ten men lost by that.

The 20th, 21st, 22nd, and 23rd. I worked laying out the alignment of the streets of the town and assigning lots. The four families I brought are housed and are busy clearing the land. Part of my crew I am sending back in the pinnaces to the *Palmier.*

The 24th. Five of M. de Tonty's men have come, having left him at the Tohomés; he is to come tomorrow.

Sunday, the 25th. At eleven o'clock in the morning M. de Tonty arrived with three chiefs and four distinguished men of the Chicacha, and four chiefs of the Chaqueta. I gave them the best welcome I could but postponed conversation with them till tomorrow.

The 26th. At eight o'clock in the morning I had the presents laid out that I desired to give these two nations: to each, 200 livres of powder, 200 livres of bullets, 200 livres of game-shot, 12 guns, 100 axes, 150 knives, some kettles, glass beads, gun flints, awls, and other hardware,[29] which made a considerable present indeed. After this I had them assembled. My brother De Bienville acting as interpreter, I said to them:[30] "I rejoice to see you disposed to live in peace with each other and with all the nations of the region"—after I had made them perceive the advantages to be had from good relations rather than from destroying each other, which they had been doing. I said: "The Chicacha have foolishly followed the advice of the English,

---

[29]MS.: "et autres clincailleries." The modern word is *quincaillerie.*

[30]This long oration that Iberville spoke to the Chickasaws and Choctaws is written in indirect discourse in both the MS. and the Margry text. Because it extends for a page and a half as one sentence held together loosely by means of the greatest number of subordinating *que*'s that I recall seeing, I have changed the style of discourse to direct, in an attempt to recover exactly what Iberville spoke through his interpreter.

who have no other objective than to work their destruction by
inciting the Chicacha and the Chaqueta[31] to make war on each
other so that the English can get slaves,[32] whom they send
away to other countries to be sold. One proof that the English
are not your friends, but are seeking only to destroy you is, as
you well know, that your enemies have taken Chicacha prisoners, whom the English of St. Georges[33] bought, as they bought
the Chaqueta, and whom they sent off to the islands to be
sold—far from sending them back home, as they should have
done. You Chichacha can observe that during the last eight to
ten years when you have been at war with the Chaqueta at the
instigation of the English, who gave you ammunition and thirty
guns for that purpose, you have taken more than 500 prisoners
and killed more than 1,800 Chaqueta. Those prisoners were
sold; but taking those prisoners cost you more than 800 men,
slain on various war parties, who would be living at this
moment if it had not been for the English. The Chaqueta see it
well—and the Chicacha ought to see it, too,—that the Englishman is to blame for the loss of your dead brothers. And the
ultimate plan of the Englishman, after weakening you by
means of wars, is to come and seize you in your villages and
then send you to be sold somewhere else, in faraway countries
from which you can never return, as the English have treated
others, as you know. To prevent all these calamities, you must
no longer listen to the Englishman.

"And, if you do not drive him from your villages, the French
and you cannot be friends with one another, and I shall engage
in no trading with you. I shall arm with guns all the Chaqueta,
the Mobilians, and the Tohomés as I have already begun to
arm the Nadchés and the other nations that are our allies. Far
indeed from preventing the Illinois from making war on you, I

---

[31]Here I have replaced ambiguous pronouns with the nouns Chicacha and
Chaqueta. Elsewhere for the sake of clarity, I have made similar alterations,
but only when I could be certain of the noun the ambiguous pronoun had
replaced.

[32]For the Charles Town traffic in slaves, see Crane, *Frontier*, pp. 112–13.

[33]The most southerly of the Windward Islands, close to South America, just
north of Trinidad and Tobago.

shall incite them to it. Certainly you see that you will be in no
condition to hold out against so many nations; you will suffer
the sorrow of seeing yourselves killed at the gates of your
villages, along with your women and children.

"But, if you drive the Englishman from your villages, who
likes nothing except blood and slaves, I will have a village built
between the Chicacha and the Chaqueta, as you want it, where
you will find all kinds of goods to be bartered for skins of
buffalo, deer, and bear—those are the slaves I want. You will
feed yourselves and all your families on the meat of the animals
you kill. To get them will not cost you your lives."

I had them told, after their manner of speaking, several other
things that aimed solely at driving the English out and ruining
them in the minds of the Chicacha. They promised me to drive
the Englishman out provided I would engage in trading with
them, about which we came to an agreement over prices. Then
I gave a gun, a blanket, a hooded cloak, an ax, two knives,
some powder, and bullets to a Chicacha as payment for the
Chaqueta slave he had taken away from the Englishman and
given to M. de Tonty. I armed with guns all the chiefs of the two
nations and their men and gave each a hooded cloak, a shirt,
and additional trifles. Next I gave them the presents for their
nations. I promised the Chicacha to warn at once all the
nations, our allies, to go in war no more among the Chicacha
and promised to send some of my men with the Chicacha to
escort them safely to their country, from which my men would
go on to the Illinois and bring back their men held as prisoners
by the Illinois and have the Illinois make peace. For their part,
the Chicacha would induce the Conchaques and the Alaba-
mon[s] to make peace with the Chaqueta, the Tohomés, and
the Mobilians, to come to the French fort, and to listen to the
English no more. If they did not do so, they could assure
themselves that our friends the Apalaches—whose tomahawks
I controlled—would make cruel war against them, which I had
so far prevented. All these Indians seemed to me quite satisfied
and disposed to live in peace.

Toward afternoon, the Sieur de Bécancour arrived with a
loaded pinnace, having left Châteaugué with his pinnace to

unload the smack into the warehouse I have had built on the little river 1 league from the mouth of La Mobile and 11 leagues from the harbor.[34] We are naming it Rivière-aux-Chiens.

I had the Chaqueta and the Chicacha make a count of the men of their nations, family by family. The Chicacha are 580 huts, 3 to 4 men to the hut, making at least 2 thousand men, of whom 7 to 8 hundred are armed with guns. I am not counting the young men 16 to 18 years old.

The Chaqueta, in three different villages, are 1090 huts, at 3 to 4 men to each, making about 3800 to 4000 men. Of these regions they are the Indians that are the best built. They have the Iroquois bearing and the style of warriors.

The Chicacha have additional people on the Ouabache River, in two villages, where they have about 120 men. From the main village of the Chicacha to that of the Chaoenons, which is on the bank of the Carolina River,[35] 40 leagues from the town of Charles Town, the Chicacha reckon six days' journey by the shortest route; from the Chicacha to the mouth of the Ouabache River,[36] it is 25 to 30 leagues by land. From the Chicacha to the Chaqueta, it is about 40 to 45 leagues south by west; from the Chaqueta to the Tohomés, 55 to 60 leagues south-southeast. The Chaqueta are possibly at 33°30' north or 34° at most.

The 16th. In the morning, I sent the Sieur de Bécancour back with the pinnace loaded with the men of my crew, whom I am sending back to the *Palmier*.

---

[34]The harbor is Port Massacre, between Île Massacre (now Dauphin) and Pelican Island, which made the little harbor that supplied a safe anchorage for big ships from France. Since 1969, after the hurricane Camille struck the Gulf Coast, the only remnant of Pelican Island has been some shoals. From the sand dunes at the Isle Dauphine Country Club—high ones—I cannot even see white water above the shoals. But 270 years have passed since Port Massacre first became the distant harbor for La Mobile at Twenty-Seven-Mile Bluff.

[35]This river, here called Carolina, appears to me to be the Tennessee River, which Crane says both Couture and Bellefeuille took on their journey to Charles Town. *Frontier*, pp. 43, 66, 70, and 90.

[36]Because the Ohio River became the Wabash after its confluence with the Wabash, this passage, with its early-eighteenth-century nomenclature, must refer to the main Chickasaw landing on the Mississippi River, called the Chickasaw Bluffs, the site of Memphis.

I then had five Canadians get ready to go with the Chicacha and the Chaqueta back up La Mobile River as far as the place where the Indians want a post established, which is 12 to 15 leagues from their village. I also ordered three of the Canadians to go on from there, with two Chicacha, to the Illinois to ask them for the Chicacha held there as prisoners and to notify them to make no further war on the Chicacha, as they are our allies, as well as to tell them I am holding back their tomahawk, which the Governor of Canada sent M. de Courtemanche[37] to tell them to raise against the Chaouenons, whom I intend to attract to the Mississipi or La Mobile. They approached me about that through Bellefeuille.[38] The Chaouenons are the single nation to fear, being spread out over Carolina and Virginia in the direction of the Mississipi. I shall speak at greater length about that in my separate report.

I took advantage of this occasion to write the Grand Vicar of Quebec, who is at the Tamaroua, to send missionaries to the Chicacha and the Chaqueta as soon as he can; sending missionaries will help keep them in the alliance. I am writing the same to the Superior of the Jesuits, who is there, in case he has some missionaries there. At the same time I wrote, in like manner, to M. Davion, a missionary priest at the Tonicas, to inform his Indians about the peace in effect between all the nations and to notify the Chaquechouma, who have withdrawn from their territory, to return to their village, which is 3

---

[37]Augustin Le Gardeur de Courtemanche was an ambassador, soldier, and commandant on the Labrador Coast. Nora T. Corley portrays him as a man of considerable ability. With little or no resources in men and arms, he once faced 800 angry Eskimos. His relations with Indians were generally good (*DCB*, s.v. "Le Gardeur de Courtmanche, Augustin").

[38]Bellefeuille, a *coureur de bois*, who, like Couture, knew the route to Charles Town, was a man persuasive with Indians. He was supposed to know nine or ten Indian tongues. Naturally Bellefeuille would be a valuable man to have at La Mobile; and he was indeed one of the first persons to be assigned lots at Twenty-Seven-Mile Bluff after the town had been laid out in the spring of 1702. Bellefeuille had made the journey to Carolina with Soton; but there the English of the assembly rebuffed his offer of trade. Crane, *Frontier*, p. 66 ff.

to 4 leagues from the place where the post will be established on the upper part of La Mobile.[39]

I likewise wrote M. Foucos,[40] a missionary priest at the Acansa, to inform the Indians that I have had the Chicacha make peace. I wrote the same to M. de St. Cosme,[41] a missionary priest at the Nadeché,[42] so that no war party will be sent against the Chaqueta. The letters will be carried to them by Chicacha from the villages situated, in a circuit, 50, 60, and 100 leagues from one another. They are reached by wide, well-beaten roads, on which one can ride on horseback.

Of the five men I had sent off with these Indians, only two will return to the fort by canoe, after thoroughly exploring the river and the country. With the Chief of the Chicacha I also sent young St. Michel,[43] who speaks Ouma fairly well, which is

---

[39]Here Iberville writes as though the Mobile River led to northwest Alabama. If he had absorbed more information, he would have placed the Tombigbee River or one of its branches in northwest Alabama. Here is evidence that the French still had much to learn about the Indian tribes and the rivers of this area, although they were learning very fast indeed.

[40]Nicolas Foucault, who was a member of the Seminary of Quebec, was killed by the Coroas Indians in 1702. In 1700 he was chosen to work with the Abbé Marc Bergier at the Tamaroas. Later, on the Lower River, the travelers hired Coroas paddlers, who murdered l'Abbé Foucault because they coveted what they took to be valuables that the priest had with him (*DCB,* s.v. "Foucault, Nicolas").

[41]Jean-François de Saint-Cosme, priest of the Seminary of Quebec and founder of the Sainte Famille mission at the Tamoroas (Illinois); b. January 1667 at Lauson and murdered by the Chitimacha Indians in 1706. Celine Dupré, the author of the biographical article in *DCB* (s.v. "Buisson de Saint-Cosme, Jean-François"), gives a dignified account of St. Cosme's being the lover of the sister of the Great Natchez Sun; she bore the child, named St. Cosme, that in 1729 as the young chief of the Natchez Indians organized and led the massacre of the French at Natchez. When the priest left the Tamoroas and moved downriver, he served as missionary to the Natchez. His failure as a missionary was probably owing to his ineptness at learning Indian languages.

[42]MS.: "Nadeche." These Indians are the Natchez.

[43]St. Michel was a member of the first group of cabin boys brought to the Mississippi by Iberville on the first voyage. See Richebourg Gaillard McWilliams, *Fleur de Lys and Calumet: Being the Pénicaut Narrative of French Adventure in Louisiana* (Baton Rouge, 1953), pp. 73–76 for the way St. Michel was later used in a plot hatched by the Choctaws.

the same language as Chicacha or very close to it, so that he will get used to that language.

Toward afternoon I left in my felucca to return to my ship. Three leagues from the fort I happened upon Châteaugué with his pinnace loaded with eighty barrels of powder, and I came on and spent the night 8 leagues from the fort.

The 28th. A stiff gale blew from the southwest, with rain. I took soundings in the channel of the river, finding everywhere a depth of 5½ and 6 feet. I came on and spent the night at Rivière-aux-Chiens, where I found the Sieur de Grandville with the *Palmier*'s longboat, busy unloading the smack.

The 29th. In the morning I sent this smack back to the ship, and we went there with all the longboats and pinnaces. The ketch, which I had sent to the Mississipi, is not back yet, nor is the vessel that I sent to Vera Cruz, which is overdue.

Because the wind was south-southwest, I could not come out with the *Palmier*. I had the smack loaded with the goods that were in the warehouse, to transport them to Rivière-aux-Chiens. Because the master who was on it was not capable of taking it and because I had no other person to put on it, I considered it for the good of the king's service to put on board an officer to supervise the safe transportation of all [the king's][44] goods and to supervise the men in their work on whatever voyages the smack has to make.

I have, accordingly, chosen the Sieur de Beccancour, sub-lieutenant on the *Renommée*, who is very capable and skillful in his profession and who has taken great pains with all the work assigned to him.

The 31st. The smack left for La Mobile in a westerly wind. I got the *Palmier* out by warping. On the bar I found no less than 21 and 22 feet of water.

The 1st of April. About noon, I reached Pensacola. There is no news here of the smack I sent to Vera Cruz or of the launch the commandant sent to the Apalaches for provisions. For the

---

[44]MS.: "tous ses effets," in which *ses* could be a poor spelling of *ces*, as Margry, 4:521, gives it. But the MS. reading *ses*, "his," makes a clear reading in the sense of "the king's."

past two months this garrison could not have subsisted except for me.

The 10th. The Spanish launch arrived without provisions, having failed to find any. At the Apalaches[45] there are only 8 families, who raise cattle, and one detachment of 25 soldiers, under a lieutenant, from the garrison of Château St. Augustin.

The 18th. The smack arrived from Vera Cruz toward evening. It had sailed on the . . . The hooker, which is supposed to bring this garrison what it needs, is still at Vera Cruz and will not sail till May. Down there, they were enjoying great peace of mind, not troubling themselves about this garrison's lack of food; they were content to send, in the smack, one month's supply of provisions, which will not last till the arrival of the hooker. So here I am, ready to sail. I am only waiting for the ketch, which is at the Mississipi.

The 19th. The ketch arrives from the Mississipi loaded with the *voyageurs'* beaver-skins and common peltries.

The 20th, 21st, 22nd, and 23rd we spent in stowing the beaver in the ships, in attending to all business, and in getting the smack ready to be sent back to La Mobile.[46]

Judging by the inventory and the issuance of provisions for the garrison at Fort de la Mobile, which I see in M. de la Salle's memorandum, it appears that, including the provisions the Spaniards are to give back, there is left no more than a six

---

[45]In 1699–1702 Apalachee was a community of *rancheros*, Fr. *éleveurs* or possibly *habitans*, living near the junction of the St. Marks and Wakulla rivers, only a short distance inland from the most northern waters of Apalachee Bay. By 1739, according to the Federal Writers' Project, the fourth fort, a stone one, was built "on the apex of a peninsula formed by the junction of the St. Marks and Wakulla" (*Florida: a Guide to the Southernmost State* [New York, 1956], p. 486). On a map without signature or date, but attributed to Delisle, and drawn after Natchitoches was established on the Red River, the settlement between the St. Marks and Wakulla rivers is marked "Sᵉ Marie d'Apalache detruit en 1705 [or 1703] par les Alibamous." Between the two rivers, just north of the confluence, is shown a tiny rectangle that I take to be the fort destroyed or the village named Ste. Marie d'Apalache. For this map and the legend quoted, see *A Book of Old Maps Delineating American History from the Earliest Days Down to the Close of the Revolutionary War,* comp. and ed. Emerson D. Fite and Archibald Freeman (New York, 1969), p. 176.

[46]Margry, 4:522, and Moodie dropped part of this paragraph.

months' supply. As I do not see how ships can come from France by that time and as the Spanish commandant assures me that he has been informed that he will get no more than the six months' supply ordinarily brought him on each trip, and because, that being so, it will be difficult for him to return the 100 cwt. of flour I lent him out of the provisions for the garrison at La Mobile, I am deciding to order M. Bienville to send the smack to Vera Cruz to buy provisions. The commandant is writing the viceroy by this smack, asking for the flour and the bacon he is due.

The 27th. The weather being favorable for sailing out of the harbor, we weighed anchor at five o'clock in the morning to go out of the harbor and set the course for Havana, which we reached at night on May 7th. There we found M. de Nesmond, M. de Châteauregnaud[47] having gone to Vera Cruz.

The 17th. In the morning I left Havana after taking on some meat and vegetables, which I needed for my crew, and set the course for France. I reached the Belle Isle roadstead in a stiff gale from the west and southwest and anchored while waiting for fair weather to go on to Rochefort.

On board the *Renommée*
June 20, 1702, at six o'clock   D'IBERVILLE
in the evening.

---

[47]Iberville's comment on these two Frenchmen shows that he knows, and that the minister will know, what they are doing in Havana and in the Gulf of Mexico; accordingly, I reason that they are André de Nesmond, a marquis commanding a French squadron, and François Louis de Rousselet, Marquis de Châteaurenault, another squadron commander. For information about documents in which their names appear, see Waldo G. Leland, *Guide to Materials for American History in the Libraries and Archives of Paris,* vol. 1 (Washington, D.C., 1932), Index and especially p. 63.

Bibliography

Sources of the Text of the Journals

Iberville's First Voyage: Archives Nationales, Marine: Série 4 JJ, Dossier No. 14. Journal of the *Badine:* "Journal du voyage fait Par d'Hibervile a la coste Meridionale de Floride en 1699." This manuscript carries Iberville's autograph at the end. At one time this manuscript was identified as Service Hydrographique de la Marine, Carton 14, no. 2. On microfilm.

Iberville's Second Voyage: Bibliothèque Nationale, MSS. fr., N.A. 9296. Journal of the *Renommée,* her first voyage: "Journal du Voyage du Chevalier d'Iberville sur le vaisseau du Roi La Renommée en mil six cent quatre vingt dix neuf, depuis le Cap Français jusqu'à la côte du Mississipi et son retour." This manuscript does not have Iberville's autograph anywhere, and I take it to be only an excellent copy of the manuscript that Iberville sent to the Minister of Marine, which I have failed to locate. It may be lost forever. But there may be another copy of this manuscript. On microfilm.

Iberville's Third Voyage: Archives Nationales, Marine B⁴ 23. Journal of the *Renommée,* her second voyage: "Journal du sieur d'Iberville depuis le 15ᵉ. décembre 1701 jusqu'au 27ᵉ avril 1702." This manuscript carries Iberville's autograph at the end. On microfilm.

Margry, Pierre, comp. and ed. *Découvertes et Établissements des Français dans l'Ouest et dans le Sud de l'Amérique Septentrionale (1614–1754).* 6 vols. Paris: Imprimerie D. Jouaust, 1879–1888. This important compilation of documents written in French about French exploration and settlement in the province of Louisiana, the middle third of the area now occupied by the United States, was printed by means of a subsidy of $10,000 appropriated by the Congress under the influence of a lobby of which the historian Francis Parkman was the most persuasive. Even though Pierre Margry had many faults as scholar, I believe that he produced a work to which many writers are deeply indebted. Margry printed in French all three of Iberville's journals, as shown immediately below.

1. "Journal de la *Badine* (31 décembre 1698 – 31 mai 1699)." Provenience: Dépôt de la Marine, 4:131–209.

2. "Journal de d'Iberville Commandant Le Vaisseau La *Renommée* Dans Son Second Voyage Au Mississipi (22 novembre 1699 – 28 mai 1700)." Provenience: Dépôt de la Marine, 4:393–431. Immediately after Iberville's second journal is printed a "Copie du journal du voyage de M. de Bienville, des Taensas au village des Yatachés par les terres (22 mars – 18 mai 1700)." Provenience: Dépôt de la Marine et Archives du Ministère de la Marine. Actually, Iberville made Bienville's journal of his overland journey from the Taensas to the Yatachés a part of his own journal. Perhaps Margry should have given one journal for the two (4:393–444). In the manuscript of the Journal of the *Renommée* (her first voyage), the Bienville journal, with a medium-sized heading, is made a part of Iberville's journal of his second voyage.

3. "Journal du Sieur D'Iberville [commanding the *Renommée* (her second voyage) on his third voyage to the Mississipi] (15 décembre 1701 – 27 avril 1702)." Provenience: Archives du Ministère de la Marine.—Fonds des Campagnes, 4:503–23.

Moodie, Edith, trans. "The Journals of Iberville's Three Voyages to the Mississippi as Given in Pierre Margry's Text Collated with Manuscripts Identified Immediately Below, Rendered from French to English." Unpublished manuscripts in the Burton Collection of the Detroit Public Library. The French manuscripts used in the collation are identified as follows: First Voyage, Service Hydrographique de la Marine, Carton 14, no. 2; Second Voyage, Service Hydrographique de la Marine, Carton 14, no. 3; and Third Voyage, Archives Nationales B, Marine 23, Folio 315. The three Burton Manuscripts are on microfilm. *Note:* Edith Moodie was assigned the task of translating the Margry text and collating the printed text with manuscripts in Paris archives. Rarely did she forget to collate the manuscript with the printed text; but sometimes she did and thus failed to catch important errors in Margry.

Letters, Mémoires, Reports, etc.,
Almost All Being in Print

Bégon à Villermont, June 30, 1699. BN MSS. fr. 22807:201.
Bienville to Pontchartrain, Port Dauphin, October 27, 1711. In *Mississippi Provincial Archives*, 3 (Jackson, Miss., 1932): 158–71.

Campbell, Captain James, to the Earl of Loudoun, Mobile, Dec. 15, 1763. In Robert R. Rea, "A New Letter from Mobile," *The Alabama Review* 22 (July 1969):230–37.

[Chasteaumorant] M. de Chasteaumorant au Ministre de la Marine, la Rade de Groye, June 23, 1699. In Margry, 4:103–16.

[D'Iberville]. Lettre de d'Iberville au Ministre de la Marine, June 18, 1698. In Margry, 4:51–57.

D'Iberville au Ministre de la Marine, on board the *Badine*, February 17, 1699. In Margry, 4:100–03.

D'Iberville au Ministre de la Marine, La Rochelle, June 29, 1699. In Margry, 4:116–28.

[D'Iberville]. Lettre de d'Iberville au Ministre de la Marine, des Bayogoulas, February 26, 1700. In Margry, 4:360–67.

Ducasse au Ministre de la Marine, Léogane, January 13, 1699. In Margry, 4:92–95.

Liste des officiers de marine choisis par le Roy pour servir sur les frégate et fluste cy-après nommées, armées à Rochefort, Marly. August 24, 1699. In Margry, 4:335.

Liste des officiers de Marine choisis pour servir sur la *Badine*, armée à Rochefort, Marly, June 10, 1698. In Margry, 4:50–51.

Mémoire de la Coste de la Floride et d'une partie du Mexique. In Margry, 4:308–23.

Mémoire pour servir d'instruction au sieur d'Iberville, capitaine de frégate légère, commandant la *Renommée*, Fontainebleau, September 22, 1699. In Margry, 4:348–54.

[Sauvole]. Recueil que j'ai pris sur mon journal de ce qui s'est passé de plus remarquable depuis le départ de M. d'Iberville, du 3 mai 1699 jusqu'en 1700. In Margry, 4:447–62.

Springer, Bernice C., Chief of the Burton Historical Collection, Detroit Public Library, to Viola W. Harper, Reference Librarian of the University of South Alabama, Detroit, February 22, 1971.

General Bibliography, Chiefly Secondary Sources

Bannon, John Francis, ed. *Bolton and the Borderlands*. Norman: University of Oklahoma Press, 1964.

Bolton, Herbert Eugene. "The Epic of Greater America," *American Historical Review* 38 (April 1933): 448–74.

———. *The Spanish Borderlands*. New Haven: Yale University Press, 1921.

————, and Thomas Maitland Marshall. *The Colonization of North America 1492–1783*. New York: The Macmillan Co., 1920.

Caldwell, N. W. "Charles Juchereau de St. Denys: A French Pioneer in the Mississippi Valley," *Mississippi Valley Historical Review* 28 (March 1942): 563–80.

Clark, Charles Upson. *Voyageurs, Robes Noires, et Coureurs de Bois*. New York: Institute of French Studies, Columbia University, 1934.

Cohen, David W., and Jack P. Greene, eds. *Neither Slave Nor Free: The Freedman of African Descent in the Slave Societies of the New World*. Baltimore: The Johns Hopkins University Press, 1972.

Columbia Lippincott Gazetteer of the World. Edited by Leon E. Seltzer. New York: Columbia University Press, 1962.

Cortés, Hernando. *Five Letters of Cortés to the Emperor, 1519–1526*. Translated by J. Bayard Morris. New York: W. W. Norton and Company, 1962.

Crane, Verner W. *The Southern Frontier, 1670–1732*. First published in 1929. Ann Arbor: The University of Michigan Press, 1956.

Crouse, Nellis M. *Lemoyne d'Iberville: Soldier of New France*. Ithaca, N.Y.: Cornell University Press, 1954.

Delanglez, Jean, S.J. "The French Jesuits in Lower Louisiana (1700–1763)." Ph.D. dissertation, Catholic University of America, 1935.

Dibble, Ernest F., and Earle W. Newton, eds. *In Search of Gulf Coast Colonial History*. Pensacola: Historic Pensacola Preservation Board, 1970.

————. *Spain and Her Rivals on the Gulf Coast*. Pensacola: Historic Pensacola Preservation Board, 1971.

Du Ru, Paul, S.J. *Journal of Paul du Ru*. Translated and edited by Ruth Lapham Butler. Chicago: Caxton Club, 1934.

Dunn, Marie S. "A Comparative Study: Louisiana's French and Anglo-Saxon Cultures," *Louisiana Studies* 10 (Fall 1971): 131–69.

Eccles, W. J. *Canada Under Louis XIV, 1663–1701*. Toronto: McClelland and Stewart, 1964.

————. *France in America*. New York: Harper and Row, 1969.

Federal Writers' Project. *Florida: A Guide to the Southern-most State*. 8th printing of the 1939 edition. New York: Oxford University Press, 1956.

Frégault, Guy. *Iberville le conquérant*. Montréal: Société des Éditions Pascal, 1944.

————. *Pierre Le Moyne D'Iberville*. Montréal: Fides, 1968.

Genovese, Eugene, and Elizabeth Fox Genovese. "The Slave Economies in Historical Perspective," *Journal of American History* 66 (June 1979): 7–23.

Giraud, Marcel. *Histoire de la Louisiane Française*. Vol. 1, *Le Règne de Louis XIV (1698–1715)*. Paris: Presses Universitaires de France, 1953.

Hamilton, Peter J[oseph]. *Colonial Mobile*. A reprint of the 2nd edition, 1910, from the original plates. Mobile: The First National Bank of Mobile, 1952.

Hanke, Lewis, ed. *Do the Americas Have a Common History? A Critique of the Bolton Thesis*. New York: Alfred A. Knopf, 1964.

Higginbotham, [Prieur] Jay. *Fort Maurepas: The Birth of Louisiana*. Mobile: Colonial Books, 1968.

———. *The Mobile Indians*. 2nd edition. Mobile: Duvall's Books, 1966.

———. *Old Mobile: Fort Louis de la Louisiane*. Mobile: Museum of the City of Mobile, 1977.

———. "Who Was Sauvole?" *Louisiana Studies* 7 (Summer 1968): 144–48.

———, trans. and ed. *The Journal of Sauvole*. Mobile: Colonial Books, 1969.

Hodge, Frederick Webb. *Handbook of American Indians North of Mexico*. 2 vols. Bulletin 30 of the Bureau of American Ethnology. Washington, D.C.: Smithsonian Institution, 1907 and 1910.

Holmes, Jack D. L. "Dauphin Island's Critical Years: 1701–1722," *Alabama Historical Quarterly* 29 (Spring and Summer 1967): 39–63.

———. "Naval Stores in Colonial Louisiana and the Floridas," *Louisiana Studies* 7 (Winter 1968): 295–309.

"Journal de la Frégate Le *Marin*," in Margry, 4:211–89. (In notes cited as Journal of the *Marin*.)

Kniffen, Fred B. *Louisiana: Its Land and People*. Baton Rouge: Louisiana State University Press, 1968.

Leland, Waldo G. *Guide to Materials for American History in the Libraries and Archives of Paris*. 2 vols. Washington, D.C.: The Carnegie Institution of Washington, 1932 and 1943.

Lemieux, Donald J. "The Mississippi Valley, New France, and French Colonial Policy," *Southern Studies* 17 (Spring 1978): 39–56.

Leonard, Irving A., trans. and ed. *Spanish Approach to Pensacola*. Albuquerque, New Mexico: The Quivira Society, 1939.

McDermott, John Francis. *A Glossary of Mississippi Valley French, 1673–1850*. Washington University Studies, n.s., Language and Literature, no. 12. St. Louis: Washington University, 1941.

McGovern, James R., ed. *Colonial Pensacola*. Hattiesburg, Miss.: University of Southern Mississippi Press, 1972.

McGowan, James T. "Planters without Slaves: Origins of a New World Labor System," *Southern Studies* 16 (Spring 1977): 5–26.

McWilliams, Richebourg Gaillard. "Iberville at the Birdfoot Sub-
delta." In John Francis McDermott, ed., *Frenchmen and French
Ways in the Mississippi Valley*. Urbana, Ill.: University of Illinois
Press, 1969.

———. "Iberville and the Southern Indians," *The Alabama Review* 20
(October 1967): 243–62.

———, trans. and ed. *Fleur de Lys and Calumet: Being the Pénicaut
Narrative of French Adventure in Louisiana*. Baton Rouge: Louisiana State University Press, 1953.

Margry, Pierre, comp. and ed. *Découvertes et Établissements des Français dans l'Ouest et dans le Sud de l'Amérique Septentrionale, (1614–
1754)*. 6 vols. Paris: Imprimerie D. Jouaust, 1879–1888.

Morison, Samuel Eliot. *Admiral of the Ocean Sea*. Boston: Little,
Brown and Company, 1942.

O'Gorman, Edmundo. "Do the Americas Have a Common History?"
In *Points of View*. Washington: The Pan American Union, 1941.

Parkman, Francis. *Count Frontenac and New France under Louis XIV*.
Boston: Little, Brown and Company, 1880.

Peckham, Howard H. *The Colonial Wars*. Chicago: University of
Chicago Press, 1964.

Phares, Ross. *Cavalier in the Wilderness: The Story of the Explorer and
Trader Louis Juchereau de St. Denis*. Baton Rouge: Louisiana State
University Press, 1952.

Prescott, William H[ickling]. *History of the Conquest of Mexico*. 2 vols.
Philadelphia: J. B. Lippincott Co., 1873.

Read, William A. *Louisiana Place-Names of Indian Origin*. Louisiana
State University and Agricultural and Mechanical College Bulletin,
19, n.s., no. 2 (February 1927). 72 pp.

———. *Louisiana-French*. Louisiana State University Studies no. 5.
Baton Rouge: Louisiana State University Press, 1931.

Smith, James Morton, ed. *Seventeenth Century America: Essays in
Colonial History*. Chapel Hill: University of North Carolina Press,
1959.

Surrey, N. M. Miller. *The Commerce of Louisiana during the French
Régime, 1699–1763*. New York: Columbia University, Longmans,
Green and Co., Agents, 1916.

Swanton, John R. *The Indians of the Southeastern United States*.
Bureau of American Ethnology Bulletin 137. Washington, D.C.:
Smithsonian Institution, Government Printing Office, 1946.

Tepaske, John J., ed. *Three American Empires*. New York: Harper
and Row, 1967.

Thomas, Alfred B. "Colonial United States History: A New Point of

View." Unpublished manuscript written in 1963. Copy in possession of Tennant S. McWilliams, Birmingham, Alabama.

Willey, Gordon Randolph. *Introduction to American Archaeology.* 2
vols. Englewood Cliffs, N.J.: Prentice-Hall, [1966–1971].

Wilson, Samuel, Jr. "Colonial Fortifications and Military Architec-
ture in the Mississippi Valley." In John Francis McDermott, ed.,
The French in the Mississippi Valley. Urbana: University of Illinois
Press, 1965.

Maps

"Carte d'une partie des côtes de la Floride et de la Louisiane . . . pour
le service des vaisseaux Francais. Par ordre de M. de Sartine . . .
1778." [Paris]. The Rucker Agee Map Collection, Birmingham
Public Library.

Coast and Geodetic Survey. "Choctawhatchee Bay." Chart 185.
Issued June, 1886.

Delisle, Guillaume. "Carte du Mexique et de la Floride," 1703.

[Des Barres, Joseph Fredrich Walsh]. "The North East Shore of the
Gulph of Mexico," [London], January 1, 1779. (Florida State University librarians in charge of this map considered it to be of the first
issue from Des Barres's plate.)

DuBois, Abraham. *La geographie moderne* . . . A la Haye, chez
Jacques van den Kieboom [and] Gerard Black, 1736, v. 3, p. 842.
The Rucker Agee Map Collection.

Fer, Nicolas de. "Le Golphe de Mexique, et les provinces et isles qui
l'environe comme sont la Floride au nord . . . par N. de Fer . . .
1717 . . . Paris." The Rucker Agee Map Collection.

Fer, Nicolas de. "Les Costes aux environs de la Riviere de Misisipi,
decouvertes par Mʳ de la Salle en 1683 et Reconnues par Mʳ le
Chevallier d'Iberville en 1698 et 1699 . . . par N. de Fer, Geographe
de Monseigneur le Dauphin." 1701. The Rucker Agee Map Collection.

Fite, Emerson D. and Archibald Freeman, comps. and eds. *A Book of
Old Maps Delineating American History from the Earliest Days Down
to the Close of the Revolutionary War.* New York: Dover Publica-
tions, Inc., 1969.

Florida Bureau of Topographical Engineers. "The State of Florida . . . " 1846.

Florida State Road Department. "General Highway Map: Okaloosa
County, Florida," April 1953.

Mitchell, S. Augustus, pub. "Map of the States of Louisiana, Mississippi, and Alabama." Philadelphia, 1835. The Rucker Agee Map Collection.

National Geographic Society, Cartographic Division. "West Indies," Atlas Plate 23, December 1962.

The Royal Illustrated Atlas of Modern Geography. London: A. Fullerton and Co., 1819.

United States Geological Survey. "Destin Quadrangle, Florida." 1970.

Index

Surgère, La Rochefoucault de, 20n,
25n, 33, 42–43, 48–49, 60, 85,
91–92, 96, 119, 135

Tabasque (Tabasco), 100
Taensa Indians, 8–9, 70, 72–75,
109, 127, 146–47; Iberville
describes village of and ritualistic
sacrifice of infants following
destruction of temple, 128–31
Tamaroua Indians, 117, 175, 176n
Tangibao (Tangipahoa) Indians, 61,
75
Tasenocogoula River, 71, 72
Tenerife: meridian used by Iberville
in calculating longitude east
around the earth, 19n, 105n
Théloël (Thecloël) Indians, 47, 72n;
tribes comprising Natchez or
Théloël nation, 73
Thierry, Catherine (mother of
Iberville), 1
Thysia Indians, 73. See also Tiou
Indians
Tiou Indians, 74n, 143
Tohomé Indians, 141, 143, 158,
172–73; visited by Iberville in
vicinity of La Mobile French
settlement, 169
Tombigbee River, 73n, 176n
Tonica (Tunica) Indians, 8, 73,
74n, 109–10, 133, 145, 175
Tonti, Henri de, 6, 8, 12, 54n,
59–60, 61n, 62, 64, 67n, 70, 76,
89, 107, 117–20, 133, 144n, 145,
163; his important letter to La
Salle recovered from
Mougoulascha chief, 87–88;
brings Chaqueta and Chicacha
chiefs to Iberville at La Mobile
French settlement, 171

Toutymascha Indians, 47
Treaty of Ryswick, 3–4
Twenty-Seven-Mile Bluff, 11, 161n

Vera Cruz, 4, 33, 53, 94, 162,
177–79
Vilautré, 91
Virginia, state of, 175
Voyageurs, 132, 134; granted
permission by Iberville to settle
at La Mobile and on the
Mississippi for trapping and
trading, 165–66
Vyspe Indians, 74n

Wabash River. See Ouabache River
War of the League of Augsburg.
See King William's War
War of the Spanish Succession
(Queen Anne's War), 7, 12
William III (of England), 2
Windward Passage, 23n

Yagueneschyto Indians, 47, 64n
Yataché Indians, 71, 152; Bienville
at their village, 153
Yayecha, 154
Yazoo River, 73n, 74n, 143n
Yezito Indians, 71
York Fort, 2
Yuahés Indians, 152